HUBER'S OBSERVATIONS ON BEES

TRANSLATED BY
C. P. DADANT

EX-
LIBRIS

FRANCIS HUBER

New Observations Upon Bees

BY

FRANCIS HUBER

1814

Translated from the French

BY

C. P. DADANT

(Editor of the American Bee Journal)

AMERICAN BEE JOURNAL

HAMILTON, ILLINOIS, U. S. A.

1926

INTRODUCTION BY THE TRANSLATOR

The writer of this has both editions of Huber's "Nouvelles Observations," in the French language, dated 1792 and 1814. He also possesses two of the four so-called "original" translations into English of this famous work, the second (1808) and the third (1821). Reading them and comparing them with each other and with the French original, he discovered that they are far from complete. They appear to be different from each other, for they begin and end with different wording. But some of the most absurd errors in translation or type-setting are repeated in each. For instance, in the eighth letter, the words "strong hive" were printed as "strange hive" and this ridiculous printer's error is repeated in each edition of the translation, showing that they are a copy of each other, with just enough changes to make it appear that they are original translations. Moreover, the English translation has but 5 plates instead of 12 in the original French editions. It is very incomplete, being very much abridged in many parts.

At the suggestion of leading students and beekeepers in America, of whom I will name only two, Dr. E. F. Phillips and Mr. E. R. Root, this complete translation was made. It is useless to recall how important a work Huber's "New Observations" has been. Many people imagine that they have discovered things in beekeeping that this wonderful man had already described, with the help of his faithful wife and devoted secretary, Burnens, for Huber was blind.

The translator's intention is not to make money out of it, but only to have the credit of a correct translation of this wonderful book. Let me add here, that credit must be given to Mr. Graham Burtt of England for his help in the translation of one chapter.

C. P. DADANT.

TABLE OF CONTENTS

VOLUME I

VOLUME II

CHAPTER I

CHAPTER II

CHAPTER III

CHAPTER IV

TABLE OF CONTENTS

VOLUME I.

PREFACE

In publishing my observations upon honeybees, I will not conceal the fact that it was not with my own eyes that I made them. Through a concourse of unfortunate accidents, I became blind in my early youth; but I loved sciences, I did not lose the taste for them when I lost the organs of sight. I caused the best works on physics and natural history to be read to me: I had for reader a servant (Francis Burnens, born in the canton of Vaud), who became extraordinarily interested in all that he read to me: I judged readily, from his remarks upon our readings, and through the consequences which he knew how to draw, that he was comprehending them as well as I, and that he was born with the talents of an observer. This is not the first example of a man who, without education, without wealth, and in the most unfavorable circumstances, was called by nature alone to become a naturalist. I resolved to cultivate his talent and to use it some day for the observations which I planned: with this purpose, I caused him to reproduce at first some of the most simple experiments of physics; he executed these with much skill and intelligence; he then passed to more difficult combinations. I did not then possess many instruments, but he knew how to perfect them, to apply them to new uses, and, when it became necessary, he made, himself, the machines which we needed. In these divers occupations, the taste which he had for the sciences soon became a veritable passion, and I hesitated no longer to give him my entire confidence, feeling sure to see well when seeing through his eyes.

The continuation of my readings having directed me to the beautiful memoirs of Mr. de Réaumur upon bees, I found in this work so beautiful a plan of experiments, observations made with so much art, so wise a logic, that I resolved to study especially this celebrated author, to shape my reader and myself at his school, in the difficult art of observing nature. We began by studying bees in glazed hives, we repeated all the experiences of Mr. de Réaumur, and we obtained exactly the same results, when we used the same processes. This agreement of my observations with his own gave me extreme pleasure, for it proved to me that I could depend absolutely upon the eyes of my pupil. Emboldened by his first trial, we attempted to make upon the bees some entirely new experiments; we devised divers hive constructions of which no one had ever thought, and which presented great advantages, and we had the good fortune to discover remarkable facts which had been unobserved by Swammerdam, Réaumur and Bonnet. These facts I publish in this work: there is not one of them that we have not seen over and again several times, during the eight years in which we have occupied ourselves with researches upon bees.

One cannot have a correct idea of the patience and skill with which Burnens executed the experiments which I am about to describe: it often happened that he followed, for 24 hours, without allowing himself any relaxation, without taking rest or food, a few worker bees of our hives, which we suspected of being fertile; in order to detect them in the laying of eggs. At other times, when it was necessary to examine all the bees which inhabited a hive, he did not have recourse to the operation of a bath, which is so simple and easy, because he had noticed that a sojourn in water disfigures the bees to a certain point, and does not enable one to perceive the little differences of structure which we wanted to ascertain; but he would take all the bees, one after another, in his fingers, and examine them with attention, without fearing their anger: it is true that he had acquired such dexterity, that he usually avoided the strokes of the sting; but he was not always so lucky, and when he was stung, he continued his inspection with the most perfect calm. I often upbraided myself for putting his courage and patience to so hard a test, but he was as interested as I in the success of our experiments, and through the extreme desire which he had to become informed of the results, he counted as nothing the trouble, the fatigue and the temporary pains of the stings. Therefore, if there is any merit in our discoveries, I must divide the honor with him; it is a great satisfaction for me to insure this reward for him, by acknowledging the justice of it publicly.

Such is the faithful account of the circumstances in which I found myself; I realize that I have to do much to secure the confidence of naturalists; but in order to be more sure of obtaining it, I will take the freedom of a little self-conceit. I communicated successively my principal observations upon bees to Mr. Bonnet; he found them correct, he advised me to publish them and it is with his approval that I publish them under his patronage. This testimony of his approval is so glorious for me, that I could not forego the pleasure of informing my readers of it.

I do not ask that I be believed upon my word: I will recount our experiments and tell all the precautions taken: I will detail so exactly the processes that we have employed, that all the observers will be enabled to repeat these experiments; and if then, as I do not doubt, they secure the same results as I did, I will have the consolation of knowing that the loss of my eyesight did not render me altogether useless in the progress of Natural History.

VOLUME I.

New Observations Upon Bees.

By FRANCIS HUBER

1814

FIRST LETTER

Upon the Fecundation of the Queen-Bee.

Pregny, August 13, 1789.

Sir, when I had the honor of giving you, at Genthod, an account of my principal experiments upon bees, you expressed the desire that I should write all the details and that I should send them to you, so that you might judge them with more attention. I therefore hastened to extract the following observations from my journal. Nothing could be more flattering for me than the interest you are kind enough to take in the success of my researches. Therefore permit me to remind you of the promise you have made to suggest new experiments to undertake.

After having for a long time watched the bees in glazed hives, constructed in the way indicated by Mr de Réaumur, you perceived, Sir, that their shape was not favorable to the observer, because these hives are too wide, the bees building in them two rows of parallel combs, and consequently all that happens between those combs is lost for the observer: from this correct remark, you advised the use for naturalists of much narrower hives, the panes of which should be so close together that there would be room between them for only one row of combs. I followed your advice, I made hives an inch and a half only in thickness and I had no trouble in hiving swarms in them. But we cannot rely upon the bees to construct a single comb; they are taught by nature to build parallel combs; it is a law from which they never derogate, when they are not constrained by some particular disposition: therefore if left to themselves in our thin hives, as they could not build two parallel combs in the length of the hive, they would construct several small ones perpendicular to it and all that would happen between them would be equally lost for the observer: one must therefore arrange the combs beforehand. I have them placed so that their plane is perpendicular to the horizon and their lateral surfaces three or four lines from the panes of the hive, on each side. This distance gives the bees sufficient freedom, but prevents them from collecting in too thick clusters upon the surface of the combs. With these precautions, the bees establish themselves easily in such narrow hives; they do their work with the same assiduity and order, and as there are no cells which are not exposed to view, we are sure that they cannot conceal any of their actions.

It is true that by compelling these bees to be content with a habitation in which they could build but one single row of comb, I had, to a certain point, changed their natural condition, and this circumstance might alter their instinct more or less. Therefore, to obviate any kind of objection, I devised a hive which, without losing the advantage of thin hives, approached the shape of the common hives, in which bees construct several parallel rows of combs. I will give here the description in a few words.

I procured several small frames of pine, a foot square, and an inch and a quarter thick; I caused them to be all joined together with hinges, so that they might open and close at will, like the leaves of a book, and I had the two outside frames covered with panes of glass, representing the covers of the book. When we used hives of this shape, we had a comb of cells fastened within each of those frames; we then introduced the number of bees needed for each particular experiment; then,[1] by opening successively the different frames, we inspected, several times each day, each comb on its two sides: there was not a cell, therefore, in which we could not examine what took place at any moment; I might almost say that there was not a single bee with which we did not get personally acquainted. In fact, this construction is nothing but the union of several narrow hives, which may

[1] Plate I. Explanation. The book hive is composed of the putting together of 12 frames placed vertically and parallel to one another.

Fig. 1 represents one of these frames: the uprights fg, fg, should be 12 inches in length, and the cross pieces ff, gg, 9 or 10 inches; the thickness of the uprights and of the cross pieces should be 1 inch and their width 1¼ inches. It is important that this last measurement be exact.

aa, piece of comb which serves to direct the bees in their work.

bb, bb, pegs which serve to fasten the comb within the frame: there are four on the other side which do not show in this cut, but figure 4 shows how they are to be placed.

d, movable cross piece which serves also in supporting the comb.

ee, pegs driven into the uprights under the movable cross piece to support it.

Figure 2 represents a book hive, composed of 12 frames all numbered. Between the 6th and 7th frames are 2 boards each with shutter which may divide the hive into two equal parts, but which are to be used only when wanting to separate the hive in two for the making of an artificial swarm. They are designated by a a.

b b, boards which close the ends of the hive, with shutters.

There are openings at the lower end of each frame; all must be closed with the exception of Numbers 1 and 12; but they must be disposed so as to be opened at will.

Figure 3 exhibits the hive as an open book in part, to show that the frames of which it is composed may be joined together, and open like the leaves of a book. a a, are shutters which close it at each end.

Figure 4 is the same as figure 1 shown in a different way.

a a, piece of combs to direct the work of the bees.

bb, bb, pegs arranged in wedge shape to hold the comb within the frame.

c c, end of two slats which serve in holding the comb, the upper one stationary, the lower one movable.

be separated at will: I acknowledge that bees must not be examined, in such a hive, before they have fixed their combs securely in the frames; otherwise they might fall out of the frames, upon the bees, crush or maim some of them and irritate them to such a point, that the observer could not avoid stings, which are always unpleasant and sometimes dangerous: but they soon become accustomed to the situation; they are in some way tamed by it, and at the end of three days one may open the hive, carry away parts of combs, substitute others, without the bees exhibiting too formidable signs of displeasure. Kindly remember, sir, that when you visited my retreat, I showed you a hive of this shape which had been a long time in experiment, and that you were much astonished at the peaceableness with which the bees permitted us to open it.

I have repeated all my observations in hives of this shape and the results were exactly the same as in the thinnest hives. I thus believe that I have obviated all the objections that might be made upon the supposed inconveniences of my flat hives. Besides, I have no regret of having repeated all my work; by going over the same observations several times, I am much more certain of having avoided error, and I have found in these hives (which I will call book or leaf hives) several advantages which make them very useful in the economic treatment of bees. I will detail them afterwards, if you permit me.

I come now, Sir, to the particular object of this letter, the fecundation of the queen-bee.[2]

I will first examine, in a few words, the different opinions of naturalists on the peculiar problem which this fecundation presents; I will mention to you the most remarkable observations which their conjectures caused me to make, and will then describe the new experiments through which I believe that I have solved the problem.

Swammerdam, who had observed bees with constant assiduity, and had never been able to see a real mating of a drone with a queen, was satisfied that mating was unnecessary for the fecundation of the eggs; but as he noticed that the drones exhaled, at certain times, a very strong odor, he imagined that this odor was an emanation of the *aura seminalis*, or the aura seminalis itself, which penetrating the body of the female, operated fecundation. He became confirmed in this conjecture, when he dissected the organs of generation of the males; he was so struck with the disproportion which they present, compared with the organs of the female, that he did not believe that copulation was possible; his opinion upon the influence of the odor of the drones had the advantage that it explained very plausibly their prodigious multiplication. There are often 1,500 to 2,000 of them in a hive, and, according to Swammerdam, it was necessary that they be there in great numbers, that the emanation proceeding from them be sufficiently intense or energetic to effect fecundation.

2 I do not dare insist that my readers, in order to better comprehend what I have to say, should read the memoirs of Mr. de Réaumur upon bees and those of the Lusatian Society, but I urge them to study the extract that Mr. Bonnet has given of them in his work, tome X of the octavo edition, and tome V of the quarto edition. They will find in it a short and clear summary of all that naturalists had hitherto discovered on those bees.

Mr. de Réaumur has already refuted this hypothesis by just and conclusive reasoning; but he has not made the sole experiment which could verify or overturn it in a decisive manner. It was necessary to confine all the drones of a hive in a box perforated with very minute holes, which would allow the passage of the odor, without permitting the passage of the organs of generation; place this box in a well peopled hive, but entirely deprived of males of either large or small size, and observe the result. It is evident that, after having thus disposed matters, if the queen had laid fertilized eggs, Swammerdam's hypothesis would have acquired much probability, and on the contrary, it would have been entirely overthrown, if the queen had not laid any eggs or only sterile ones. We made this experiment as I have just indicated it, and the queen remained barren. It is therefore certain that the odor of the drones is insufficient to impregnate her.

Mr. de Réaumur had a different opinion: he believed that the fecundity of the queen-bee was the result of actual mating; he enclosed a few drones with a virgin queen, in a glass sand-box; he saw her make many advances to the males, but, as he could not see any connection sufficiently intimate to call it a mating, he made no decision, leaving the question open. We have repeated the experiment after him, we enclosed, at different times, virgin queens, with drones of all ages, we made the experiment in all seasons; we saw the advances made by the queen: we have even at times thought that we detected between them a sort of union, but so short and imperfect that it was not likely that it had operated fecundation. However, as we did not wish to neglect anything, we confined to her hive the queen which had been approached by the male and observed her for several days. She was imprisoned for more than a month, she did not lay a single egg during that time, therefore she had remained sterile. Those momentary junctions do not operate fecundation.

In the *Contemplation de la Nature*, part XI, chapter XXVII, you have reported the observations of an English naturalist, Mr. de Braw. They appeared made with accuracy and seemed, at last, to clear the mystery of the fecundation of the queen-bee.[3] This observer, favored by chance, one day perceived, at the bottom of some cells containing eggs, a whitish liquid, of spermatic appearance, distinct at least from the jelly which the workers usually gather around the newly hatched worms. Curious to learn its origin, and conjecturing that it was drops of the prolific masculine liquid, he undertook to watch in one of these hives the actions of the drones, so as to detect them at the time when they would be sprinkling the eggs. He asserts that he saw several of them insinuating the posterior part of their body in the cells, depositing the liquid there. After repeating this observation several times he undertook a long series of experiments: he confined a number of workers with a queen and a few drones in a glass bell; he supplied them with pieces of comb containing honey but no brood and he saw this queen lay eggs which the drones afterwards sprinkled and from which worms hatched. On the other hand, when he failed to enclose drones within the prison with the queen, she did not lay, or laid only sterile eggs. He did not hesitate to give, as a demonstrated fact, that the males of bees fecundate

---

[3] See Volume LXVII of the Transactions philosophiques.

the eggs of the queen in the manner of fishes and frogs, that is to say, externally after they have been laid.

This explanation appeared specious; the experiments upon which it was based appeared well made, and it especially accounted for the prodigious number of males which are found in hives. However there remained a very strong objection which the author had overlooked. Larvæ are born when there are no longer any drones. From September till April the hives are, usually, deprived of drones and notwithstanding their absence, the eggs which the queen lays in that interval are not sterile: thus they have no need, to be fertile, of the influence of the drone's sperm. Should we suppose that it is needed at a certain time of the year and that in other seasons it becomes useless?

To discover the truth amid these apparently contradictory facts, I resolved to repeat the experiments of Mr. de Braw and to take greater precautions than he had taken himself. First, I sought, within the cells which contained eggs, to see the liquid of which he speaks, and which he mistook for drops of sperm; we found, Burnens and I, several cells containing an appearance of liquid, and I must acknowledge that, during the first days, after making this observation, we had no doubt of the reality of this discovery: but we recognized the illusion afterwards, caused by the reflection of the rays of light; for we could see traces of this liquid only when the sun was sending its rays to the bottom of the cells. That bottom is usually lined with debris of different cocoons of the worms which have successively hatched in it. Those cocoons are sufficiently bright and when strongly lighted there results an illumination, which is quite deceiving. We became convinced of this when we examined the matter more closely. We detached the cells which presented this peculiarity, we cut them up in different ways and saw very clearly that there was not the least trace of liquid in them.

Although this observation inspired us with a sort of distrust of Mr. de Braw's discovery, we repeated his other experiments with the greatest care. On the 6th of August 1787, we immersed a hive and examined all the bees while they were in the bath. We made sure that there was not a single drone in it, either of the large or of the small size. We examined also all the combs and we made sure that there were neither nymph nor larvæ of males in them. When all the bees were dry we placed them all back with the queen in their hive; and transported this hive into my cabinet. As we wished them to enjoy full liberty, we did not close them up; they went into the fields and made their usual harvest; but, as it was necessary that, during the entire time of the experiment, there should be no drones among them, we adapted a glass tube to the entrance, the dimensions of which were such that two bees only could pass at once, and we watched this tube attentively during the four or five days that the experiment lasted. Had a drone appeared, we would have recognized him instantly and removed him so that the result of the experiment be not disturbed. We can affirm that not one was seen. However, the queen laid, from the first day (6th of August), 14 eggs in worker cells and all the worms hatched on the 10th of the same month.

This experiment is decisive. Since the eggs were fertile that the queen laid in a hive containing no drones, and where no drones could possibly have been introduced, it is very certain that they do not need to be sprinkled with the sperm of the drones in order to hatch.

It appears to me that no reasonable objection can be brought against this inference. However, as I have accustomed myself, in all my experiments, to seek the most trifling difficulties which might be raised against their results, I thought that Mr. de Braw's partisans would say that the bees, deprived of their drones, might seek those living in other hives, remove the fertilizing liquid from them, and bring it to their own home to deposit it upon the eggs.

It was easy to appreciate the value of this suspicion. It was only necessary to repeat the previous experiment, confining the bees in their hive so closely that not one of them could escape. You know, sir, that the bees may live for three or four months in confinement in their hive, otherwise well provisioned with honey and wax, and in which small openings have been left for the passage of air. I made this experiment on the 10th of August; I had made sure, by means of immersion, that there was not a single drone among them; they were kept prisoners, in the closest manner, for four days, and at the end of that time I found forty worms newly hatched, on their bed of jelly. I went to the length of immersing this hive again to make sure that no male had escaped my search; we examined all the bees separately and we can assure that there was not a single one which did not show us her sting. This result, coinciding with the first experiment, demonstrated that the eggs of the queen-bee are not fecundated externally.

In order to conclude the confutation of Mr. de Braw's opinion, I need only to indicate that which led him into error. In his different observations he used queen-bees with which he was not acquainted from their birth. When he saw the eggs hatch which were laid by a queen confined with males, he determined that they had been sprinkled with the prolific liquid; but to have a just conclusion, he should have ascertained that this female had never mated, and this he neglected. The fact is, that, without knowing it, he had employed in this experiment a queen which had had commerce with a male. Had he used a virgin queen and enclosed her with drones within his glass bells, at the moment of her emerging from the royal cell, he would have had an entirely different result. For even amidst this seraglio of males, she never would have laid, as I will prove in the sequel of this letter.

The Lusatian observers, and Mr. Hattorf in particular, thought that the queen was fertile, of herself, without the concourse of the males.[4] I will recall here the experiment upon which this opinion was founded.

Mr. Hattorf took a queen of whose virginity there could not be any doubt; he confined her to a hive from which he excluded all the males of the large or small size and a few days after he found in it eggs and worms. He asserts that, in the course of this experiment, no drones were introduced

4 See in Schirach's history of bees a memoir of Mr. Hattorf, entitled: Physical researches upon this question: Does the queen-bee require fecundation by drones?

within this hive, and, since in spite of their absence the queen laid eggs from which worms hatched, he concluded that she is fertile by herself.

Reflecting on this experiment, I did not find it sufficiently exact. I knew that drones pass easily from one hive to another and that Mr. Hattorf had taken no precautions to prevent any of them from being introduced within his hive; indeed he says that no males came, but he does not say by what means he made sure of this fact: even though he might have made sure that no drones of the large size had entered, it might have been possible that one of the small size had entered, escaping his vigilance, and had fecundated the queen. To clear up this doubt, I resolved to repeat the experiment of this observer, as he described it, without greater care or precautions.

I placed a virgin queen within a hive from which I removed all the drones, and left entire freedom to the bees: a few days after, I visited this hive and found newly hatched worms in it. Here then was the same result as Mr. Hattorf had obtained; but to draw similar consequences, it was necessary to make sure that no males had been introduced. It was necessary to immerse the bees and examine them separately. We performed this operation and after careful search we found four small males. It results from this, that to render an experiment decisive on this question, it is not only necessary to remove all the drones, but one must also, by some sure method, prevent any from being introduced, which the German observer had neglected to do.

I prepared to repair this omission. I placed a virgin queen in a hive from which I carefully removed all the males, and to be physically certain that none would come, I adapted to the entrance of the hive a glass tube of such dimensions that the worker bees could easily pass through, but which was too small for even a drone of the small size. Matters remained thus for thirty days; the workers, going and coming, did their usual work, but the queen remained sterile; at the end of the thirty days, her belly was as slender as at the time of her birth. I repeated this experiment several times and the result was the same.

Therefore, since a queen remains sterile which is rigorously separated from all commerce with the males, it is evident that she is not fertile by herself. So the opinion of Mr. Hattorf is ill-founded.

Hitherto, when seeking to verify or destroy the conjectures of all the previous observers by new experiments, I had acquired the knowledge of new facts; but these facts were apparently so contradictory that they rendered the solution of the problem still more difficult. While working upon Mr. de Braw's hypothesis, if I confined a queen within a hive from which I had excluded all the drones; she did not fail in fertility. On the contrary, if, while examining the opinion of Mr. Hattorf, I placed in the same conditions a queen of whose virginity I was positively certain, she remained sterile.

Embarrassed by so many difficulties, I was on the point of abandoning this subject of researches, when at last, in reflecting more attentively upon it, I thought that these apparent contradictions were due to my bringing together experiments made on virgin queens and others executed upon females which I had not observed from their birth, and which had perhaps been fecundated unknown to me. Impressed with this idea, I undertook to follow a new plan of observation, not on queens taken haphazard from my hives, but on positively virgin females, whose history was known to me from the moment of their leaving the cell.

I had a great number of hives: I removed all the reigning females and substituted for each of them a queen taken at the moment of her birth; I then divided those hives into two classes. From those of the first class I removed all the males of both large and small sizes, and adapted to the entrances a glass tube so narrow that no drone could enter, but large enough for the free ingress and egress of the workers. In the hives of the second class, I left all the drones that were there and even introduced new ones, and to prevent them from escaping, I placed on these hives, as with the first, a glass tube too narrow for the passage of the drones.

I followed with great care, for over a month, this experiment made on a large scale, and was very much surprised, at the end of that time, to see my queens equally sterile.

It is therefore absolutely certain that queens remain unfertile, even amidst a sergalio of drones, when one confines them to the hive. This result led me to suspect that the females cannot be fecundated in the interior of their hives, and that they must go out in order to receive the approaches of the males. It was easy to ascertain this by a direct experiment. As this is important, I shall relate in detail that which we made, my secretary and I, on the 29th of June, 1788.

We knew that, during the fine season, the drones usually emerge from their hives at the warmest hour of the day. It was therefore natural to conclude that, if the queens are also compelled to emerge in order to be fecundated, they would be induced to select the hour of the drones' flight.

We therefore stationed ourselves in front of a hive whose unfertile queen was five days old. It was 11 o'clock in the forenoon: the sun had been shining from its rising, the air was very warm; the drones began to fly from several hives, we then enlarged the entrance of that selected for observation; then fixed our attention upon that entrance and the bees that issued from it. We first saw a few males appear, which took flight as soon as released. Soon afterwards, the young queen appeared at the entrance of the hive; she did not fly at once. We saw her promenading on the stand of the hive for a few instants, brushing her belly with her posterior legs: neither the bees nor the males that emerged from the hive appeared to bestow any attention upon her: at last the young queen took flight. When a few feet from the hive, she turned and approached as if to examine the point from which she had left; (it seemed that she judged this precaution necessary to recognize it on her return) she then flew away, describing horizontal circles twelve or fifteen feet above the earth. We then contracted the entrance of the hive, so that she might not re-enter unobserved, and we placed ourselves in the center of the circles which she was describing in her flight, to be better able to follow her and witness all her actions. But she did not remain long in a situation so favorable for observation; soon she took speedy flight and arose out of sight: we returned immediately to our place in front of the hive, and in seven minutes we saw the young queen return and alight at the entrance of this hive from which she had emerged only once. We took her in our hands to examine her and having found no signs of fecundation upon her we allowed her to re-enter the hive. She remained inside nearly a quarter of an hour, when she appeared again; after having brushed herself as before, she took flight, turned to examine the hive, and rose so high that we lost sight of her. This second absence was much longer than the first, it was only after twenty-seven minutes that we saw her return and alight on the board. We found her then in a very different state from that in which she was after her first excursion: the posterior part of her body was filled with a whitish substance, thick and hard, the interior edges of her vulva were covered with it; the vulva itself was partly open and we could readily see that its interior was filled with the same substance. This substance very much resembled the liquid contained in the seminal vesicles of the males, completely similar to it in color and consistency[5]; but we needed a stronger proof than this resemblance, to make sure that the white liquid with which she was impregnated, was really the fecundating liquid of the drones; it was necessary that it should operate fecundation. We then allowed this queen to enter the hive and confined her there. Two days later we opened the hive and saw the proof that she was fertile. Her belly was perceptibly enlarged and she had already laid nearly a hundred eggs in worker cells.

To confirm this discovery, we made several other experiments, with the same success. I will transcribe this one from my journal: The second of July, the weather being very fine, the males came out in numbers. We set at liberty a queen which had never lived with drones (for her hive had always been entirely deprived of them.) She was eleven days old and positively not fertile; we soon saw her leave the hive, turn to examine it, and rise out of sight: she returned after a few minutes, without any exterior signs of fecundation; she flew again for the second time, at the end of a quarter hour, but with so rapid a flight that we were able to follow her for only an instant; this new absence lasted thirty minutes. The last ring of her abdomen was open and the vulva was filled with the whitish matter already mentioned. We replaced her in her home, from which we continued to exclude all males. We examined her two days later and found her fertile.

These observations at length taught us why Mr. Hattorf had obtained results so different from ours. He had had fertile queens, in hives which were deprived of drones, and he had concluded that their intercourse was not necessary for fecundation, but he had not deprived his queens from the liberty of flight and they had taken advantage of this to join the drones.

---

5 It will be shown in the following letter that what we took for drops of coagulated sperm was really the male organs, which the mating fixes into the body of the female. We owe this discovery to a circumstance that I will here relate. In order to shorten this work, perhaps I should have omitted all the accounts I give of my first observations on the fecundation of the queen-bee, and pass directly to the experiments which prove that she brings home with her the genital organs of the male; but in observations of this kind, which are both new and delicate, it is so easy to be deceived, that I believe I serve my readers by exposing candidly the errors which I committed. It is an additional proof, added to so many others, of the necessity for an observer, to repeat his experiments thousands of times, to obtain the certainty of seeing facts in their true light.

We, on the contrary, had surrounded our queens with a great number of males, and they had remained sterile, because the precautions which we had taken for confining the males to the hives had also prevented the queens from departing and seeking *outside* the fecundation which they could not obtain within.

We repeated these experiments upon queens aged twenty, twenty-five, thirty, thirty-five days. All became fertile after a single impregnation. However, we have observed some essential peculiarities in the fecundity of those queens which were fecundated after the twentieth day of their life; but we defer speaking of it until we can offer to naturalists some observations sufficiently positive and sufficiently numerous to better merit their attention.

However, allow me to add a word here. Although we did not witness a real mating between the queen and a drone, we believe that, after the details which we have just given, there will remain no doubt of the actual mating and of the need of it for fecundation. The sequel of our experiments, made with every possible precaution, appears demonstrative. The uniform sterility of queens in the hives containing no males and in those in which they were confined with males; the departure of these queens from their hives and the very conspicuous signs of impregnation which they exhibited on their return, are proofs against which no objections can stand. We do not despair of being able, next spring, to secure the last complement of this proof, by seizing the female at the very instant of copulation.

Naturalists had always been much embarrassed to account for the great number of drones found in most of the hives and which seem to be only a burden on the community of bees, since they fulfill no functions there. But we may now begin to discern the intention of nature in multiplying them to such a extent: since fecundation cannot take place within the hives, and the queen is compelled to fly in the expanse of the air to find a male who may fecundate her, it was requisite that these males be in sufficient number for the queen to have the chance of meeting one; were there only one or two drones in each hive, the probability of their issuing at the same time as the queen and of meeting her would have been very scanty and the majority of the females would have remained sterile.

But why has nature forbidden fecundation within the hives? It is a secret which has not been unveiled to us. Some favorable circumstance may enable us to penetrate it in the course of our observations. One might make divers conjectures but today we require facts and we reject gratuitous suppositions. We will remember only that the bees do not form the sole republic of insects presenting this singularity; female ants are also compelled to leave the ant-hills in order to be fertilized by the males of their species.

I dare not beg you, Sir, to communicate to me the reflections which your genius will suggest to you upon the facts that I have just related to you. I have not yet any right to this favor. But if, as I have no doubt, some new experiments to be tried come to your mind, upon the fecundation of the queen-bee or upon other points of the history of bees, be so kind as to suggest them to me: I will bring in their execution all the care of which

I am capable, and I will consider this mark of your friendship and interest as the most flattering encouragement which I may receive in the continuation of my labour.

I am, Sir, with the greatest respect,

Yours &c.

LETTER FROM MR. BONNET TO MR. HUBER UPON BEES.

You surprised me, Sir, very agreeably, with your communication upon the fecundation of the queen-bee. You had a very fortunate idea, when you surmised that she left the hive to be fecundated, and the method to which you resorted to ascertain it was very appropriate to the end.

I will remind you that the males and females of the ants mate in the air, and that after fecundation the females return to the ant-nest to deposit their eggs. Contemplation de la Nature, part XI, Chapitre XXII, note I. It would still be necessary to seize the instant when the drone unites with the queen-bee, but how can we ascertain the manner in which the copulation takes place, in the air, far from the eyes of the observer! Since you have good proofs that the liquid which moistened the last rings of the queen upon her return is the same as that which the males supply, it is more than a simple presumption in favor of mating. Perhaps it is necessary, for its operation, that the male may seize the female under the belly, which cannot easily take place except in the air. The large opening that you have observed in a certain circumstance at the extremity of the queen's belly appears to correspond with the singular volume of the sexual organs of the male.

You desire, Sir, that I should indicate some new experiments to try upon our industrious republicans; I shall do it with the greater interest and pleasure, since I know to what extent you possess the precious art of combining ideas and drawing from this combination results adapted to the discovery of new truths. A few at this moment come to my mind.

It would be suitable to try to fecundate a virgin queen artificially, by introducing, within the vagina, at the end of a hair pencil, a little of the prolific liquid of the male, taking every precaution to avoid error. You know how much artificial fecundations have been worth to us already in more than one way.

In order to make sure that the queen that left the hive for fecundation is the same one that returns to deposit eggs, it would be necessary to paint her corslet with a moisture-proof varnish. It will be well also to paint the corslet of a good number of workers to discover the duration of their life. One would succeed still better by mutilating them slightly.

In order to hatch, the little egg must be fixed almost vertically by one end near the bottom of the cell; this brings one question to mind: is it very certain that it may not hatch unless it is fixed in that position? I would not dare affirm it, and I leave the decision to experiment.

I said to you once that I long doubted the real nature of those small oblong bodies that the queen deposits in the bottom of the cells: I was inclined to consider them as minute worms that had not yet begun their development. Their very elongated shape favored my conjecture; it would be advisable to watch them with the utmost assiduity from the time of their being laid until they hatch. If one can see the shell burst open and the little worm emerge from the aperture, there will no longer be any doubt that these little bodies are real eggs.

I return to the manner in which the mating takes place. The height to which the queen and the males rise in the air prevents us from distinctly seeing what passes between them: it would then be necessary to try enclosing the hive in a room with very high ceiling. It would also be advisable to repeat the experiment of Mr. de Réaumur, who confined a queen with several males in a glass sand-box; and if, instead of a glass sand-box, one used a glass tube several inches in diameter and several feet long, perhaps one could observe something decisive.

You had the good fortune to observe some of the small queens mentioned by the Abbé Needham, but which he had not seen. It would be important to dissect with care some of these queens for the purpose of discovering their ovaries. When Mr. Riems informed me that he had confined about 300 workers in a box, with a comb that did not contain any eggs, and that some time after he had found hundreds of eggs in that comb, which he credited to the laying of the workers, I strongly recommended to him to dissect the workers: he did so, and informed me that he had found eggs in three of them. They were apparently small queens which he had dissected without knowing it. Since small drones are produced, it is not astonishing that small queens are produced also, doubtless by the same external causes.

These queens of the small size deserve to be known, for they may have great influence in divers circumstances and embarrass the observer. We should ascertain whether they grow in pyramidal cells smaller than common or in hexagonal cells.

Schirach's famous experiment on the pretended conversion of a common worm into a royal one could not be too often repeated, although the Lusatian observers have done so many times. But the discoverer maintained that the experiment succeeds only with worms three or four days old, and never with simple eggs. I would much like that this last assertion be tested.

The Lusatian observers and the one from Palatinate affirm that the common bees or workers lay only drone eggs, when they are confined upon combs containing no eggs at all: so there may be small queens that lay only drone eggs; for it is evident that those eggs, which they believed had been laid by workers, must have been produced by queens of the small size. But how can we conceive that the ovaries of those small queens contain only drone eggs?

Mr. de Réaumur informed us that we may prolong the life of chrysalids by keeping them in a cold place, such as an ice-house: it would be advisable to try the same experiment upon the eggs of the queen-bee and upon the nymphs of drones and workers.

Another interesting experiment would be to remove all the combs composed of common cells, leaving only those made of cells intended for drones. One would ascertain whether the eggs which the queen would lay in those large cells would produce workers of a larger size. But it is quite probable that the deprivation of common cells would discourage the bees; because they need this sort of cells for their honey and wax. Perhaps however, if we removed only a part of these common cells, the mother might be compelled to lay common eggs in drone cells.

I should also desire that an attempt be made to gently remove from a royal cell the worm which is housed in it and place it at the bottom of a common one, in which some of the royal jelly would have also been deposited.

As the shape of hives has a great influence upon the respective disposition of the combs, it would be a desirable experiment to vary their shape and internal dimensions. Nothing would be better adapted to inform us of the manner in which bees modify their work and apply it upon circumstances.

This might enable us to discover particular facts which we do not divine.

They have not yet compared with care the royal egg and the drone egg with the eggs from which common workers are produced. It would be well to make this comparison to ascertain whether these different eggs contain distinctive characters.

The pap supplied by the workers to the royal worm is not the same with that given to the common worms. Could we not endeavor to remove a little of the royal pap with a hair pencil and feed it to a common worm which would be placed in a common cell of the greater size. I have seen common cells hanging almost vertically in which the queen had laid common eggs. These cells I would prefer for the experiment which I suggest.

I have gathered, in my Memoires sur les Abeilles, divers facts which would need verification; the same would be required of my own observations; you will know, sir, how to select, among these facts, the ones which are most worthy of your attention; you have already enriched the history of bees so greatly that everything may be expected from your sagacity and perseverance. You know the sentiments with which you have inspired the Contemplator of Nature.

Genthod, August 18, 1789.

SECOND LETTER FROM MR. HUBER TO MR. BONNET.

Continuation of Observations on the Fecundation of the Queen-Bee.

Pregny, August 17, 1791.

Sir, It was in 1787 and 1788 that I made the experiments related to you in my previous letter. They seem to establish two facts upon which only vague indications had been secured previously.

1st. The queen bees are not fertile of themselves, they become so through mating with a drone.

2nd. Mating is accomplished outside of the hive, and in the air.

The latter fact was so extraordinary, that notwithstanding all the proofs which we had acquired, we keenly desired to see the queen in the act. But as she arises to a great height in this circumstance our eyes could never reach it. It was then that you advised us, sir, to cut off some part of the wings of virgin queens, to prevent them from flying as rapidly and to so great a distance. We endeavored in every manner to profit by this advice, but to our great regret, when we mutilated their wings very much, they could no longer fly, and when we cut off but a small part, it did not diminish the speed of their flight. There is, probably, a medium between these two extremes, we were unable to attain it. We tried also, upon your recommendation, to render their sight less acute, by covering a part of their eyes with an opaque varnish; this attempt was also useless. At last, we tried to artificially fecundate some queen-bees by introducing into their posterior parts the liquid of the drones.[6]

We took in this operation all imaginable precautions to insure its success, but the result was not satisfactory. Several queens were the victims of our inquisitiveness; the others which survived remained sterile nevertheless.

Although these divers attempts were fruitless, it was proved that the

---

[6] Swammerdam, who gave us the description of the ovary of the queen-bee, has left it incomplete. He says that he could not see where the egg canal emerges from the belly, nor what parts may be perceived, outside of those which he described.

"However much pain I took," says he (Bible of Nature), "to discover distinctly the vulva opening, I was unable to do so, partly because I was then in the country and did not have all my instruments with me, partly because I did not wish to force the vulva out of the abdomen of the female, for fear of damaging some other parts which I needed to examine at the same time. However, I saw plainly enough that the excretory duct of the eggs forms a muscular enlargement, at the place where it is near the last ring of the abdomen; afterwards shrinking and again enlarging when it becomes membraneous. I could not follow it farther, because I desired to preserve the venom vesicle, with the few muscles which serve for the play of the sting. But in another female, it seemed to me, that the vulva, when the bee is lying on her belly, opens in the last ring under the sting, and that it is very difficult to penetrate in this opening, unless these parts stretch and extend at the time when the bee lays."

We tried, sir, to see what indefatigable Swammerdam had failed to see; he put us on our way by indicating to us the time of laying as the most advantageous for this research: we then saw that the excretory canal of the eggs did not open directly to the outside of the body; and that the eggs, when emerging from the womb, fell in a cavity, in which they were held for a time, before issuing out of the belly through the lips of the last ring.

On the 6th of August 1787, we took out of her hive a very prolific queen: holding her carefully, overturned, by the wings, her entire belly was uncovered; she seized the extremity of it with the second pair of legs, and bringing it in this way towards her head, she bent it as much as she could, giving it the shape of a bow. This posture appeared to us opposed to free laying; by the use of a straw we compelled her to take a more natural attitude and to straighten out her belly. Pressed to lay, she could not withhold her eggs any longer: we saw her make an effort and stretch out her belly; the inferior part of the last ring spread away from the upper sufficiently to make an opening which uncovered a part of the interior of the belly. We saw the sting within its sheath in the upper part of this cavity. The queen then made further efforts, and we saw an egg emerge from the end of the ovary duct and drop into the cavity which we have mentioned; then the lips closed again and after a few instants they opened, but much less than the first time, yet sufficiently to allow the egg which we had seen, to fall out of this cavity.

females emerge from their hives to seek the males, and that they come home with the most evident signs of fecundation. Being satisfied with this discovery, we hoped for time or accident to give us decisive proof, a real mating, taking place under our eyes. We were far from suspecting a most singular discovery, which we made this year in the month of July and which gives a complete demonstration of the supposed mating.

We knew by our own observations that the sperm of the drone coagulates as soon as it is exposed to air; several experiments, by confirming this fact, left so little doubt on that score, that whenever we saw the females return with the exterior signs of copulation, we thought that we recognized the drops of the male sperm in the white substance with which their vulva was filled. We did not even think of dissecting one of those females, to make ourselves more positively certain of the fact. But this year, in order to neglect nothing and also to take note of the development which we supposed was produced in the organs of the queens by the injection of the coagulated sperm left by the drones, we undertook the dissection of several; to our great surprise, we found that what we had mistaken for the prolific liquid, was really the generative organs of the male, separated from his body at the time of copulation, and remaining planted within the vulva of the females: here are the details of this discovery.

After having resolved to dissect several queen-bees at the time when they would return to the hive with the exterior signs of fecundation, we procured several, by the Schirach method, and allowed them successively to fly out to hunt for drones; the first one that took advantage of it was caught at the instant when she was about to re-enter the hive, and without dissection, she displayed to us what we were so desirous of learning. We had seized her by her four wings, and examined the underside of her belly. Her partly open vulva showed the almost oval end of a white body which, by its volume and position, prevented the lips from closing altogether; the belly of the queen was in continuous motion; it stretched, shrank, lengthened, shortened, bent and straightened successively. We were making ready to cut open her rings, and seek, by dissection, the cause of all those motions, when we saw her bend her belly sufficiently to reach its extremity with her posterior legs, and seize, with the hooks upon her claws, that part of the white body which was within the lips of her vulva and which held them apart; she was evidently making efforts to draw it out; she soon succeeded and dropped it in our hands. We were expecting to see the shapeless mass of some coagulated liquid; but our surprise was great when we found that it was a part of the body of the drone who had made her a mother. At first we did not believe our eyes; but after having examined that substance on all sides, both with the naked eye and with a good magnifying glass, we recognized distinctly the part of a drone which Mr. de Réaumur calls the "lenticular part" or "lentil," of which I here give the description copied from his own work (Ninth Memoir upon Bees, quarto edition, page 489).

"When we open the body of a drone, either from above or from below, "we notice a substance formed from the assembling of several parts, often of "a white color surpassing that of milk: if we spread out this substance, we "find it composed principally of four oblong bodies; the two largest of these

"bodies are fastened to a sort of tortuous cord which Swammerdam called
"*the root of the penis* (Plate II fig. 1), and he gave the name of *seminal*
"*vesicles* s s, to the two white, long bodies which we have just mentioned.
"Two other bodies, oblong like these, but with a diameter only about half
"of the others, and shorter, are called by the same author *deferent vessels*
"d d. Each of these communicates with one of the seminal vesicles, near the
"spot q q, which the latter are joined to the tortuous duct r; at the other
"end of each of these deferent vessels, a slim duct is found x x, which, after
"a few curves, ends in an enlarged body t, a little larger, but difficult to
"separate from the trachæ which surround it. Swammerdam considers these
"two bodies as the testicles. So we have two bodies of considerable volume
"which join with two larger and longer ones still longer and larger. These
"four bodies have a cellular tissue filled with a whitish liquid, which may
"be forced out by pressure. The long and tortuous duct r, to which the
"two largest bodies are fastened, which are called the seminal vesicles, is
"undoubtedly the duct through which the milky liquid can escape. After
"several turns it widens or rather terminates in a sort of bladder l, i, a
"fleshy bag. This part is more or less stretched and more or less flat in
"different drones; by giving it the name of *lenticular body* or *lentil*, we de-
"scribe its appearance in all the drones whose organs have been hardened
"in alcohol. This bag l, i, is then a rounded lentil, half of whose circum-
"ference is bound by two scaly plates e i, e i, of chestnut color which follow
"the curves of its contour. A little whitish cord, on the border of the lentil,
"is visible and separates them from one another. As this lentil is oblong
"we will give its two ends the names of posterior and anterior. The an-
"terior end l, nearest to the head, is the one into which the duct r is in-
"serted, coming from the seminal vesicles. The posterior end i, nearest to
"the anus gives rise to the two scaly plates e i, e i, each of which widens
"so as to cover a part of the lentil. Below the spot where each of these
"scaly plates is widest, there is a notch which makes two rounded points of
"uneven lengths, the longer being upon the circumference of the lentil.
"Besides these two plates, there are two others n n, Fig. 2, of the same color,
"but narrower, and shorter by half, each of which is near the others, with
"their end at the same end as the others, at the posterior part of the lentil,
"fig. 2. The rest of the lentil is white and membranous; at its posterior
"end is a tube k, also white and membranous, the diameter of which is
"difficult to determine, for the membranes which compose it are visibly
"folded. At one side of this tube a fleshy body, p, is fastened which re-
"sembles a palet, one side concave with plaited edges; the other side con-
"vex; in some cases the plaits turn up and their edges project beyond the
"circumference; they form rays which give the palet the appearance of
"pretty work. This palet lies upon the lentil, and rests upon it on its con-
"cave side, but it does not adhere to it.
    "The parts which we have just mentioned, and which are the most
"visible in the body of the drones, are not those that emerge first out of the
"body, nor those that are most remarkable, outside of the body. If we con-
"sider the tube k, or the sac which begins at the posterior end of the lentil
"which separates the two scaly plates, we can easily see the part, u, which
"we have named the arch; one may see five wooly bands disposed crosswise,

"they are of tawny color, while the rest is white. This arch even seems to
"be outside of the membranous tube, for it is covered only by a very trans-
"parent membrane; at one end it almost touches the lenticular body while
"at the other it terminates where the membranous canal joins the mem-
"branes m, which are wrinkled and yellowish, making a sort of sac resting
"upon the edges of the opening from which the generative organs are to
"issue. The tawny-colored membranes mentioned are those which pressure
"forces out first, they form the elongated mass the end of which resembles
"a wooly mask. Lastly, this sac, composed of tawny membranes, holds two
"appendices c c, of reddish yellow color, even red to the tip; and these are
"the appendices which project to the outside in the shape of horns.

"When we press the belly of a drone gradually, with care, we cause
"other parts also to be ejected; these parts show themselves on the opposite
"side from their position in the body. The surface of these parts, which
"was the inside, becomes the outside; the same thing happens to them as
"to a stocking which is drawn inside out. If the opening of the stocking
"which we try to turn inside out was fixed upon a hoop, and if we began
"to evert it by beginning at the part nearest the opening, so that the heel
"and toe came last, we would have in this eversion of the stocking an exact
"illustration of the manner in which the organs of the male bee are turned
"to project outside.

"When we know the position of these parts in the interior of the body,
"it is easy to figure the order in which they must appear at their ejection.
"The tawny sac, which is nearest the opening, appears first and as a portion
"of its interior part is woolly, it provides the woolly mask. The base of the
"horns then show themselves; the arch next. When the arch is entirely
"extruded, it is necessary to increase the pressure to bring out other parts;
"for it is through the end of this arch that the lenticular body passes which
"then assumes a very lengthened appearance. In spite of this, it is easily
"recognized, and it is evident that it has been everted inside out, since we
"see, upon one of its sides, the scaly plates already described, and that the
"side on which they are seen is concave, while when in the body of the
"drone it is convex."

The lenticular body l, i, covered with the scaly plates i e, i e, is the
only one of the parts described by Mr. de Réaumur which we have found
within the vulva of the queens.

The canal r, which Swammerdam has called the *root of the penis*, is
torn after fecundation; we saw fragments of it at the place where it joins
the end l of the lentil, near its forward extremity, but we have never
found any trace of the tube k, made of folded membranes, nor of the plaited
palet p, which adheres to this tube, and which Swammerdam had called the
penis, on account of its resemblance to that of other animals, although he
did not believe that this part, which is not perforated, could fulfill these
functions. It must be that the tube k, and all that belongs to it break apart
at i, near the posterior end of the lentil, and that these parts remain within
the body of the male.

When we dissect a drone, we see, at the upper end of the canal r, two
very apparent nerves which are inserted in the seminal vesicles, and divide
among them as well as in the penis a number of ramifications.

According to Swammerdam these nerves and their ramifications may serve, at the same time, for the action of the parts, the emission of the sperm and the pleasure feeling at the instant of this emission.

We perceive also, near these two nerves, two ligaments intended to retain in place the generative organs, so that they may not be drawn out without effort, excepting however the root of the penis and the lentil which may extrude naturally and which are in fact expelled from the body of the drone during the mating.

The canal r is not stretched out in the body of the males as it is in the engraving which is shown here; but this long and tortuous duct folds upon itself several times between the vesicles s s from which it emerges to the lenticular body to which it carries the seminal liquid. So, it may unfold, extend, and lengthen as far and farther than is necessary for the lentil to move within the body of the drone, emerge from it and pass into the body of the female.

When we open the body of a drone, we see that this is possible, for if we grasp the lenticular body and try to displace it, the folds of this canal disappear, it stretches considerably, and if we draw it farther it breaks at l, close to the lentil, and precisely at the same spot where it breaks in the mating.

A more or less intense pressure may force out of the body of the drone several of the parts represented in the engraving; but they are then everted, like a glove, and show their inner side. Swammerdam and Réaumur admired this structure and described it with the greatest precision. We have also, like them, squeezed a great number of drones, we have often seen this marvelous eversion and understood how it might be operated under air pressure. But we are unable to believe that the generative parts turn inside out during the mating, as happens with an unusual pressure; for not one of the drones that we thus pressed survived after the operation: it is singular that such an extraordinary circumstance should have been unobserved by these naturalists.

We have indeed seen drones which we had not touched, in which the generative parts were inverted, but they had evidently died instantly, without being able to draw back into their body any of the parts which perhaps an accidental pressure had forced out.

Another observation gives proof also that the everting in question does not take place in natural circumstances. When we examined the lentil of which the queen had rid herself, we saw clearly that it had not been everted, since the side of it which we saw was the same as what is seen within the body of a male; we recognized this by the position of the four scaly plates, which exhibited their convexity and which covered the lentil at its posterior end; had they been everted the contrary would have been the case.

We conjectured then that these plates, intended, according to Mr. de Réaumur, to strengthen the lenticular body, might have a more important use and serve as pincers or hooks. The respective position of these plates, their appearance, their scaly consistency, the space that they occupied upon the lentil, and especially the efforts that the queen was compelled to make to rid herself of them, seemed to strengthen this conjecture: but it was verified only when we had observed the position of these parts within the body of females which we killed to satisfy our inquisitiveness. For this purpose, we prevented several of these queens from displacing and pulling from their body the organs left by the drones that had fecundated them, and dissection showed us that those plates were true pincers or hooks, as conjectured by us.

The lentil was inserted beneath the sting of the queen and pressed against the upper part of the body; it thus filled the cavity of the vulva and rested at its posterior end against the end of the vagina or excretory canal of the eggs. It was there that we saw the action and use of the scaly plates; they were a little farther apart than they are in the body of the male. They were inserted below the orifice of the vagina and pressed between them some parts which their infinitely small size did not allow us to distinguish; but the effort required to separate them and remove the lenticular body left no doubt to us of the use of those scaly hooks.

The lentils taken out of the body of males always seemed smaller than those found in the vulva of females; we also noticed, as did Mr. Réaumur, that those parts, in different drones, are not always of the same size; but we discovered another part, which escaped his notice or that of Swammerdam, which probably plays the main role in fecundation. We will mention it when giving account of the experiment which caused us to notice it.

FIRST EXPERIMENT.

On the 10th of July, we released, one after another, three virgin queens, four or five days old. Two of those queens took flight several times; their absences were short and unsuccessful; the one which we released last succeeded better, she flew three times: her first trips did not last long, but the last trip lasted thirty-five minutes. She came back in a very different condition, which permitted no doubt of the use she had made of the time; for her vulva partly open exhibited the organs, which the male had left in her body, that had fertilized her.

We caught her in one hand by her four wings, and with the other we obtained the lenticular body which she pulled out of her vulva with the claws of her posterior legs; the posterior end of this was armed with two scaly and elastic pincers; one could spread them apart, but when they were released they came back into the same position.

Towards the anterior end of the lentil, one could see a fragment of the root of the penis; this tube had broken, half a line from the lenticular body: is it fragile at that spot in order to facilitate the separation of the female from the male? One would be tempted to believe it. We allowed this queen to re-enter her hive and arranged the entrance so that she might not emerge, unknown to us.

On the 17th we opened her hive, but found no eggs there; the queen was as slender as on the day of her flight. The drone that had mated with her had evidently not fecundated her. We gave her liberty again; she took advantage of it, and after two absences, she again brought to the hive the evidences of a mating; we confined her again, and the eggs which she laid afterwards gave us evidence that the second mating had been successful, and that some drones may be more fit for mating than others.

It is however very rare that a first mating is insufficient; in the course of our numerous experiments, we have seen but two queens that needed more than one to become fertile; all the others were fertile after the first mating.

SECOND EXPERIMENT.

On the 18th, we gave liberty to a young queen, twenty-seven days old; she flew twice, her second absence lasted twenty-eight minutes, and upon her return she brought the evidence of her mating. We did not allow her to enter the hive, but placed her under a tumbler, to see in what manner she would rid herself of the male organs which prevented the closing of her vulva; she could not succeed in it, as long as she had nothing but the table and the smooth glass to rest upon. We enclosed under the glass a little piece of comb, in order to give her the same conveniences as she would have had in her hive, and to see whether, with this help, she could do without the help of the bees. She climbed promptly upon it, held to the edges of the cells with her four front legs; then stretching her two hind legs along her belly, she appeared to press it by rubbing with the legs up and down on each side, at last passing the hooks of her feet in the opening of the last ring of her abdomen, she clasped the lenticular body and allowed it to drop on the table; we took it up then: its posterior end was armed with the two scalp plates, under which, in the same direction, we saw a cylindrical body, of grayish-white color; the end of this body, farthest from the lentil appeared perceptibly larger than the end next to it; beyond this enlargement it terminated in a point; this point was double and open like the beak of a bird, which caused us to believe that this body had been broken and torn; the following experiment sustained this conjecture.

THIRD EXPERIMENT.

On the 19th we released a virgin queen four days old. She flew twice, the second absence, longer than the first, lasted thirty-six minutes; she returned with the signs of fecundation. We wanted to secure in their entirety the parts which the drone had left in her vulva; for this purpose it was necessary to prevent her from breaking them by drawing them out with her claws: after having killed her as promptly as we could, we cut open her last rings to uncover the vulva; but in depriving her of life we had not deprived her of motion; there was so much of this in these parts that the lenticular body dropped out spontaneously, and the part which we were interested in was broken as it had been the previous time; we were thus compelled to repeat the test: I will give only the results of this.

In several instances, when we separated the lenticular body from the orifice of the vagina, against which it was pressed, we found with it a white body which adhered to it by one of its extremities; the other being engaged in the excretory canal of the eggs.

This body appeared cylindrical at its end near the lentil; it became enlarged farther along, then shrunk and again enlarged more than at first; it thus formed a sort of acorn, after which it terminated in a sharp point.

These details were not perceptible with the naked eye, a magnifying glass was needed to perceive them.

The shape of this body and its position seemed to indicate that it was the special male organ, of which the lenticular body was only an appendix; but the last queen that we had under our control destroyed this conjecture.

FOURTH EXPERIMENT.

On the 20th, we liberated two virgin queens: the first one had already taken flight the previous days, but had not been fecundated; we seized her upon her return; her vulva was open and the lentil of the drone appeared between its lips: we wanted to prevent her from getting rid of it, but she removed it with her legs so quickly that we could not forestall her, and we allowed her to re-enter the hive.

The second queen liberated flew twice; her first absence was as short as usual: the second lasted about a half hour; she returned fecundated, and we caught her at her arrival. We opened her promptly after having killed her. We found the lenticular body placed as in all the queens observed before: its pincers penetrated to the base of the vulva; the dull points which terminate them appeared to be implanted under the excretory canal of the eggs; they pressed between them some parts which their infinitely small size did not permit us to distinguish: the resistance which they offered, in trying to loosen them, convinced us that these hooks serve to bring the end of the lentil against the orifice of the vagina and to hold it there. Through this precaution, of which we see examples in other insects, as the drone and the queen cannot pull apart until the requirements of nature are accomplished, the success of their union is assured.

Before disturbing these parts, we placed them under the lens of the microscope: we then saw a peculiarity which had escaped our observation: when drawing back the lenticular body, there emerged from the vagina a small body (figure 2 v), adhering to the posterior end of the lentil and located under the scaly plates. It drew back of itself within the lentil, like the horns of a snail. This part is very short, white and apparently cylindrical: there was, under the plates, a little of the seminal fluid half clotted at the bottom of the vulva. Looking farther in the vagina, we did not find any other hard substances: we pressed out much sperm: it was almost liquid, but soon clotted and became a shapeless whitish mass. This careful observation put an end to our doubts and convinced us that what we had mistaken for the characteristic organ of the drone was the semen itself which had clotted in the interior of the vagina and assumed the shape of the latter.

Thus, the only hard part that the male had introduced within the vagina of the female was this short cylindrical point which had withdrawn into the lentil when we had drawn it out. Its action and situation prove that it is there that we must seek the escape of the seminal liquid, if it is possible to find it open at any other time than during the mating.

We sought this new part in the drones and found it in the first one dissected; by pressing the seminal vesicles s s, figure 1, from above, we forced the white liquid with which they were filled to flow and run down into the root of the penis r, and into the lenticular body l, i, which was then considerably enlarged. We prevented this liquid from flowing back, and forced it forward by a renewed pressure. However, the liquid did not flow out when we pressed the lentil, but we saw, at its posterior end and under the scaly plates, a small white body, short, cylindrical and with the same appearance as that which we had found in the vagina of the queen. When we ceased to press the lentil, this part re-entered it, but reappeared every time that we pressed it.

I ask you, Sir, when you read this letter, to glance at the figure which Mr. de Réaumur has published of the sexual organs of the drones, and which I caused to be copied (Plate II); the descriptions that accompany it appear quite correct, and give a proper idea of the position of these parts. Upon examination of these figures one easily conceives the appearance which they present within the vulva of the female, when they are implanted in it after mating.

The details which I have exposed, help to fix the idea of the reader and sufficiently indicate the shape and position of the organ which I discovered and which must be considered as the penis of the male bee, of which the lentil must be only an appendix.

I have no doubt that the drones perish when they lose their sexual organs after mating. While reflecting one day upon the discovery which is the subject of this letter and upon the impossibility of witnessing a mating which takes place in the air, it seemed to us that one could add another proof to those that we had, if one could find the male which had fecundated one of our queens and catch him on his return; but we could hope for this only in case he did not die suddenly after mating, and if he had time to return to the hive.

Burnens thought that it would be easy to distinguish such a male from those that die without having mated and without having suffered any mutilation. So he condemned himself to examine, one after another, all the drones that he would find dead near the hives during the swarming season.

After long and useless researches, he found a few that had died in front of the hives and were evidently mutilated, for they had lost those of the genital parts that remain within the body of the queens. The root of the penis had protruded out of their body after mating, a piece of this canal ten or twelve lines long was hanging at the extremity of their belly and had dried there. None of the parts which pressure may force out showed itself in that case.

These observations, made with greatest care, confirmed the conjecture which I had already stated, that is: that no other part than the penis and its appendages extrudes from the body of the male during mating. They proved also that the males perish after having lost their sexual parts, and that their death is not as prompt as one might have expected.

By coming back to die at the front of the hive, they bring back, as the queen does, the evidence of their union and of a long unknown fact.

But for what reason has nature required from the drone so great a sacrifice? It is a mystery which I will not attempt to penetrate. I do not know of any similar fact in the history of animals; but as there are two kinds of insects whose mating can only take place in the air, the ephemerids and the ants, it would be very interesting to learn whether their males also lose their sexual organs in those circumstances, and whether, while making love upon the wing, like drones, the enjoyment of it is also for them a harbinger of death?

Accept the assurance of my respect, &c.

May 29th.

N. B. I have not observed the matings of ephemerids, but Mr. Degers who has witnessed them, does not speak of the males as being mutilated. So remarkable a circumstance could not have escaped him.

As to the ants, their drones lose so small a part of their sexual organs, that they are able to fecundate several females in succession, and I have made sure of this through repeated observations.

THIRD LETTER.

Continuation of the same subject. Observations on queen-bees whose fecundation is delayed.

Pregny, August 21, 1791.

Sir, I wrote you in my first letter that when the young queens were not permitted to mate until the twenty-fifth or thirtieth day after their birth, the result of this fecundation presented some very interesting peculiarities. I did not then give you the detail of these, because, at the time when I had the honor of writing you my experiments upon this subject had not been sufficiently multiplied. I have repeated them so many times since, and their results have been so uniform, that I am not afraid of announcing to you, as a positive discovery, the singular effect that retarded fecundation produces upon the ovaries of the queen. When a queen is mated within the first fifteen days of her life, she becomes able to lay worker or drone eggs; but if her fecundation is delayed up to the twenty-second day, her ovaries become viciated so that she will be unable to lay worker eggs; she will lay only male eggs.

I was occupied with researches relative to the formation of swarms, when I had, for the first time, occasion to observe a queen that laid only drone eggs. It was in June, 1787. I had found out that, when a colony is ready to swarm, the time of issue is always preceded by a very lively agitation, which first affects the queen, is then communicated to the workers, and excites among them so great a tumult that they abandon their labors and issue in disorder through all the entrances of the hive. I then knew well the cause of the queen's agitation (I will describe it in the history of swarms); but I was still ignorant how this delirium is communicated to the workers and this difficulty interrupted my work. To solve it, I thought of seeking, by direct experiments, whether when the queen was greatly agitated, even at other times than that of swarming, her agitation would be communicated similarly to the workers. I enclosed a queen in a hive, at the time of her birth, and prevented her issuing, by contracting the entrances in such a manner that they would be too narrow for her. I had no doubt that she would make great efforts to escape, whenever she would feel the imperious desire of joining the males, and that this impossibility might throw her into a kind of delirium. Burnens had the patience of observing this captive queen for thirty-five days. Every morning, towards 11 o'clock, when the sunshine invited the males to issue from the hives, he saw her traverse every corner of her habitation seeking an issue: but as she found none, her useless efforts threw her each time into an extraordinary agitation, the symptoms of which I shall describe elsewhere, and by which all the common bees were affected.

During the course of this long imprisonment, the queen did not go out a single time, she could not then be fecundated. On the thirty-sixth day, I at last set her at liberty; she quickly took advantage of it and soon returned with the most evident marks of fecundation. Satisfied with the success of this experiment for the particular object I had proposed, I was far from hoping that she would supply me also with the knowledge of a remarkable fact. How great was my surprise, when I found that this female, which began to lay, as usual, forty-six hours after mating, did not lay worker eggs, but only drone eggs, and that she continued, afterwards, to lay only this kind of eggs!

At first, I exhausted myself in conjectures upon this singular fact; but the more I reflected on it, the more did it seem inexplicable. At last, by attentively meditating on the circumstances of this experiment, it appeared to me that there were two points which I should try to weigh separately. On the one hand, this queen had suffered from long imprisonment; on the other hand, her fecundation had been extremely retarded. You know, sir, that queen-bees usually have commerce with a male on the fifth or sixth day after their birth, and this one had not mated until the thirty-sixth day. I do not put great weight upon the supposition that this imprisonment had been the cause of this result. In natural conditions queen-bees fly out only to seek the males, a few days after birth: during the remainder of their life, excepting for the departure of swarms, they remain voluntary prisoners: it was therefore unlikely that captivity should have produced the result which I was trying to elucidate. However, as one must neglect nothing in so new a subject, I desired to ascertain whether it was the length of confinement or retarded fecundation which brought about the singularity which I had observed in the laying of this queen.

But this was not an easy task. To discover whether captivity, and not retarded fecundation, had vitiated the ovaries of the queen, it would have been necessary to allow a queen to mate, while retaining her a prisoner; this could not be done since queen-bees never mate inside of the hive. For the same reason it was impossible to delay her mating without keeping her a prisoner. I was long embarrassed by this difficulty: at last I devised an apparatus which was not exactly what I wanted, but which filled the purpose fairly.

I took a queen, at the end of her metamorphosis; I placed her within a well supplied hive, stocked with a sufficient number of workers and males. I contracted the entrance, so that it would be too narrow for the queen, but wide enough to give the workers free passage. At the same time, I made another opening for the passage of the queen and adapted to it a glass tube communicating with a large glass box measuring eight feet on each face. The queen could at all times come to this box, fly about and sport, breathing a better air than within the hive, in which nevertheless she could not be fecundated; for, although the males could also fly within this enclosure, the space was too limited for any mating between them. You know, sir, that the experiences which I have related to you show that the mating takes place only high in the air. I therefore found in this apparatus the advantage of retarding fecundation, while the queen had sufficient liberty that her condition of life was not too remote from the natural state. I followed this experiment for fifteen days. The captive female emerged from her hive every morning, when the weather was nice; she sported in her glass prison, and flew about with ease and much motion. She did not lay during this time, for she had no connection with a male. At last, on the sixteenth day, I set her at liberty: she flew from the hive, rose into the air and came back with all the signs of fecundation. Two days afterwards she began laying: her first eggs were worker eggs and from that time on, she laid as much as the most fertile queens.

It thence follows, first, that captivity does not alter the organs of queen-bees.

Second. That when fecundation takes place within the first sixteen days after their birth, they lay eggs of both sorts.

This first experiment was important; it rendered my task more simple, by pointing out to me clearly the method to be pursued; it absolutely precluded the supposed influence of captivity and left nothing to seek but the effects of a longer delayed fecundation.

For this purpose, I repeated the previous experiment; but instead of giving her liberty to the virgin on the sixteenth day, I detained her until the twenty-first day; she flew then, rose in the air, was fecundated and returned to her home. Forty-six hours afterwards, she began to lay, but it was male eggs, and although very prolific, she never laid any other kind. During the remainder of the year 1787, and the two following years, I occupied myself with experiments on retarded fecundation and constantly had the same results. It is therefore true that, when the mating of queen-bees is delayed beyond the twentieth day, there is but a semi-fecundation, if one may thus call it: for instead of laying both worker eggs and male eggs, those queens lay male eggs only.

I do not aspire to the honor of explaining this strange fact. When the continuation of my observations on bees made known to me the fact that there are sometimes queens that lay only drone eggs, I sought for the proximate cause of this singularity, and ascertained that it was due to retarded fecundation. The proof that I acquired is demonstrative, for I can always prevent queens from laying worker eggs by delaying their fecundation until the twenty-second or twenty-third day. But what is the remote cause of this fact, or in other words, why does retarded fecundation prevent queens from laying worker eggs? It is a problem upon which analogy throws no light; in all the physiological history of animals I do not know of any observation bearing the least similiarity to it.

This problem appears still more difficult, when we know how things happen in natural circumstances, that is, when fecundation has not been delayed. The queen then lays worker eggs 46 hours after mating and continues, for the space of 11 months, to lay almost only these. It is usually only at the end of these 11 months that she begins a considerable and uninterrupted laying of eggs of drones.[7] When, on the contrary, fecundation is retarded beyond the 20th day, the queen begins to lay drone eggs from the 46th hour, in considerable numbers, and never lays any others during her entire life. Since she lays only worker eggs, during the first 11 months in a natural condition, it is clear that the worker eggs and the drone eggs are not indiscriminately mixed in her oviducts: doubtless they occupy a situation corresponding to the laws that regulate her laying: those of workers are first, those of drones are behind them; it appears that the queen cannot lay drone eggs until she has discharged all the worker eggs that occupy first place in her oviducts. Why then is this order inverted by retarded impregnation? How does it happen that all the worker eggs that the queen should have laid, if fecundated in time, are withered and disappear, without obstructing the passage of the drone eggs, which occupy only second place in the ovaries?

This is not all: I ascertained that a single mating is sufficient to fertilize all the eggs that a queen will lay in the course of two years at least: I have even reason to believe that this single act of fecundation is sufficient for the fertilization of all the eggs that she will lay during her life, but I have full evidence only for the two years. This fact, which is already very remarkable in itself, renders the influence of retarded fecundation still more difficult to conceive. Since a single mating is sufficient, it is clear that the masculine liquid acts from the first moment upon the eggs that the queen is to lay for two years. According to your principles, sir, it gives them that degree of *animation* which afterwards determines their successive development; after having received this first impulse of life, they grow, ripen, so to speak, progressively, until the day when they will be laid: and as the laws of laying are invariable, as the eggs laid during the first 11 months are always eggs of workers, it is clear that those eggs, which are to appear first, are also the first to mature; thus in the natural state, the space of 11 months is necessary for the male eggs to acquire the growth which they must have at the time they are laid. This consequence which seems to me direct, renders the problem insoluble in my eyes. How can the male eggs which must grow slowly during 11 months, acquire at once their full development in the space of 48 hours, when fecundation has been retarded beyond 21 days, and by the effect of this delay alone? Observe, I beg you, that the supposition of the successive growing of eggs is not gratuitous: it is upon the principles of sound physics: besides, to be convinced that it is well founded, it is only necessary to glance at the figure given by Swammerdam of the ovaries of the queen: we see there that the eggs in that part of the oviduct contiguous to the vulva of the queen, are much farther advanced, larger than those contained in the part more remote of the same oviduct. The difficulty which I mention remains therefore in full force. It is an abyss wherein I am lost.

The only known fact which seems to have a semblance of connection

---

[7] It appears that this period is not strict, and that the epoch of the great drone laying may be accelerated or delayed according to atmospheric circumstances more or less favorable to bees and to their crops.

with those just mentioned is the state in which some vegetable seeds are found, which, although outwardly in good preservation, lose the faculty of germinating, through age; it might be, similarly, that the eggs of workers retain for only a short time the property of being fecundated by the seminal liquid, and that, after this period, which might be fifteen or eighteen days, they may be so disorganized as to be no longer susceptible of being animated by this liquid. I realize, sir, that this comparison is very imperfect; and besides that it explains nothing; it does not even put us in the way of making any new experiments; I will add but one reflection.

Up to this time, no effects had ever been observed of retarded fecundation upon the females of animals, excepting its rendering them absolutely sterile. The queen-bees offer us the first example of a female upon which this delay still leaves the faculty of engendering males. As no fact is unique in nature, it is very probable that we should find the same peculiarity in some other animals. So it would be a very curious object of research to observe insects under this new point of view. I say insects, for I do not conceive that anything similar would be found in other species of animals. It would even be necessary to begin these experiments upon the insects most analogous to bees, such as wasps, woolly bumblebees, mason bees, all kinds of flies, etc. Some experiments might afterwards be made upon butterflies; finding perhaps some animal upon which retarded fecundation would produce the same effect as upon bees. If this animal were of a greater size than the bees, dissection would be easier, and we could discern what happens to the eggs, whose retarded fecundation prevents their development. At least we might hope that some fortunate circumstance would lead us to the solution of the problem.[8]

I now return to the recital of my experiments.

In May 1789, I took two queens at the time when they were going through their last metamorphosis; I placed one of them in a leaf hive, well stocked with honey and wax, and sufficiently peopled with workers and males. The other was placed in a similar hive from which all the drones had been removed. I arranged the entrances of these hives for the freedom of the worker bees, but too narrow for the passage of females and drones. I kept those queens prisoners for 30 days. After that time, I liberated them. They departed eagerly and came back fecundated. In the beginning of July, I examined the two hives and found much brood: but this consisted entirely in worms and nymphs of males; there was not a single nymph, not a single worm, of a worker. Both queens laid without interruption until autumn, and uniformly eggs of drones. Their laying ended during the first fortnight of November, as did that of the queens of my other colonies. I was very desirous of ascertaining what would become of them in the ensuing spring; whether they would resume their laying, whether a new fecundation would be necessary, and, in case they should lay, of what sort their eggs would be; but as their hives were already much weakened

---

8 The experiments which I suggest in this paragraph remind me of a singular reflection of Mr. de Réaumur. Speaking of viviparous flies, he says it might not be impossible for a hen to give life to a living chick, if after fecundation, the eggs that she might lay were retained for 20 days in her oviducts. (See Réaumur sur les Insects, tome IV, Mémoire 10.)

I feared that they might perish during the winter. Fortunately, we succeeded in preserving them, and, as early as April, they recommenced their laying: through the precautions we had taken we were sure that they had not received new approaches of the male; their eggs were still drone eggs.

It would have been very interesting to follow farther the history of these females, but, to my great regret, their workers abandoned them on the 4th of May, and on that same day we found both the queens dead. Yet there were no moth worms in the combs to cause any disturbance to the bees, and the honey was still fairly abundant, but, as in the course of the previous year no workers had been born, and as winter had destroyed many, they found themselves in too small numbers to engage in their ordinary labors, and in their discouragement they deserted their hives to join the neighboring hives.

I find, in my journal, the detail of a multitude of experiments on the retarded fecundation of queen bees: it would be an endless task to transcribe them all here: I repeat that there was not the least variation in the principal result and every time and whenever the mating of the queens was delayed beyond the 21st day, they laid none but male eggs. Therefore, sir, I will limit myself to expound to you those of my experiments which have taught me some remarkable facts not yet mentioned.

On the 4th of October 1789, a queen hatched in one of my hives: we placed her in a leaf hive. Although the season was well advanced there were still many males in the hives. It was important to learn whether, at this time of the year, they could equally effect fecundation, and, in case of success, whether the laying, begun in the middle of autumn, would be interrupted or continued during the winter. So we allowed this queen to leave the hive. She did, but made 24 fruitless trips before returning with the signs of fecundation. At last, on the 31st of October, she was more fortunate, she came back with most evident marks of the success of her amours; she was then 27 days old, so that her fecundation had been much delayed. She should have begun laying 46 hours afterwards, but the weather was cold and she did not lay; which, let me say it in passing, proves that refrigeration of the temperature is the principal cause of the suspension of the queens' laying in autumn. I was very impatient to learn whether, on the return of spring, she would prove fertile, without the need of a new union. The means of ascertaining this was easy; for it only required contraction of the entrance of her hive, so that she might not escape. I confined her from the end of October until May. In the middle of March we examined her combs, and found many eggs, but as they were laid in cells of the small size, we had to wait a few days to pass judgment. On the 4th of April, we again examined the hive and found a prodigious quantity of nymphs and worms. They were all of drones; the queen had not laid a single worker egg.

Here, as in former experiments, delayed fecundation had rendered the queen bee incapable of laying eggs of workers. This result is the more remarkable that the laying of the queen began four months and a half after fecundation. The term of 46 hours which usually elapses between mating and laying is therefore not a rigorous term; the interval may be much longer if the weather grows cold. Lastly, it follows from this experiment that: even when the cold retards the laying of a queen fecundated in autumn, she will begin to lay in spring without the need of a new mating.

I may add that the queen whose history I have just given was of astonishing fecundity. On the first of May, we found, in her hive, besides 600 males in full development, 2438 cells, containing eggs, larvæ or nymphs of drones. Thus, she had laid, during March and April, more than 3,000 male eggs, or about 50 per day. Unfortunately, she perished shortly afterwards and we were unable to continue our observations: I had intended to calculate the number of drone eggs that she would lay during the year, and compare it with eggs of the same sort that queens lay whose fecundation has not been retarded. You know, sir, that the latter lay about 2,000 male eggs in spring; and a second laying less considerable in August; in the intervals they lay almost exclusively worker eggs. It is otherwise with females whose mating has been delayed, for they produce no worker eggs; for 4, 5, or 6 months in succession they lay male eggs uninterruptedly, and in such great numbers that, in this short time, I presume that they give birth to more drones than a female whose fecundation has not been retarded would produce in the course of two years: I much regretted having been unable to verify this conjecture.

I should also, Sir, describe to you the remarkable manner in which the queens that lay only drone eggs deposit them sometimes in the cells. They do not always place them upon the lozenges forming the bottom of the cells, but often deposit them upon the lower side, two lines from the mouth. The reason of this is that their belly is shorter than those of queens whose fecundation has not been retarded, their posterior extremity remains slender, while the first two rings next the corslet are extraordinarily enlarged: it results from this that, when they dispose themselves for laying, the anus cannot extend down to the lozenges at the bottom of the cells: the enlargement of the rings not permitting it; and consequently the eggs must remain attached to the part reached by the anus. The larvæ proceeding from these spend their vermicular state in the same place, which proves that bees are not entrusted with the care of transporting the eggs of the queen, as had been presumed. But in this case they follow another plan; they lengthen the cells in which eggs are thus placed 2 lines beyond their opening.[9]

Permit me, Sir, to digress a moment from my subject, to narrate to you an experiment, the result of which seems interesting. I said that the bees are not intrusted with the care of transporting eggs, misplaced by their queen, into convenient cells; and even judging by the sole fact which I mention here, you will think me well entitled to deny this feature of their industry. However, since several writers have affirmed the contrary and have even claimed our admiration of workers in conveying the eggs, I must prove to you clearly that they are mistaken.

I had a glass hive constructed of two stories: I filled the upper story with combs of large cells and the lower with combs of small cells. These two stories were separated from one another with a sort of division or

[9] This observation also teaches us that the eggs of bees need not be fixed by one end at the bottom of the cells in order to be fertile.

diaphragm, which left on each side a sufficient space for the passage of the workers from the one story to the other, but too narrow for the queen. I stocked this hive with a good number of bees, and confined in the upper story a very prolific female that had just lately finished her great laying of male eggs. Therefore, this female had only worker eggs to lay; she was compelled to deposit them in large cells, since there were none of the other sort about her. You will divine, sir, the aim which I proposed in thus disposing matters. My reasoning was very simple. If the queen lays worker eggs in large cells and if the workers are charged with transporting them when misplaced, they would not fail to take advantage of the liberty allowed them to pass from one story to the other; they would seek the eggs deposited in large cells and carry them to the lower story, containing the cells suitable for them. If, on the contrary, they left the worker eggs in the large cells, I should obtain certain proof that they are not entrusted with transporting them.

The result of this experiment excited my curiosity deeply. We watched the queen of this hive and her bees, for several days in succession, with sustained attention. During the first 24 hours, the queen obstinately refused to lay a single egg in the large cells which surrounded her; she examined them one after another, but passed on without insinuating her belly within any of them: she seemed restless, distressed; she traversed the combs in all directions; the weight of her eggs appeared to burden her, but she persisted in withholding them rather than deposit them in cells of unsuitable diameter. Her bees, however, did not cease to pay her homage and treat her as a mother. I even saw, with pleasure, that when she approached the edges of the partition which separated the two stories, she gnawed them to try to enlarge the passage; the workers also labored with their teeth, and made efforts to enlarge the entrance to her prison, but ineffectually. On the second day, the queen could no longer retain her eggs, they escaped in spite of her, she dropped them at random. Yet, we found 8 or 10 of them in the cells, but they had disappeared the following day. We then conceived that the bees had transported them into the lower cells, we sought them with the greatest care; but I can assure you that there was not a single one there. On the 3d day the queen again laid a few eggs, which disappeared as the first. We again sought them in the small cells but they were not there. The fact is that the workers eat them, and that is what deceived the former observers who claim that they transport them. They noted the disappearance of the misplaced eggs from the cells, and without farther investigation asserted that the bees place them elsewhere; they take them indeed, but not to transfer them; they eat them.

Thus, nature has not entrusted the bees with the care of placing the eggs in appropriate cells; but she has given the females themselves enough instinct to know the nature of the egg which they are about to lay and to place it in a suitable cell. Mr. de Réaumur had already observed this, and in this my observations agree with his. It is therefore certain that, in the natural state, when fecundation has been timely and the queen has not suffered from any circumstance, she does not err in the choice of the different cells in which she is to deposit her eggs: she does not fail to lay those of workers in the small cells and those of males in the large cells.—

I am speaking here, Sir, of what happens in natural conditions.—This distinction is important, for we do not find the same unerring instinct, in the behavior of females whose mating has been too long delayed; they make no selection of cells in which they are to lay. This fact is so true, that when I first observed the queens whose fecundation had been delayed, I often made mistakes on the kinds of eggs that they were laying; when I saw them lay indistinctively in both small and large cells, I thought that the eggs laid in the small cells were worker eggs: I was thus very much surprised, at the time of their transformation into nymphs, to see them close up the cells with convex cappings, exactly similar to those that they place upon the cells of males: they were, in fact, males; those that were born in small cells were drones of the small size; those that were born in large cells became large drones.—I warn those who wish to repeat my experiments upon queens laying only male eggs, that they must expect to see those queens deposit drone eggs in worker cells.

Moreover, here is a curious observation: these same females, whose fecundation has been delayed, sometimes lay drone eggs in royal cells. When I give the history of swarms, I shall show, that, in a natural condition, when the queens begin their great laying of male eggs, the workers construct numerous royal cells: there is probably a secret relation between the production of those eggs and the formation of those royal cells: it is a law of nature from which the bees never derogate. It is not surprising, therefore, that cells of this sort are constructed in hives governed by queens laying drone eggs only. Neither is it singular that these queens should deposit in royal cells the eggs of the only kind that they are able to lay, for in general their instinct seems altered. But what I cannot comprehend is that the bees take the same care of male eggs deposited in royal cells, as of the eggs that would become queens; they give them a more abundant food, they build up the cells as if containing a royal worm; they work upon them, in fact, with such regularity that we have been frequently deceived, ourselves. More than once we opened one of these cells, after they had sealed them, in the persuasion of finding royal nymphs, but it was always a drone nymph that was lodged there. Here the instinct of the workers appear defective. In the natural state, they distinguish the worms of males from those of common bees, since they never fail to give a particular cover to the drone cells. Why then do they no longer distinguish the drone worms, when they are placed in royal cells? This fact deserves much attention. I am convinced that, in order to understand the laws of the instinct of animals, we must carefully observe the cases where this instinct appears to err. (See note 1 of the 12th letter.)

Perhaps in beginning this letter, Sir, I should have given an abstract of the observations which other naturalists have made previously, on queens laying only male eggs; but I shall here repair this omission.—In a work entitled, Histoire de la reine des abeilles, translated from the German by Blassière, there is printed a letter which Mr. Schirach wrote you in date of April 15, 1771, in which he speaks of several of his hives, the brood of which changed into drones. You remember, sir, that he ascribed this accident to some unknown vice in the ovaries of the queen in these hives; but he was far from suspecting that retarded fecundation caused this vice of the ovaries. He justly felicitated himself on having discovered a method of preventing the dwindling of hives in this case; this was very simple, it consisted in removing the queen that laid male eggs only, and substituting another whose ovaries were not vitiated. But to make this substitution, it was necessary to procure queen-bees at will, and the discovery of this secret was Mr. Schirach's. I will speak of it in the following letter. You see by this detail that all the experiments of the German naturalist tended to the preservation of the hives whose queens laid only male eggs and that he did not attempt to discover the cause of the vice in their ovaries.

Mr. de Réaumur also says a word, somewhere, concerning a hive in which he had found many more drones than workers, but he advances no conjectures upon this fact; he adds only, as a remarkable circumstance, that the males were tolerated in that until spring of the following year. It is true that bees governed by a queen laying only drone eggs, or by a virgin, preserve their drones several months after they have been massacred in the other hives. I cannot ascribe a reason for this, but it is a fact that I have witnessed many times during the long course of observations that I undertook upon queens with retarded impregnation. In general, it appeared that as long as a queen lays male eggs, her bees do not destroy the drones that live in the hive in the insect form.

Accept, sir, the acknowledgment of my respect, &c.

FOURTH LETTER

On Schirach's Discovery.

Pregny, August 24, 1791.

Sir, When you were induced, in the edition of your works, to give an account of Schirach's beautiful experiments on the conversion of common bees' worms into royal ones, you invited naturalists to repeat them. Indeed, so important a discovery required the confirmation of several testimonials. I therefore hasten to inform you that all my researches establish its truth. During the 10 years that I have been studying bees, I repeated Schirach's experiment so many times, with such uniform success, that I cannot raise the least doubt. Therefore, I consider as a positive fact, that when bees lose their queen, and still have in their hive some worker's worms, they enlarge several of the cells in which they are located, feed them, not only with a different kind of food, but in greater amount, and that the worms reared in this manner, instead of changing to common bees, become real queens. I beg my readers to think over the explanation which you have given of so new a fact, and the philosophical consequences that you deduced from it. Contemplation de la Nature, par. XI, chap. XXVII.

I will limit myself, in this letter, with giving you some details upon the shape of the royal cells which the bees build around the worms destined for the royal state. I will terminate by discussing a few points upon which my observations differ from those of Mr. Schirach.

When bees lose their queen, they perceive it very quickly and in a few hours undertake the necessary work to repair their loss.

They first select the young worker worms, which are to receive the proper care to convert them into queens, and at once begin to enlarge the cells in which they are lodged. Their mode of proceeding is curious. In order to make it most intelligible, I will describe their work upon a single cell, which will apply to all those that contain worms intended for queens. After having selected a worker worm, they sacrifice three of the contiguous cells; taking away the worms and the pap and build around this one a cylindrical enclosure; its cell thus becomes a perfect tube, with rhomboidal base, for they do not tamper with the pieces of this base; if they damaged it they would uncover the three corresponding cells on the opposite side of the comb, and therefore would sacrifice the worms that inhabit them, which is unnecessary and which nature has not permitted. They therefore leave the rhomboidal base and are content with raising a cylindrical tube around the worm, which is thus placed horizontally, like the other cells of the comb. But this habitation is adapted to the intended royal worm for only the three first days of its existence; it requires a different situation for the other two days, during which it will still remain a worm. During these two days, which constitute so small a portion of the duration of its existence, it must live in a cell of nearly pyramidal form, the base of which is at the top and the point at the bottom. It seems that the workers are aware of this, for after the worm has completed its third day, they prepare the place to be occupied by its new lodging, gnawing away some of the cells located below the cylindrical tube, they mercilessly sacrifice the worms that are in them, and use the wax which they have just gnawed away to construct a new pyramidal tube which they solder at right angles to the first, working it downwards. The diameter of this pyramid decreases insensibly from its base, which is wide, down to the point. During the two days that the worm inhabits it, there is constantly a bee with her head more or less inserted in the cell: when a worker leaves it, another takes her place. They lengthen the cell as fast as the worm grows, they bring food, which they place before its mouth and around its body in a sort of band around it. The worm, which can only move in a spiral direction, turns incessantly to take the food before its head: it insensibly descends and at length arrives near the mouth of the cell: it is at this time that it must transform into a nymph. The care of the bees is no longer necessary: they close its cradle with an appropriate substance, and in proper time it undergoes its two metamorphoses.

Schirach holds that bees never select other than *3 days old worms*, to give them the "royal education": I have ascertained, on the contrary, that this operation succeeds as well on worms aged only *2 days*. Permit me to relate at full length the evidence which I have acquired of this: it will demonstrate, at the same time, both the reality of the conversion of worker worms into queens, and the little influence which their age has upon the success of the operation.

In a hive deprived of its queen, I caused to be placed some pieces of combs containing worker eggs and already hatched worms of the same kind. The same day, the bees enlarged several of the worm cells, and changed them to royal cells, giving to the worms in them a thick bed of jelly. We then removed 5 of the worms placed in those cells, and Burnens substituted for them 5 worker worms which we had witnessed hatching from the egg 48 hours previously. Our bees did not appear aware of this exchange: they

fed the new worms as well as those selected by themselves; they continued
enlarging the cells in which they were placed, and closed them at the usual
time; they then incubated these 5 cells during 7 days, at the end of which
time we took them away to preserve alive the queens which would be produced from them. Two of these queens emerged almost at the same moment,
they were of large size and well formed in every respect. The three other
cells having passed the term without any queen emerging, we opened them
to ascertain their condition; we found a dead queen in nymph state in one
of them, the other two were empty, the worms in them had spun their silk
cocoons but had died before getting to the nymph state, and showed only a
dried up skin. I can conceive nothing more conclusive than this experiment:
it demonstrates that bees have the power of converting the worms of
workers into queens, since they succeeded in procuring them by operating
on the worms of workers which we ourselves had selected: it is equally
demonstrated that, for the success of the process, it is not necessary that
the worms be three days old, since those which we entrusted to the bees were
only two days old.

Nor is this all: bees can convert into queens worms still younger. The
following experiment taught me that, when they have lost their queen, they
destine worms only a few hours old to replace her. A hive in my possession,
deprived of female, had not had any eggs or worms for a long time: I gave
them a queen of the greatest fecundity; she soon began to lay in the worker
cells; I kept her in that hive a little less than 3 days, and removed her
before any of her eggs were hatched: the following day, that is the fourth
day, Burnens counted 50 small worms, the oldest of which were hardly 24
hours old. However, several of them were already destined for queens, which
was proved by the bees depositing around them a much greater provision of
jelly than is supplied to common worms. The following day, the worms
being nearly 40 hours old, the bees had enlarged their cradles; they had converted their hexagonal cells into cylindrical cells of the greatest capacity;
they still labored at them the following days and closed them on the fifth
day from the hatching of the worms. Seven days after the sealing of the
first of these royal cells, we saw a queen of the largest size emerge from
it. This queen rushed towards the other royal cells and endeavored to
destroy the nymphs or worms that were in them. I shall narrate the effects
of her fury, in another letter.

You see, Sir, from these details, that Mr. Schirach had not yet sufficiently
varied his experiments, when he asserted that, in order to become converted
into queens, the worms of workers should be 3 days old. It is undoubted
that the operation is equally successful, not only with worms 2 days old,
but even with those that are only a few hours old.

After having made the researches which I have just described, to verify
Mr. Schirach's discovery, I desired to ascertain whether, as this observer
claims, the only means which the bees have of procuring a queen is to give
the common worms a certain kind of food and rear them in larger cells.
You have not forgotten that Mr. de Réaumur had very different ideas upon
this. "The mother," said he, "must lay and does lay eggs from which bees
fit to become mothers must in their turn proceed. She does so and we will
show that the workers know what she is to do. The bees, to which mothers

are so precious, seem to take great interest in the eggs which are to supply them, and consider them as very important: they construct particular cells in which they are to be deposited, &c. When a royal cell is only just begun, it has the shape of a cup, or more precisely of an acorn cup, from which the acorn has dropped, &c, &c."

Mr. de Réaumur did not suspect the possiblity of the conversion of a common worm into a queen, but he conceived that the mother bee laid a particular species of eggs in the royal cells, from which came worms that should be queens in their turn. On the contrary, according to Mr. Schirach, bees always having the possibility of procuring a queen, by rearing worker worms 3 days old in a particular manner, it would be unnecessary for females to have the faculty of laying royal eggs; such prodigality of means did not appear to him consistent with nature's laws: therefore he asserts in proper terms that the mother bee does not lay royal eggs in cells prepared to that end: he considers the royal cells only as common ones, enlarged by the bees at the moment when the included form is destined to become a queen; and he adds that, in any case, the royal cell would be too deep for the belly of the mother to reach its bottom to deposit an egg.

I admit that Mr. de Réaumur does not say anywhere that he had seen the queen lay in the royal cell; however he had no doubt of this, and after all my observations I see that he had guessed correctly. It is quite certain that, at certain times of the year, the bees prepare royal cells, that the queens lay eggs in them, and that from these eggs worms hatch which become queens.

Mr. Schirach's objection concerning the length of the royal cells proves nothing: the queen does not wait till they are finished, to lay in them; she deposits her eggs in them when they are only sketched and have the shape of an acorn cup. This naturalist, dazzled by the brilliancy of his discovery, did not see the whole truth; he was the first to perceive the resource which nature granted to the bees, for repairing the loss of their queen, and too soon persuaded himself that she had provided no other means for the birth of females. His error arose in not observing the bees in sufficiently narrow hives. Had he used hives such as mine he would have found a confirmation of the opinion of Mr. de Réaumur, in every one that he opened in the spring. In that season, which is the season of swarms, hives in good condition are governed by a prolific queen. One finds in such hives royal cells of a different shape from those which the bees build around worker eggs, which they destine to become queens. They are large cells, attached to the comb by a pedicle, and hanging vertically like stalactites; such, in a word, as Mr. de Réaumur has described. The females do not wait, to lay in them, until they are at full size; we have surprised several depositing the egg, when the cell was only as an acorn cup; the workers never lengthen them until the egg has been laid in them; they enlarge them as fast as the worm grows, and close them when it is about to transform into a royal nymph. It is then true that, in spring, the queen deposits, in the royal cells previously prepared, eggs from which insects of her own sort will hatch. Nature has thus provided a twofold means for the multiplication and conservation of the species of bees.

I have the honor, &c.

FIFTH LETTER

Experiments Proving That There Are, Sometimes, in the Hives, Worker
Bees Which Lay Fertile Eggs.

Pregny, August 25, 1791.

Sir, The singular discovery of **Mr. Riem**, concerning the existence of
fertile workers appeared very doubtful to you.[10]

You have suspected that the eggs, ascribed to workers by this naturalist,
were really laid by small queens, which had been mistaken for workers on
account of their small size.   However you did not state decisively that
Mr. Riem was mistaken; and in the letter which you did me the honor of
addressing to me, you invited me to seek, through new experiments, whether
there are truly in the hives worker bees capable of laying fertile eggs.   I
have made those experiments, Sir, with great care; you will judge of the
degree of confidence which they merit.

On the 5th of August 1788, we found eggs and worms of drones in two
of my hives, which had both been deprived of queens for some time.   We
saw there also the first rudiments of several royal cells, appended like stalactites at the edges of the combs.   In those cells were some male eggs.   As
I was perfectly certain that there was no queen of the large size among the
bees of these two hives, it was evident that the eggs that were there, the
number of which increased every day, had been laid, either by queens of
the small size, or by fertile workers.   I had reason to believe that it was
actually common bees that laid them; for we often observed bees of the
latter kind introducing the posterior part of their body into the cells,
assuming the same attitude as the queen when she is about to lay.   But
notwithstanding all our efforts, we had never been able to seize one in this
position to examine her more closely; and we did not wish to assert anything until we had been able to hold in our fingers one of the bees that had
been laying.   We therefore continued our observations with the same
assiduity, hoping that, by some fortunate hazard or in a moment of dexterity, we could secure one of those bees.   For more than a month, all our
endeavors failed.

Burnens then proposed to me to make upon those two hives an operation which required so much courage and patience that I had not dared
mention it to him, although the same plan had occurred to me.   He proposed
to examine, separately, all the bees in these hives, to discover whether
some small queen had not insinuated herself among them, which had
escaped our first researches.   This experiment was very important, for if we
did not find any small queens, we would acquire the demonstrative evidence
that the eggs whose origin we were seeking had been laid by simple workers.

To accomplish with all possible exactness an operation of this nature,
immersing the bees was not sufficient.   You know, Sir, that the contact of
water stiffens their exterior parts, that it alters to a certain point the shape
of their organs; and as the small queens much resemble the workers, the

---

[10] See Contemplations de la Nature New edition, in-4, Part XI, page 265.

slightest alteration in their shape would not have permitted us to distinguish, with sufficient precision, to which species those that were immersed belonged. Therefore, it was necessary, to take each bee, one at a time, in the hives, alive, in spite of their anger, and observe their specific character with the greatest care. This is what Burnens undertook and executed with inconceivable dexterity. He spent 11 days in this operation, and during the entire time scarcely allowed himself any other relaxation than that required for the relief of his eyes. He took in his hands every one of the bees that composed these two hives, examined carefully their proboscis, their posterior legs, their sting; he found none that did not possess the characters of the common bee; that is to say, the little basket on the posterior legs, the long tongue and the straight sting. Having previously prepared glass cases containing combs, he placed each bee into one of them after having examined her: needless to say that he kept them confined; this precaution was indispensable, for the experiment was not yet ended; it was not sufficient to make sure that they were worker bees, it was also necessary to see whether any of them would lay eggs. So, we inspected, for several days, the combs which we had given them, and we shortly noticed newly laid eggs from which drone worms hatched in due time.

Burnens had held between his fingers the bees that produced them, and as he was positive that he had handled only common bees, it was demonstrated that there are, sometimes, in the hives, fertile workers.

After having verified Mr. Riem's discovery by so decisive an experiment, we replaced all the bees that we had examined, into very thin glass hives; these hives which were only an inch-and-a-half thick could contain but a single row of combs; they were thus very favorable for observation. We no longer doubted that, by persisting in watching our bees, we should surprise one of the fertile ones in the act of laying, and seize her. We desired to dissect her, compare the state of her ovaries with those of queens, and take note of the difference. At length, on the 8th of September, we had the good fortune to succeed.

A bee was noticed in a cell, in the position of a laying female; we did not give her time to leave the cell; we promptly opened the hive and seized that bee; she had all the external characteristics of common bees; the only difference we could recognize, and a very slight one, was that her belly was smaller and more slender than those of the other workers. We dissected her and found her ovaries smaller, more fragile, composed of a less number of oviducts than the ovaries of queens; the filaments which contained the eggs were exceedingly fine and exhibited slight swellings at equal distances. We counted 11 eggs of sensible size, some of which appeared ready to be laid. This ovary was double, like that of a queen.

On the 9th of September, we seized another fertile worker, the instant she laid, and dissected her. Her ovary was still less developed than that of the preceding one, we counted only 4 eggs that had reached maturity. Burnens extracted one of these eggs from the oviduct which held it, and succeeded in fixing it by an end on a strip of glass: we may say in passing that this indicates that it is in the oviducts themselves that the eggs are coated with the viscous liquid with which they come to light and not in their passage under the spherical sac, as Swammerdam believed.

During the remainder of this month, we found still in the same hives 10 fertile workers, which we also dissected. We distinguished easily the ovaries in most of those bees; in a few, however, we found no trace of them; the oviducts of the latter were apparently but imperfectly developed, and more skill than we had yet acquired in dissecting was necessary for their discovery.

Fertile workers never lay eggs of common bees; they lay only drone eggs. Mr. Riem had already observed this singular fact, and in this regard, all my observations confirm his own. I shall only add to what he says that fertile workers are not absolutely indifferent in the choice of the cells for depositing their eggs. They always prefer to lay them in large ones, and lay in small cells only when they do not find any of a larger diameter; but they have this in common with queens whose fecundation has been retarded that they also lay eggs in royal cells.

When speaking, in my third letter, of those females that lay only drone eggs, I recorded my surprise that bees bestow such care upon those deposited in royal cells, the assiduity with which they feed the worms which hatch from them, and the sealing under which they enclose them when nearing the term of their growth; but I do not know, Sir, why I forgot to tell you that, after having sealed those cells, the workers braid (guilloche) them and incubate them until the last transformation of the males which they contain. Their treatment of the royal cells in which fertile workers have laid eggs of drones, is very different; they begin, indeed, by bestowing every care upon the eggs and the worms that inhabit them; they close the cells in suitable time; but they never fail to destroy them 3 days after having sealed them.

After having successfully finished these experiments, I had still to discover the cause of the development of the sexual organs of fertile workers. Mr. Reim did not engage in this interesting problem, and at first I feared that I might have no other guide to its solution than my conjectures. However, after long reflection, I perceived, in the connection of the facts of which this letter gives the details, a light to indicate the progress to be followed in this new research.

Since the beautiful discoveries of Mr. Schirach, it is beyond all doubt that the common bees are originally of the female sex; nature has given them the germs of ovaries; but she has permitted their expansion only in the particular case where those bees receive, in their worm form, a special food. So we must examine, especially, whether our fertile workers have received this special food, in the worm state.

All my experiments convinced me that bees capable of laying are born only in hives that have lost their queen. In such case, they prepare a large quantity of royal jelly, to feed the worms destined to replace her. Therefore, if fertile workers are born only in these circumstances, it is evident that they appear only in the hives whose bees prepare royal jelly. It was upon this circumstance, Sir, that I bent all my attention. It induced me to suspect that when bees give the royal treatment to certain worms, they, by accident or by a particular instinct the principle of which I do not know, drop some small particles of royal jelly into the cells next to those containing the worms intended for queens. The worms of workers that have accidentally received small doses of so active an aliment, must be more or less influenced by it: their ovaries must acquire some sort of development; but this development will be imperfect. Why? Because the royal food has been administered only in small doses, and besides, the worms in question having lived in cells of the smaller diameter, their parts could not enlarge beyond the ordinary proportions. The bees born from those worms will therefore have the size and all the exterior characters of simple workers; but they will have in addition the faculty of laying a few eggs, solely from the effect of the small portion of jelly mixed with their other food.

In order to judge of the correctness of this explanation, it was necessary to follow the fertile workers from their birth, to investigate whether the cells in which they are raised are constantly in the vicinity of the royal cells, and whether the pap fed to them is mixed with particles of the royal jelly. Unfortunately this part of the experiment is very difficult to perform. When pure, the royal jelly is recognized by its tartish and pungent taste, but when mixed with some other substance, its savour is imperfectly distinguished. I therefore confined myself to the examination of the location of the cells in which fertile workers are born. As this is important, allow me to describe one of my experiments in detail.

In June 1790, I observed that the bees in one of my thinnest hives had lost their queen for several days, and that they had no means of replacing her, since they had no worker's worms. I gave them a small piece of comb every cell of which contained a worm of this sort. As early as the following day, the bees lengthened several of those cells, to the shape of royal cells, around the worms which they intended for queens. They also bestowed some care upon the worms in the adjoining cells. Four days afterwards, all the royal cells were sealed, and with much gratification we counted 19 small cells which had also been perfected and were sealed with a flat capping. In these were the worms which had not received the royal treatment; but as they had grown in the vicinity of the worms destined for replacing the queen, it was very interesting for me to observe what would become of them. It was necessary to watch the moment of their last transformation. In order not to miss it, I removed those 19 cells and placed them into a grated box which was introduced among the bees; I also removed the royal cells; for it was very important that the queens that were to come should not disturb or complicate the results of my experiment. Another precaution was here required: it was to be feared that the bees, being deprived of the fruit of their labor, and the object of their hope, should become discouraged: therefore I supplied them with another piece of comb containing worker brood, expecting to remove this new brood, without mercy, when the time came. This plan succeeded marvelously; the bees, while bestowing their care upon these latter worms, forgot those which I had removed.

When the time arrived of the last transformation of my 19 cells, I caused the grated box in which they were enclosed to be examined each day, several times, and at length found six bees exactly similar to common bees. The worms in the remaining 13 cells perished without metamorphosis.

I then removed from my hive the last piece of brood which had been placed there to prevent the discouragement of the workers; I put aside the queens born from the royal cells, and after having painted the thorax of my six bees red, after having amputated their right antenna, I placed them all 6 in the hive, where they were well received.

You readily conceive my object, Sir, in this course of operations. I knew that there was no queen of either large or small size among my bees: if, then, in the continuation of the observation, I should find newly laid eggs in the combs, how very likely that they had been laid by one or the other of my 6 bees. But to attain absolute certainty, it was necessary to take them in the act of laying, and some ineffaceable mark was required to distinguish them.

This arrangement was fully successful. Indeed we soon perceived eggs in the hive; their number increased daily; the worms that hatched from them were all of the drones sort; but a long interval elapsed before we could catch the bees that laid them. At length, by dint of assiduity and perseverance, we perceived one introducing her posterior part into a cell; we opened the hive and caught this bee; we saw the egg that she had deposited; and in examining her we recognized readily, by the remnant of red upon her thorax and the privation of the right antenna, that she was one of the 6 reared under the vermicular state in the vicinity of the royal cells.

I no longer doubted the correctness of my conjecture; I do not know, however, Sir, whether this demonstration will appear as rigorous to you as it does to myself; but here is my reasoning: If it is certain that the fertile workers are always born in the vicinity of royal cells, it is no less certain that this vicinity is, in itself, an indifferent circumstance; for the size and shape of those cells can have no effect upon the worms in the surrounding cells; there must be something more to this: We know that the bees bring to the royal cells a particular food; we also know that the influence of this pap is very powerful upon the ovaries; that it alone can develop this germ; we must necessarily suppose that the worms placed in the adjacent cells have had a portion of this food. This is what they gain by vicinity to the royal cells; the numerous bees going to the latter pass over them, stop and drop some portion of the jelly destined for the royal worms. I believe that this reasoning is consistent with the principles of sound logic.

I so often repeated the experiment just described, and I have weighed all the circumstances with so much care, that I succeed in producing fertile workers in my hives, whenever I please. The method is simple. I remove the queen from a hive; the bees undertake to replace her at once, by enlarging several cells containing the brood of workers, and giving royal jelly to the worms in them; they also let fall small doses of this pap upon the worms located in the adjacent cells, and this food causes a certain development in their ovaries. Fertile workers are always produced in hives where the bees labor to replace their queen; but it is very rare to find them, because they are attacked and destroyed by the young queens reared in the royal cells. In order to save them, we must remove their enemies; we must take away the royal cells before the worms located in them have undergone their last transformation. Then the fertile workers, finding no rivals in the hive at the time of their birth, will be well received there, and if we take the trouble to mark them with some distinctive sign, we will see them, a few days afterwards, laying male eggs. Thus, the whole secret of the process consists in removing the royal cells at the proper time; that is, as soon as they are sealed and before the young queens have left them.[11]

I shall add but a word to this long letter. There is nothing very surprising in the birth of fertile workers, when one has meditated upon the consequences of Schirach's beautiful discovery. But why do these bees lay eggs of males only? I conceive that they lay a small number because their ovaries have had but an imperfect development; but I cannot distinguish why all their eggs are of the male sort. I do not understand any better of what use they are in the hives; and I have not hitherto made any experiments on the mode of their fecundation.

Accept, Sir, the assurance of my respect, &c.

SIXTH LETTER

On the Combats of Queens; on the Massacre of Males and on what Happens in a Hive When a Strange Queen Is Substituted for the Natural One.

Pregny, August 25, 1791.

Sir, Mr. de Réaumur had not witnessed everything relative to these industrious insects, when he composed his history of bees. Several observers, and particularly those of Lusatia, discovered a number of important facts that had escaped him; and I, in my turn, made divers observations which he did not foresee; however, and it is a very remarkable thing, not only all that he expressly declares he saw has been verified by succeeding naturalists, but even all his conjectures have been found just; the German observers, Messrs. Schirach, Hattorf, Riem, sometimes contradict him in their memoirs; but I can assure you that, when they combat the experiments of Mr. de Réaumur, it is they who are almost always mistaken; of which I can cite several examples. The one which I will mention to-day will give me the occasion of detailing some interesting facts.

Mr. de Réaumur observed that when a supernumerary queen is either born or supplied to a hive, one of the two soon perishes: he had not actually witnessed the combat in which she falls, but he conjectured that there is a mutual attack and that the empire remains to the stronger or the more fortunate. On the other hand, Schirach, and after him Riem, hold that the worker bees assail the stranger queens and kill them with their stings. I do not comprehend by what hazard they were able to make this observation; for, as they used only thick hives, containing several rows of parallel combs, they could at most only perceive the commencement of hostilities: bees move fast when they fight; they run in every direction, glide between the combs, thus concealing their movements from the observer. For my part, Sir,

[11] I have often seen queen-bees, at the moment of their birth, begin by attacking the royal cells and afterwards the common cells adjoining. When I first observed this fact, I had not yet observed fertile workers, and I could not understand the motive of the fury of the queens against these common cells; but now I conceive that they distinguish the sort of bees enclosed in them, and that they must have against them the same instinct of jealousy, or the same feeling of aversion, as against the nymphs of queens proper.

though using the most favorable hives, I have never seen any combat between
the queens and the workers; but often between the queens themselves.

I had one hive in particular containing at the same time 5 or 6 royal
cells, each inclosing a nymph; the oldest of them first accomplished her
transformation.   Scarcely ten minutes from the time of her leaving her
cradle, she visited the other closed royal cells; she threw herself with fury
upon the first: by dint of labor she succeeded in opening the tip, we saw
her tearing the silk of the cocoon with her teeth; but probably her efforts
did not succeed to her satisfaction, for she abandoned this end of the royal
cell and began at the other extremity, in which she managed to make a
larger aperture; when it was large enough she turned to introduce her belly
into it; she made several motions until she succeeded in striking her rival
with a deadly sting.   Then she quitted the cell, and the bees which had been
spectators of her labor, enlarged the breach that she had made and drew
out the body of a dead queen scarcely out of its envelope of a nymph.

Meanwhile, the victorious young queen attacked another royal cell and
made in it also a large opening, but she did attempt to introduce her
extremity into it; this second cell did not contain an already developed
queen, ready to emerge from her shell; it contained but a royal nymph: it is
therefore apparent that, under this shape, the nymphs of queens inspire their
rivals with less furore; but they do not escape death any better, for whenever a royal cell has been opened before its time, the bees extract its contents,
under whatever form, worm, nymph or queen; so after the victorious queen
left this second cell, the workers enlarged the opening which she had
effected and extracted the enclosed nymph; lastly the young queen attacked
a third cell, but did not succeed in opening it: she labored languidly appearing fatigued by her first efforts.   At that time we needed queens for some
particular experiment, so we resolved to carry away the other royal cells
which had not yet been attacked, to shelter them from her anger.

We next wished to see what would happen if two queens emerged from
their cells at the same time and in what manner one of them would perish.
We made upon this subject an observation which I find in my journal in
date of May 15, 1790.

Two queens emerged from their cells, on that day, almost at the same
moment, in one of our thin hives.   As soon as they perceived each other
they rushed upon one another, with the appearance of great anger, and placed
themselves in such position that the antennæ of each were caught in the teeth
of her rival; their heads, corslets and bellies were opposed to each other, they
had but to bend the posterior extremity of their bodies to pierce one another
with their stings and both die in the combat.   But it appears that nature
has not ordained that both combatants perish in the duel, but rather that
when they find themselves in the position just described (that is belly to
belly), they recede at once with the greatest precipitation.   Thus, when the
two rivals felt that their posterior parts were about to meet, they disengaged
themselves and each ran away.   You will observe, Sir, that I repeated this
observation very often; it leaves no doubt, and it appears that, in such a
case, one may penetrate the intention of nature.

There must be but one queen in a hive; therefore it is necessary, if by
chance a second one is born or appears, that one of the two should be put to

death. This could not be permitted to the workers because, in a republic composed of so many individuals, a simultaneous consent cannot be supposed to exist, it would frequently happen that a group of bees would pounce upon one of the females, while a second group would massacre the other, and the hive would be deprived of queen. Therefore it is necessary that the queens themselves be entrusted with the destruction of their rivals. But as, in these combats, nature demands only one victim, she has wisely provided that, at the moment when, from their position, both combatants might lose their lives, both should be so greatly alarmed, that they think only of flight, without using their stings.

I know that we run risk of erring, when minutely seeking the final causes of the most trifling facts; but in this, the aim and the means appeared so clear that I have ventured to advance this conjecture. You will judge better than I, Sir, whether it is well founded; let me return to my digression.

A few minutes after our two queens separated, their fear ceased, and they again seeked each other; soon they noticed one another and we saw them rush together: they again seized each other as before, and placed themselves in the same position: the result was the same; as soon as their bellies met, they disengaged themselves and fled. During all this time the workers were much agitated and the tumult appeared to increase when the adversaries separated; at two different times, we saw them stop the queens in their flight, seize their legs and hold them prisoners for more than a minute. Lastly, in a third attack, the more rabid or stronger of the queens darted upon her rival when the latter did not see her; she seized her with her teeth at the base of the wing; then rose above her and brought the extremity of her belly upon the last rings of her enemy, which she readily pierced with her sting; quitting hold of the wing which she held, she withdrew her sting; the vanquished queen fell, dragged herself languidly, quickly lost her strength and soon expired. This observation proves that virgin queens engage in single combats. We next wished to discover whether fertile queens or mothers entertained against each other the same animosity.

On the 22d of July, we selected, for this observation, a thin hive whose queen was very fertile, and as we were curious to learn whether she would destroy the royal cells, as virgin queens do, we placed 3 of these closed cells in the center of her comb. As soon as she perceived them, she rushed upon the group which they formed, pierced them at the base, and did not leave them until the nymphs in them were exposed. The workers which, hitherto, had been spectators of this destruction, now came to remove the nymphs, they avidly took the pap which remained at the bottom of the cells, and sucked also the fluid from the abdomen of the nymphs, and finally destroyed the cells from which they had been drawn.

We next introduced into this hive a very prolific queen, whose corslet we had painted to distinguish her from the reigning queen: a circle of bees quickly formed around this stranger, but their intention was not to welcome or caress her, for they insensibly so accumulated around her, and surrounded her so closely, that in a minute she lost her liberty and found herself a prisoner. It is a remarkable circumstance here, that, at the same time, other workers collected around the reigning queen and restrained all her motions: we saw the instant when she was about to be confined like the stranger. It would seem that the bees foresaw the combat in which the two queens were about to engage, and were impatient to behold the issue of it; for they retained them prisoners only when they appeared to withdraw from each other, and if one of the two, less restrained in her motions seemed desirous of approaching her rival, all the bees forming those clusters gave way to allow them full liberty for the attack; but returned and enclosed them again if the queens appeared disposed to run.

We have very often witnessed this fact: but it presents so new and extraordinary a trait in the policy of bees, that it must be seen again a thousand times to dare assert it positively. I would recommend, Sir, that the naturalists attentively watch the combats of queens and particularly the role played by the workers. Do they seek to accelerate the combat? Do they excite the fury of the combatants by some secret means? How is it that, although accustomed to bestow care upon their own queen, there are circumstances in which they stop her when she prepares to avoid an impending danger?

A long series of observations would be necessary to solve these problems. It is a vast field for experiments, the result of which would be infinitely curious. Pardon my frequent digressions; this subject is deeply philosophical but your genius would be required, Sir, to handle and present it: I will proceed with the description of the combat of our queens.

The cluster of bees that surrounded the reigning queen having permitted her to move slightly, she appeared to advance towards that part of the comb where her rival stood; all the bees then receded before her; gradually the multitude of workers that separated the two adversaries dispersed; until only two remained, who also departed and allowed the two queens to see one another: at that instant the reigning queen rushed upon the stranger, seized her with her teeth at the bast of the wings, and succeeded in fixing her against the comb without any possibility of resistance or motion; next she curved her belly and pierced with a deadly stroke this unhappy victim of our curiosity.

Lastly, to exhaust every combination, we still had to discover whether there would be a combat between two queens, one of which would be fertile and the other virgin, and what would be the circumstances and the issue.

We had a glass hive, whose queen was a virgin 24 days old; we introduced into it a very prolific queen, putting her on the opposite side of the comb, that we might have time to see how the workers would receive her: she was soon surrounded with bees who confined her. However, she was confined but a moment; as she was pressed with the necessity of laying, she dropped her eggs and we could not see what became of them; the bees certainly did not place them in the cells, for on inspection we found none. The group surrounding this queen having dispersed a little, she advanced towards the edge of the comb and soon found herself very near the virgin queen. At first sight, they rushed on one another; the virgin queen got on the back of her rival, and gave her several stings in the belly, which struck only the scaly part and did her no harm; and the combatants parted: a few minutes after they returned to the charge; this time the fecundated queen mounted on the back of her rival, but she vainly sought to pierce her, the sting did not enter the flesh; the virgin queen disengaged herself and fled; she succeeded yet to escape from another attack, in which the fertile queen had the advantage of position. These two rivals appeared of equal strength, and it was difficult to foresee to which side victory would incline, until at last, by a successful hazard, the virgin mortally wounded the stranger, and she expired at the moment.

The stroke had penetrated so deeply that she was at first unable to withdraw her sting and was drawn down by the fall of her enemy. We saw her make many efforts to disengage her spear: she succeeded only by turning on the extremity of her belly as on a pivot. It is probable that the barbs of the sting were bent by this motion, and lying spirally around the stem, thus came out of the wound that they had made.

I believe, Sir, that these observations will no longer leave you any doubts upon the conjecture of our celebrated Réaumur. It is certain that if several queens are introduced into a hive, one alone will preserve the empire, the others will perish from her attacks, but the workers will at no time attempt to use their stings against the foreign queen. I conceive what has misled Messrs. Schirach and Riem; but to explain it, I must relate, at considerable length, a new trait in the policy of bees.

In the natural state of hives, several queens may be found, born in royal cells constructed by the bees; they will remain there until a swarm has formed, or until a combat between those queens decides to which the throne shall appertain; but excepting this case, there never can be supernumary queens, and if an observer wishes to introduce one, he can accomplish it only by force, that is, by opening the hive. In a word, in the natural state, a foreign queen can never insinuate herself there, for the following reasons.

Bees place and preserve a sufficient guard, night and day, at the entrance of their habitation: those vigilant sentinels examine all that present themselves, and as if distrusting their eyes, they touch, with their flexible antennæ, every individual endeavoring to penetrate the hive, and the various substances put within their reach, which, to be said in passing, leaves but little doubt of the antennæ being the organ of feeling. If a stranger queen appears, the guards seize her on the instant; to prevent her from entering, they lay hold of her legs or her wings with their teeth, and crowd so closely around her that she cannot move; gradually other bees come from the interior of the hive and join this cluster, making it still more compact; all their heads are turned towards the center where the queen is enclosed, and they cling with so much eagerness, that the ball formed by them may be taken up and carried about a few moments without their perceiving it; it is utterly impossible that a foreign queen, so closely enveloped and confined, be able to penetrate in the hive. If the bees retain her too long imprisoned, she perishes, her death probably caused by hunger, or deprivation of air: it is very certain at least that she is not stung: in only one single instance did we see the stings of the bees turned towards a queen thus imprisoned, and it was through our fault; moved by her situation, we endeavored to remove her from the center of the ball that surrounded her; the bees became enraged at once, darted their stings and a few strokes killed her. It is so certain that those stings were not intended for her that several workers were themselves killed; and it was certainly not their intention to kill one

another. Had we not interfered, they would have been content with confining the queen, and would not have massacred her.

To return to Mr. Reim, it was in a similar circumstance that he saw the
workers eagerly pursuing a queen; he thought that they designed to pierce
her with their stings, and concluded that the common bees were entrusted
with the destruction of supernumerary queens. You have quoted his observation in the Contemplation de la Nature, part XI, chap. 27, note 7, but you
see, Sir, from the details which I have just given, that he was mistaken; he
did not know of the attention with which the bees watch what happens at
the entrance of their hives, and he was entirely ignorant of the means which
they take to prevent the entrance of supernumerary queens.

After having ascertained that in no case do the workers kill supernumerary queens with their stings, we were curious to learn how a strange
queen would be received in a hive deprived of the reigning one; to elucidate
this point, we made a multitude of experiments the details of which would
too much lengthen this letter; I shall only relate the principal results.

When we remove the queen from a hive, the bees do not perceive it at
first; they do not interrupt their labors, they care for their young; they
do all the ordinary operations, with the same tranquillity; but after a few
hours, they become agitated; all appears in tumult in their hive; a singular
hum is heard; they leave their young, run over the surface of the combs
with impetuosity and appear in delirium; they evidently discover that the
queen is no longer among them. But how do they perceive it? How do the
bees on the surface of one comb know that the queen is not on the next
comb?

While speaking of another trait in the history of our bees, you have
yourself, Sir, proposed these same questions; I am assuredly not yet in position to answer them, but I have collected a few facts which may facilitate
the discovery of this mystery by the naturalists.

I do not doubt that this agitation arises from the knowledge they have
of the loss of their queen; for as soon as she is returned to them, calm is
restored instantly among them, and what is very singular is that they recognize her; this expression, Sir, must be accepted strictly. The substitution of
another queen does not produce the same effect, if she is introduced in the
hive within the first 12 hours after the removal of the reigning queen. In
such case, the agitation continues, and the bees treat the stranger just as
they do when the presence of their own queen leaves nothing for them to
desire; they seize her, envelope her all around, and keep her a long time
captive in an impenetrable cluster; usually she dies, either from hunger or
deprivation af air.

When 18 hours elapse before a strange queen is substituted for the
reigning queen removed, she is at first treated in the same manner, but the
bees that surround her are sooner weary; the ball which they form around
her becomes less compact; gradually they disperse and the queen is at last
liberated; we see her walk with weak and languishing steps: sometimes she
dies within a few minutes. We have seen queens escape in good health from
an imprisonment of 17 hours, and end with reigning in the hives where they
had been so ill-received at first.

But if we wait 24 or 30 hours, to substitute a strange queen for the removed queen, she will be well received and will reign from the moment of her introduction in the hive.[12]

An absence of 24 or 30 hours is thus sufficient to cause the bees to forget their first queen. I abstain from conjectures.

This letter being filled only with descriptions of combats and lugubrious scenes: I should give you, in closing, the account of some more pleasing and interesting fact relative to their industry. However, to avoid returning to duels and massacres, I shall here subjoin my observation upon the carnage of the males.

You remember, Sir, that all the observers of bees agree in saying that,

[12] I speak here of the good reception given after an interregnum of 24 hours, by the bees to a strange queen substituted for their natural queen; but as this word reception is rather vague, it is proper to enter into some details to determine the sense which I give it.—On the 15th of August of this year, I introduced into one of my glass hives a fertile queen 11 months old. The bees had been deprived of queen for 24 hours, and in order to repair their loss, had already commenced the construction of 12 royal cells of the kind described in one of the preceding letters.—At the time when I placed this strange female upon the comb, the bees near her touched her with their antennæ, passed their trunks over all parts of her body, and gave her honey; then they made way for others that treated her in exactly the same way. All those bees vibrated their wings at the same time and ranged in a circle around their sovereign. Hence resulted a sort of agitation which gradually communicated to the workers situated on the same side of the comb, and induced them to come and see, in their turn, what was happening. They soon arrived, broke through the circle formed by the first, touched the queen with their atennæ, gave her some honey, and after this little ceremony they retired behind the others and enlarged the circle. They vibrated their wings, fidgeted without disorder, without tumult, as if experiencing some very agreeable sensation.—The queen had not yet left the spot where I had put her, but after a quarter-hour she began to walk. The bees, far from opposing her motion, opened the circle in the direction which she took, followed her, and stood in a line about her. She was oppressed with the need of laying and dropped her eggs. Lastly, after an abode of 4 hours, she began to deposit male eggs in the large cells that she met.

While these events passed on the surface of the comb where I had placed the queen, all was perfectly quiet on the opposite side: it appeared as if the workers there were unconscious of the arrival of a queen in their hive; they worked with great activity upon the royal cells as if ignorant that they no longer needed them; they cared for the royal worms, brought jelly to them, &c. But, at length, the new queen passed to their side; she was received by them with the same eagerness that she had experienced from their companions on the first side of the comb; they stood in line, gave her honey, touched her with their antennæ; and what proves better that they treated her as a mother was their immediate desisting from work at the royal cells; they removed the royal worms and ate the pap which they had accumulated around them. From this moment the queen was recognized by all her people, and behaved in her new habitation as she would have done in her native hive.

These details appear to give a fairly correct idea of the manner in which the bees welcome a strange queen, when they have had time to forget their own. They treat her exactly as if she was their natural queen, except that, in the first instant there may be more warmth, or if I dare so express, more demonstrations. I am conscious of the impropriety of these expressions, but Mr. de Réaumur has in some manner consecrated them: he does not hesitate to say that the bees give their queen care, respect and homage, and from his example, these same expressions have escaped most authors who have spoken about bees.

at a certain period of the year, the workers expel and kill the drones. Mr. de Réaumur speaks of these executions as a horrible slaughter, indeed, he does not assert expressly that he has witnessed it; but what we have seen is so consistent with his statement, that there is no doubt of his having seen the details of this massacre.

It is usually in the months of July and August that the bees get rid of the drones. Then we see them chase them and pursue them to the inner parts of the hives, where they collect in numbers; and as at the same time we find a great many drone bodies on the ground in front of the hives, it does not appear doubtful that the workers, after having expelled them, kill them with their stings. However, we do not see the sting used upon them, on the surface of the combs; they are content with pursuing them and driving them away. You say this yourself, Sir, in the new notes which you added to the Contemplation de la Nature (Note 5, Chapter XXVI, part XI), and you seem disposed to think that the drones, reduced to retire in a corner of the hive, perish there from hunger. This conjecture is very probable. Still it might be possible that the carnage took place in the bottom of the hive, and had been unobserved, because that part is dark and escapes the observer's eye.

To appreciate the justice of this suspicion, we conceived the idea of having the stand which supports the hive made of glass, and placing ourselves under it, to see what passed on the scene. We constructed a glazed table, upon which we placed 6 hives, stocked with swarms of the previous year, and lying under it, we sought to discover how the drones lost their lives. This invention succeeded admirably. On the 4th of July, 1787, we saw the workers massacre the drones, in 6 swarms, at the same hour and with the same peculiarities. The glazed table was covered with bees that appeared full of animation, rushing upon the drones as they came to the bottom of the hive; they seized them by the antennæ, by the legs, or the wings; and after having dragged them about, or so to speak, quartered them, they pierced them with their stings, directed between the rings of the belly; the moment when this formidable weapon reached them was always that of their death; they stretched their wings and expired. However, as if the workers had not considered them as dead as they appeared to us, they would again strike them, so deeply that they had much trouble in withdrawing their stings, and had to turn round upon themselves, to succeed in withdrawing them.

On the next day, we resumed the same position, to observe these same hives, and witnessed new scenes of carnage. During 3 hours, we saw our furious bees destroy the males. They had massacred all their own on the previous evening; but on that day they attacked the drones driven from the neighboring hives that took refuge in their home. We saw them also tear from the cells a few remaining larvæ of males; they greedily sucked all the fluid from the abdomen, and then carried them out. The following days no drones appeared in those hives.

These two observations seem to be decisive, Sir; it is incontestable that nature has charged the workers with the killing of the males at certain times of the year. But by what means does she excite their fury against them? This also is one of those questions which I will not attempt to answer. However, I have made an observation which may lead some day to the solution of the problem. The bees never kill the males in the hives deprived of queens; on the contrary they find there a safe asylum, while a horrible massacre prevails in other places; they are tolerated and fed, and a great many are seen, even in January. They are also preserved in the hives which, without a queen properly so called, have among them some individuals of that sort of bees that lay eggs of males, and in those whose *half fertile* queens, if I may so express it, engender only drones. Therefore, the massacre takes place only in the hives whose queens are completely fertile, and it never begins until the season of swarms is past.

I have the honor of being &c.

SEVENTH LETTER.

Continuation of the Experiments on the Reception of a Stranger Queen:
Observations of Mr. de Réaumur Upon This Subject.

Pregny, August 30, 1791.

Sir, I have often told you how much I admired Mr. de Réaumur's memoirs upon bees. I am glad to repeat that, if I have made any progress in the art of observing, I am indebted for it to the profound study of the works of this excellent naturalist. In general his authority is so powerful that I can hardly trust my own experiments when the results are different from those obtained by him. So, when I find myself in opposition to the historian of bees, I repeat my experiences, vary the processes, examine with the utmost caution all the circumstances that might mislead me, and never interrupt my labors until I have acquired the moral certainty of not being mistaken. With the help of these precautions, I have recognized the correctness of Mr. de Réaumur's eyes, and I have a thousand times seen, that if certain experiments seemed to combat them, it was from incorrect execution. Yet, I must except some cases, in which my results have been constantly different from his. Those exposed in my previous letter, on the manner in which the bees receive a strange queen in place of their accustomed one, are of that number.

After having removed the queen of a hive, if I at once substituted a strange one, the usurper was ill-received, they surrounded her, balled her, and often ended by smothering her. I could succeed only, in making them adopt a new queen, by waiting 20 to 24 hours, to introduce her. At the end of that time, they appeared to have forgotten their own queen, and received with respect any female put in her place. Mr. de Réaumur says, on the contrary, that if we remove the queen from the bees and give them another at once, she will be well received. To prove this, he gives the details of an experiment, that one should read in his own work (Quarto edition, tome V, page 258); I will give only an extract from it: he induced four or five hundred bees to leave their hive and enter a glass box, in which he had fixed a small piece of comb towards the top; at first they were much agitated; to quiet them he tried to offer them a new queen. From that time, the tumult ceased, and the foreign queen was received with due respect.

I do not contest the result of this experiment, but in my opinion it does not warrant the conclusion drawn by Mr. de Réaumur: the apparatus employed removed the bees too far from their natural situation, to enable him to judge of their instinct and dispositions. In other circumstances, he has himself seen that bees reduced to small numbers lose their industry, their activity, and imperfectly continue their ordinary labors. Thus their instinct is modified by each operation that reduces them to too small a number. To render such an experiment truly conclusive, it should then be made in a populous hive, removing from that hive her native queen, and immediately substituting a stranger; I am persuaded that, in such a case, Mr. de Réaumur would have seen the bees imprison the queen, ball her for 15 or 18 hours at least, and often end by suffocating her. He would not have witnessed a favorable reception of a strange queen, until he had waited 24 hours before introducing her in the hive, after the removal of the native queen. No variation took place in the result of my experiments in this regard: their number and the attention with which they were made make me presume that they merit your confidence.

In another passage of the Memoir already quoted (page 267) Mr. de Réaumur affirms that *the bees having a queen with which they are pleased are nevertheless disposed to give the best possible reception to a strange female seeking refuge among them*. In my previous letter, I have related to you, Sir, my experiments on this fact; their success was very different from that of Mr. de Réaumur. I have proved that the workers never use their stings against any queen, but this is far from a welcome to a stranger queen; they retain her within their ranks, they press her in their ranks and appear to give her freedom only when she prepares to combat the reigning queen. But this observation can be made only in our thinnest hives. Those of Mr. de Réaumur had at least 2 parallel combs; and through this disposition he could not see some very important circumstances which influence the conduct of the workers when they are given several females. He mistook for caresses the circles which they form at first around a strange queen; and if the queen advanced a little between the combs, it was impossible for him to see that those rings, which were always contracting, ended in the restraint of the female enclosed within them. Had he used thinner hives, he would have seen that what he supposed to be the signs of a welcome was but the prelude of a real imprisonment.

I am reluctant to say that Mr. de Réaumur was mistaken; but I cannot admit with him that in certain occasions the bees tolerate in their hives a plurality of females. The experiment upon which he bases this assertion cannot be considered decisive. In the month of December he introduced a strange queen in a glass hive placed in his cabinet, and confined her there. The bees could carry nothing out, the stranger was well received; her presence awakened the workers from their torpidness, into which they did not relapse. She excited no carnage, the number of dead bees on the bottom board did not sensibly increase, and no dead queens were found. In order to draw from this observation any consequence favorable to the plurality of queens, it was necessary to ascertain whether the hive still had its native queen, when the new queen was introduced; the author neglected this precaution; it is very probable that the hive which he mentions had lost its queen, since the bees were languid, and the presence of a stranger restored their activity.

I hope, Sir, that you will pardon this slight criticism. Far from seeking faults in the works of our celebrated Réaumur, I had the greatest pleasure when my observations agreed with his, and more especially when my experiments justified his conjectures. But it was necessary to point out the cases in which the imperfection of his hives led him into error and to explain from what reasons, I did not see certain facts in the same manner that he did. I desire especially to merit your confidence and I am aware that I need the greatest efforts when I must combat the historian of the bees. I confide in your judgment, Sir, and ask you to accept the assurance of my respect, &c.

EIGHTH LETTER

Is the Queen Bee Oviparous? Researches Upon the Manner in Which the Worms of the Bees Spin Their Cocoons. What Is the Influence of the Size of the Cells Upon the Bees That Hatch in Them?

Pregny, September 4, 1791.

Sir, I shall gather together in this letter several isolated observations, relative to divers points of the history of bees in which you desired me to engage. You desired me to seek whether the queen be really oviparous. Mr. de Réaumur has not decided this question, he even says that he never saw a worm hatch; he only affirms that worms are found in cells where eggs were deposited three days previously. You understand, sir, that in order to seize the moment when the worm emerges from the egg, we must not confine ourselves to observations within the hive; for the continual motion of the bees does not permit us to see precisely what passes at the bottom of the cells. The eggs must be taken out, placed upon a strip of glass under the microscope, and every change which they undergo attentively watched.

There is still one other precaution to take: as a certain degree of heat is necessary for them to hatch, if the eggs were too soon deprived of it, they would wither and perish. The only method to succeed in seeing the worm come out, consists therefore in watching the queen while she lays, marking the eggs which she has just deposited so as to recognize them, and remove them from the hive to place them upon a strip of glass, only an hour or two before the three days elapse. Thus the worms will certainly hatch, for they will have enjoyed the necessary heat as long as possible. Such is the course which I followed. Here is the result.

In the month of August we removed a few cells, containing eggs laid three days previously; we cut down the walls of all those cells and placed upon a glass slide the pyramidal bottom on which the eggs were fixed. Slight motions of curving and of straightening were soon perceptible in one of the eggs; at first the lens did not show us any external organization on the surface of the egg; the worm was entirely concealed by its pellicle: we placed it then upon the focus of a very powerful lens; but while we were preparing this apparatus, the worm burst the imprisoning membrane, and cast off a part of its envelope; we saw it torn and crumpled on some parts of its body and more particularly upon its last rings; the worm, by lively action, curved and straightened itself alternately and occupied 20 minutes in concluding the casting off of its skin; its lively exertions ceased then, it lay down, bent its body in a curve and seemed to take a needed rest. This worm proceeded from an egg laid in a worker cell and would have become a worker.

We next directed our attention upon the moment when a male worm was to hatch. We exposed it to the sun on a glass slide, and with the help of a good lens we discovered 9 rings of the worm under the transparent pellicle of the egg; this membrane was still entire; the worm was completely motionless: we distinguished the two longitudinal lines of the tracheæ, and many of their ramifications. We did not lose sight of the egg a single instant and this time noticed the first motions of the worm. The large end curved and straightened alternately and almost touched the base upon which its point was fixed. These efforts burst the membrane first at the upper part, towards the head, then on the back, and afterwards in all the parts successively. The crumpled pellicle remained in lumps on different parts of the body, then fell off. So it is positive that the queen is oviparous.

Some observers state that the workers care for the eggs laid by the queen before the worms hatch, and it is true that, at any time that we examine the hive, we always see workers with their head and thorax inserted in the cells containing eggs and remaining motionless in that position for several minutes. It is impossible to see what they do, because their body conceals the interior of the cell. But it is easy to ascertain that, when they assume this attitude, they are not caring for the eggs. If we enclose eggs in a grated box at the moment when the queen has laid them, and deposit them in a strong hive, so they may have the necessary degree of heat, they hatch at the usual time, just as if they had been left in the cells. So they have no need of particular care from the bees to hatch them.

I have reason to believe that, when the workers enter the cells and remain there 15 or 20 minutes, it is only to repose from their flight and their labors. My observations on this subject are very definite. You know, Sir, that bees sometimes construct cells of irregular shape against the panes of the hive; these cells, glazed on one side, are very convenient to the observer, since all that passes within them is exposed. I have often seen bees enter such cells when nothing could attract them there; they were finished cells and yet contained neither eggs nor honey. Therefore the workers came thither only to enjoy some instants of rest. Indeed, they would remain for 15 or 20 minutes in them, so motionless, that one might have thought them dead, had not the dilation of their rings showed that they were breathing. This need of repose is not special with the workers, the queens also, sometimes, enter the big male cells and remain long motionless. This attitude prevents the bees from paying full homage to them; yet, even in these circumstances, the workers do not fail to circle around them and to brush the part of their belly which remains uncovered.

The drones do not enter the cells, when they wish to rest, but they cluster against one another on the combs, and sometimes remain in this position for 18 or 20 hours, without the slightest motion.

As it is important, in several experiments, to know exactly the length of time that the three sorts of worms exist, before assuming their ultimate shape, I shall here subjoin my particular observations on this subject.

Worm of worker. Three days in the egg state, five days in the worm state, at the end of which time the bees close its cell with a wax covering; the worm then begins to spin its silk cocoon, in which operation 36 hours are consumed. Three days later, it metamorphoses into a nymph and spends seven days and a half in this form; so it reaches its last state, that of a bee, on the 20th day of its life, counting from the moment the egg was laid.

The royal worm also passes 3 days in the egg, and 5 as a worm: after these 8 days, the bees close its cell and it begins at once to spin its cocoon, which operation occupies 24 hours. It remains in complete repose during the 10th and 11th day and even during 16 hours of the 12th. Then it transforms into a nymph and spends 4 days and a third in this shape. Thus it is in the 16th day of its life that it reaches the state of perfect queen.

The male worm. Three days in the egg, six and a half as worm: it changes into a winged insect only the 24th day after the laying of the egg.

Although the worms of bees are apod, they are not condemned to absolute immobility in their cells: they advance in a spiral. This motion, so slow during the first 3 days that it can hardly be perceived, afterwards becomes more evident: I have seen them perform two complete revolutions in an hour and three quarters. When the end of their metamorphosis approaches, they are only two lines from the orifice of the cell. The position which they assume is always the same, they are bent in an arc. It follows that, in the horizontal cells, such as those of workers or of drones, the larvæ are perpendicular to the horizon; on the contrary, in the royal cells, the worms are placed horizontally. It might be thought that the difference of position has great influence on the increment of the various larvæ, yet it has none. By reversing combs containing common cells of brood, I brought the worms to a horizontal position, but they did not suffer in their development. I have also turned the royal cells so that their worms were placed vertically, and their growth was neither less speedy nor less perfect.

I have paid a great deal of attention to the manner in which the worms spin the silk of their cocoons, and I witnessed in this matter new and interesting peculiarities. The worms of workers and of males spin complete cocoons in their cells, that is, closed at both ends and surrounding the whole body; the royal worms, on the other hand, spin only incomplete cocoons, that is, they are open at the posterior part and envelope only the head, thorax and first ring of the abdomen. The discovery of this difference in the shape of the cocoon, which may at first seem too minute, gave me extreme pleasure, as it evidently shows the admirable art with which nature connects the various traits of the industry of bees.

You remember, Sir, the proofs which I have given you of the mutual aversion of queens, of their combats, and of the animosity with which they seek to destroy one another. When there are several royal nymphs in a hive, the first one transformed into a queen attacks the others and pierces them with her sting. But she could not succeed in this, if they were enveloped in a complete cocoon. Why? Because the silk that the worms weave is so strong that the cocoon is of a close tissue, and the sting could not penetrate through it; or if it did, the queen could not withdraw it, because the barbs would be retained by the meshes of the cocoon, and she would thus perish, a victim of her own fury. Thus, that she may destroy her rivals, it is necessary that their posterior parts be uncovered; the royal nymphs must therefore weave incomplete cocoons; take note, please, that it is the last rings which must remain uncovered, for they are the only part which the sting can penetrate; the head and the thorax are covered with scaly plates which it cannot pierce.

Hitherto, Sir, observers have called for our admiration of nature, in her care for the multiplication and preservation of the species, but in the facts which I relate, we must admire also her precautions in exposing certain individuals to a mortal danger.

The details on which I have just entered clearly indicate the final cause of the opening which the royal worms leave in their cocoons, but they do not show us whether it is in obedience to a particular instinct that they do so, or whether the widening of their cells prevents them from stretching the threads in the upper part. This question interested me very much. The only way to decide it was to observe the worms while they spin, which could not be done through their opaque cells: it occurred to me to dislodge them and introduce them into glass tubes, which I had caused to be blown in exact imitation of the different kinds of cells. The most difficult part was to draw them from their habitation and place them into these new domiciles. Burnens performed this operation with much address; he opened in my hives several sealed royal cells; selecting the time when we knew that they were about to begin their cocoons, he took them out cautiously, and introduced one in each of my glass cells, without doing them any harm.

We soon saw them prepare their work: they began by stretching the anterior part of their body in a straight line, leaving their posterior part curved, thus forming an arc of which the longitudinal sides of the cell were tangents, and afforded two points of support. Being sufficiently supported in this position, their head was next brought to the different parts of the cell which it could reach, and carpeted the surface with thick silk. We noticed that they did not stretch their threads from one wall to the other, which they could not do, because, being obliged to sustain themselves by keeping their posterior rings curved, the free and movable part of their body was not long enongh to admit of their mouth fixing threads upon diametrically opposite sides. You have not forgotten, Sir, that the royal cells are in the shape of a pyramid, the base of which is broad, with a long and thin point. Those cells are placed vertically in the hives, with their base at the top, and the point below. In this position, you will conceive, the royal worm can sustain itself only when the curve of its posterior part secures two points of support, and it cannot obtain this support unless it rests upon the lower part or near the point. Thus, if it wanted to ascend towards the wide end, to spin a thread, it could not reach both walls, because too far apart. It could not touch one side with its tip, the other with its back, consequently it would tumble down. I made positively sure of this by placing a few royal worms in glass cells that were too large, and the diameter of which was greater towards the point than in ordinary cells: there they were unable to sustain themselves.

These first experiments prevented the supposition of a particular instinct in royal worms. They proved that, if they spin incomplete cocoons, it is because they are compelled to do so by the form of their cells. However, I desired to have a still more direct proof. I placed worms of this same kind in cylindrical glass cells, or portions of glass tubes resembling common cells, and I had the pleasure of seeing these worms spin complete cocoons, as the worms of workers do.

Lastly, I placed common worms in very wide cells, and they left their cocoon open. It is thus demonstrated that the royal worms and the worker worms have exactly the same instinct, the same industry, or in other words, when placed in similar circumstances, they conduct themselves in the same manner. I will add here that the royal worms, artificially lodged in cells of such a shape that they are able to spin complete cocoon, undergo all their metamorphoses equally well. The obligation which nature has imposed upon them, to leave their cocoon open, is not necessary to their development, it has no other object than that of exposing them to the danger of death under the strokes of their natural enemy: a very new and truly singular observation.

In order to complete the history of the worms of bees, I must relate the experiments that I have made on the influence which the size of the cells has upon them. It is to you, Sir, that I am indebted, for the suggestion of the experiments needed upon this interesting subject.

As we often find in the hives males that are smaller than usual, and also sometimes queens of a smaller size than they should be, it was desirable to determine in general to what degree the cells in which bees have passed the first period of their existence has influence upon their size. With this view, you advised me to remove from a hive all the combs composed of common cells, leaving only those composed of large cells. It was evident that if the eggs of common bees, which the queen laid in those cells, would produce workers of a larger size, we should conclude that the size of the cells had a decided influence on that of the bees.

The first time I made this experiment it was unsuccessful because moths having invaded the hive discouraged my bees: but I repeated it and the result was remarkable.

I removed from one of my finest glazed hives all the combs composed of common cells, leaving only those composed of drone cells, and in order to have no vacant room in it, I added more combs of the same kind. It was in June, the season most favorable to bees. I expected those bees to quickly repair the damage produced in their hive by this operation, that they would work upon the breaches made and fasten the new comb to the old; but I was much surprised to see that they did not begin work. I observed them for several days, in the hope that they would resume activity. But this hope was disappointed. Indeed they did not fail in their respect to their queen, but except in this their behavior was quite different from what it is usually: they remained clustered on the combs without exciting any sensible heat; a thermometer placed among them rose only to 22° though it was at 20° in the open air.[13] In a word they appeared to be in the greatest discouragement.

The queen herself, though very fertile, and though she must have been

[13] This is the Réaumur scale, corresponding to 81° and 77° F.

oppressed with the need of laying, hesitated a long time, before depositing any eggs in the large cells; she dropped them, rather than lay them in unsuitable cells. However, on the second day we found six which had been deposited regularly. Three days after, the worms had hatched and we followed their history. The bees commenced to feed them, they did not appear very eager at this work, yet I was in hopes that they would continue to care for them. I was mistaken, for on the following day all the worms disappeared and the cells were empty. Dismal silence reigned in the hive, only a few bees took wing, those that returned had no pellets on their legs: all was cold and inanimate. To promote a little motion, I supplied the hive with a comb of small cells, full of male brood of all ages. The bees, which had obstinately refused to work in wax for 12 days, did not unite this comb to their own; however their industry was awakened in a manner that I had not foreseen; they removed all the brood from this comb, cleaned out the cells and made them ready to receive new eggs; I do not know whether they expected their queen to lay in them, but if they did, they were not disappointed: from this moment the female no longer dropped her eggs; she came to this new comb and laid such a number of eggs that we found 5 or 6 together in several of the cells. I then removed all the combs of large cells, to put small cells in their place and this operation restored their complete activity.

The circumstances of this experiment seem worthy of attention; they prove first that nature has not left to the queen the choice of the eggs which she is to lay; it is ordained that at certain times of the year the female should lay male eggs; she is not permitted to invert this order. You have seen, Sir, in the third letter, that another fact led me to the same consequence, and as this was very important, I was delighted to see it confirmed by a new observation. I repeat therefore that the eggs are not indiscriminately mixed in the ovaries of the queen, but arranged so that, at a certain season, she can lay only a certain kind. So, it would be vain, at the time of the year when the queen should lay the eggs of workers, to attempt forcing her to lay drone eggs by filling her hive with large cells; for by the experiment just described we see that she prefers to drop her worker eggs haphazard, rather than place them in unsuitable cells, and that she will not lay male eggs. I do not yield to the pleasure of granting this queen discernment or foresight, for I perceive a sort of inconsistency in her conduct. If she refused to lay the eggs of workers in large cells because nature taught her that their size is not proportioned to the size or the need of the common worms; why did she not learn also that she should not lay several eggs in the same cell? It appeared much easier to rear a single worker worm in one large cell than several of the same kind in a small cell. The supposed discernment of the queen is not very much enlightened. The most prominent feature of industry here appears in the common bees of this hive. When I gave them a comb of small cells filled with male brood, their activity was awakened; but instead of caring for this brood, as they would have done in other circumstances, they destroyed these worms and nymphs, and cleaned out the cells, so that the queen, oppressed with the need of laying, be enabled to deposit her eggs. Could we allow them either reason or sentiment, this would be an interesting proof of their affection for her.

The experiment here detailed at length, not having fulfilled my object in determining the influence of the size of the cells upon that of the worms, I devised another which was more successful.

I selected a comb of large cells containing eggs and worms of males. I caused all of these worms to be removed from their pap, and Burnens substituted worms one day old, taken from worker cells, then gave this comb to be cared for to bees that had a queen. The bees did not abandon these substituted worms; they sealed the cells with an almost flat capping very different from that which they place on the cells of males, which shows that, although these worms were in large cells, they were well aware that they were not drone worms. This comb remained in the hive for eight days from the time the cells were sealed. I then had it removed to examine the nymphs which it contained. They were worker nymphs, in a more or less advanced state; but as to size and shape they were exactly similar to those that make their growth in the smaller cells. I concluded that the worker worms do not acquire greater size in large than in small cells. Although I made this experiment only once, it appears decisive. Nature which has intended the workers to grow in cells of a certain dimension, undoubtedly ordained that they should receive in them the full development of their organs: a greater space would be useless to them; and they do not reach greater size in spacious cells than in those that are intended for them. If there were cells, in the combs, of a smaller size than common cells, and if the queen should lay worker eggs in them, it is probable that the bees reared in them would attain a less size than the ordinary workers, because they would be cramped in those cells, but it does not ensue that a large cell should give them an extraordinary size.

The effect produced on the size of drones by the diameter of the cells which their worms inhabit may serve as a rule to judge of what must happen to worker worms in similar circumstances. The large male cells have all the space required for the full extension of their organs. Thus, even if we reared drones in still larger cells, they would grow no larger than ordinary drones. We have the proof of this in those that are produced by queens whose fecundation has been retarded. You will remember, Sir, that these queens sometimes lay drone eggs in royal cells: the drones reared in such cells, much more spacious than those provided for them by nature, are no larger than ordinary males. Thus it is correct to say that whatever be the size of the cells in which bees are reared, they will not acquire a larger size than is proper to their kind; but if they grow in smaller cells than those intended for them, as their growth will then be checked they will not attain the usual size.

I had proof of this in the following experiment: I had a comb composed of drone cells and another of worker cells, both occupied with drone worms. Burnens took worms from the small cells and placed them in the large cells on the bed of jelly which had been prepared for them: in return he introduced into the small cells worms which had hatched in the larger ones, and gave both to the care of a hive whose queens laid only male eggs. The bees were not disquieted by this displacement, they took equal care of the worms and when they reached the time of metamorphosis, they gave to both kinds of cells the convex covering which they usually place upon the cells of males.

Eight days afterwards we removed these combs and found, as I had expected, large drone nymphs in the large cells and small males in the small ones.

You pointed out to me, Sir, another experiment, which I made with great care, but which met with an unexpected obstacle. To appreciate the degree of influence of royal food upon the development of worms, you desired me to remove a little of this pap with the end of a pencil and to feed it to a larva of workers in a common cell. Twice I attempted this operation without success, and I am certain that it can never succeed, for the following reason:

When bees have a queen and we put in their charge worms in cells in which we have placed royal jelly, they promptly remove those worms and greedily eat the pap upon which they were placed. When, on the contrary, they are deprived of queen, they change the common cells containing these worms into royal cells of the largest size; then the worms which were to be only common bees are infallibly converted into queens.

But there is another situation in which we can judge of the influence of the royal jelly, administered to worms in common cells. I described these details to you at length in my letter upon the existence of fertile workers. You have not forgotten, Sir, that these workers owe the development of their sexual organs to particles of royal jelly with which they were fed while in the worm shape. For want of new observations more directly upon this subject, I refer you to the experiments described in my 5th letter.

Accept the assurance of my respect, &c.

NINTH LETTER.

On the Formation of Swarms.

Pregny, September 6, 1791.

Sir, I can add a few facts to the information which Mr. de Réaumur has given us on the formation of swarms.

In his history of bees, this celebrated naturalist says, that it is always or almost always a young queen that heads a swarm; but he did not assert the fact positively; he had some doubts and here are his own words:

"Is it very certain, as we have supposed until now, in coincidence with all who have treated of bees, that the colony is uniformly headed by a young mother? May not the old mother become disgusted with her habitation? Or may she not be impelled, by peculiar circumstances to abandon all her possessions to the young female? It would be in my power to solve this question otherwise than by probabilities, had not mishaps destroyed the bees of hives whose queens I had marked with a red spot on the corslet."

These expressions seem to indicate that Mr. de Réaumur suspected that the old queens sometimes head the swarms. From the following details, you will see, Sir, that his conjectures were fully justified.

The same hive may cast several swarms, in the course of spring and the fine season. The old queen is always at the head of the first colony that goes; the others are conducted by the young queens. Such is the fact which

I shall prove in this letter; it is accompanied with remarkable circumstances, which I shall not neglect.

But before beginning this account, I must repeat that which I have stated many times, that one must use leaf or flat hives to see what belongs to the industry and instinct of the bees. When we allow them to build several parallel combs, we can no longer observe what passes constantly between them; or if we wish to see what they have built we must dislodge them by water or smoke, a violent proceeding which leaves nothing in natural conditions, disturbs the instinct of the bees, and exposes the observer to mistaking simple accidents for permanent laws.

I now proceed to the experiments proving that an old queen always conducts the first swarm.

I had a glass hive composed of 3 parallel combs, placed in frames closed like the leaves of a book: the hive was fairly well peopled, and abundantly supplied with honey and comb, with brood of all ages. I removed its queen, on the 5th of May 1788: on the 6th I transferred to it all the bees of another hive, with a fertile queen at least a year old. They entered readily and without fight and were generally well received. The old inhabitants of the hive, which, since the removal of their queen had begun 12 royal cells, also gave the fertile queen a good reception; they offered honey to her, and made regular circles around her; however there was a little agitation in the evening, but confined to the surface of the comb upon which we had put the queen and which she had not quitted. All remained perfectly quiet on the other side.

On the morning of the 7th, the bees had destroyed their 12 royal cells. Order continued to reign in the hive; the queen laid alternately male eggs in the large cells and worker eggs in the small ones.

Towards the 12th we found our bees busy building 22 royal cells of the kind described by Mr. de Réaumur, that is, the bases not in the plane of the comb, but suspended by pedicles of different length, like stalactites, on the edge of the passages made by the bees through the combs. They resembled the cup of an acorn, and the longest were not to exceed two and a half lines (about 1/5 inch) from the bottom to the orifice.

On the 13th, the queen's belly appeared to us to be more slender than when she was introduced in the hive: but she still laid some eggs, both in worker and male cells. We also surprised her this day, at the moment when she was laying in one of the royal cells: she first dislodged the worker employed there, by pushing her away with her head; then after having examined the bottom, she introduced her belly into it, by supporting herself with her anterior legs on one of the adjoining cells.

On the 15th, the queen appeared still more slender; the bees continued to care for the royal cells, which were unequally advanced: some to 3 or 4 lines, while others were already an inch in length; thus proving that the queen had not laid in all those cells at the same date.

On the 19th, when we least expected it, the hive swarmed; we were warned of it only by the noise which it made in the air: we hastened to collect it and placed it in a prepared hive; though we had overlooked the circumstances of its departure, the particular object of this experiment was fulfilled, for on examination of all the bees of the swarm, we became convinced that it had been led by the old queen, the one which we had introduced on the 6th of the month, which we had made easy to recognize by the deprivation of one of her antennæ. Observe that there was no other queen in this colony. In the hive which she had left we found 7 royal cells, closed on the end but open on the side and entirely empty. Eleven more were sealed and some others newly begun; but there was no queen left in the hive.

The new swarm next became the object of our attention: we observed it during the rest of the year, during the winter and the following spring, and in April, we had the satisfaction to see another swarm issue, with this same queen that had conducted one in the previous month of May, of which I have just spoken.

You see, Sir, that this experiment is positive. We used an old queen, placed her in the hive at the time of her laying of drone eggs: we saw the bees accept her, and at that time begin the building of royal cells. The queen laid in one of those cells under our eyes, and lastly left this hive with a swarm.

We repeated this observation several times with equal success. Thus it appears incontestable that it is always the old queen that leads the first swarm out of the hive; but she leaves it only after having deposited eggs in the royal cells from which young queens will hatch after her departure. The bees prepare these cells only when they see the queen laying male eggs, and this is attended by a remarkable fact, namely, that after termination of this laying, her belly is notably diminished; she can fly more easily, whereas, previous to the laying of male eggs, her belly is so heavy that she can hardly drag it along. Therefore it is necessary that she should lay them, to be able to undertake a journey which sometimes may be very long.

But this single condition is not sufficient; it is also necessary that the bees be very numerous in the hive; they should be superabundant, and it may be said that they are aware of it, for if the hive is scantily peopled, they will not build any royal cells at the time of the laying of male eggs, which is the only period when the old queen is able to conduct a colony. We acquired the proof of this in an experiment made on a very large scale.

On the 3d of May 1788, we divided in two each of 18 hives whose queens were about a year old; so each portion of those hives had but half of the bees that were there before the division: 18 of those half hives were thus without queens; but in the space of 10 or 15 days, the bees made up this loss and secured new females: the other 18 had very fertile queens. They soon began to lay male eggs, but the bees, seeing themselves in small number, did not construct any royal cells and none of the hives swarmed. Therefore, if the hive containing the old queen is not very populous, she remains in it till the subsequent spring; and if the population is then sufficient, the bees will construct royal cells, as soon as the queen begins her laying of male eggs; she will deposit eggs in them and will issue at the head of a colony, before the birth of any young queens.

Such is, Sir, an abridged abstract of my information upon swarms, led by old queens; excuse the lengthy details upon which I am about to enter, on the history of royal cells, which remain in the hive after the departure of the queen. Everything relative to this part of the history of bees was hitherto very obscure; a long course of observations, protracted during several years, was necessary to partly remove the veil concealing these mysteries; it is true that I was indemnified by the pleasure of seeing my experiences reciprocally confirmed; but owing to the assiduity which they required, these researches were very laborious.

Having established, in 1788 and 1789, that queens a year old conducted the first swarms and that they left in the hive worms or nymphs which were to transform into queens in their turn, I undertook, in 1790, to profit by the goodness of spring, to observe all that relates to these young queens; I shall now extract the principal experiments from my Journals.

On the 14th of May, we introduced bees from 2 straw hives into a very thin, large glass hive, giving them only one queen born in the preceding year, and which had already commenced laying drone eggs in her native hive.

We introduced her on the 15th; she was very prolific; she was well received and quickly commenced to lay in small and large cells alternately.

On the 20th, we found the foundations of 16 royal cells: they were all on the edges of the passages which the bees establish in the thickness of the combs in order to pass from one side to the other; they were shaped like stalactites.

On the 27th, 10 of these cells were much enlarged, though unequal, and none had the length which bees give them when the worms are hatched.

On the 28th, previous to which the queen had not ceased laying, her belly was much reduced, but she began to exhibit agitation. Her motions soon became more lively; yet she still examined the cells as when she wants to lay in them: sometimes introducing into one the half of her belly, then withdrawing it brusquely. At other times, introducing it no deeper, she would lay an egg, placed irregularly; not fastened by one of its points to the bottom of the cell, but laid upon the center of one of the panes of the hexagon. The queen produced no distinct sound in her course, and we heard nothing different from the ordinary humming of the bees; she would pass over the body of those that were in her way; sometimes if she stopped the bees that met her stopped also, as if to consider her; they would advance brusquely toward her, strike her with their heads and climb on her back; she would then start, carrying several thus upon her; none gave her any honey, but she took some herself out of the open cells on her way; they no longer hedged around her or surround her with regular circles. The first bees that were aroused by her motions followed her running, and excited, in passing, those that were still quiet upon the combs. The path followed by the queen was noticeable, after her passage, by the agitation created, which was no longer quelled. She had soon visited every part of the hive and caused general excitement; if any places still remained tranquil, those that were agitated would arrive and communicate the excitement. The queen no longer laid in the cells, she dropped her eggs: the bees no longer cared for the young; they ran through the hive in every direction; even those returning from the field, before the agitation reached its height, no sooner entered the hive than they participated in these tumultuous motions, and neglecting to rid themselves of the pollen pellets which they carried upon their legs, ran about blindly. At last, in another moment, all the bees rushed to the entrance of the hive and the queen with them.

As it was very important for me to see the formation of new swarms in this hive, and that for that reason I wished it to remain very populous, I caused the queen to be removed at the time when she came out, so that the bees might not fly too far but would return. In fact after losing their female, they did return to the hive. To increase the population still more, I added another swarm which had issued from a straw hive on the same morning, and whose queen was also removed.

Although all the facts here related were very positive and apparently not susceptible of any error, I wished to duplicate them; I was especially anxious to discover whether the old queens always follow a similar course. So I decided to place in this hive a year-old queen, hitherto observed by me, and which had just begun to lay the eggs of males. She was introduced on the 29th. On the same day, we discovered that one of the royal cells, that the previous queen had left behind, was larger than the others; and, from its length we supposed that the included worm was 2 days old. So the egg from which it had come must have been laid on the 24th and the worm had hatched on the 27th. On the 30th, the new queen laid many eggs, alternately in large and small cells. On that day and the two following, the bees enlarged several cells into royal cells, but unevenly, which proved that they contained larvæ of different ages.

On the 1st of June, one of them was sealed, on the 2d, another. The bees also commenced several new ones. Everything was still perfectly quiet in the hive at 11 o'clock in the morning; but at mid-day, the queen changed from the utmost quiet to a very marked agitation, which insensibly was communicated to the workers in every part of their dwelling. Within a few minutes, they crowded towards the entrances and left the hive along with the queen; they settled upon the limb of a neighboring tree; I caused the queen to be sought and removed, so that the bees, deprived of her, should return to the hive, which they did. Their first care seemed to seek for their female; they were still very much excited, but at 3 o'clock all was quiet and in order.

On the 3d they resumed their ordinary labors; they cared for the young, worked within the open royal cells and also gave some attention to those that were closed: they made waved wax work on them (guilloche), not by applying wax bands upon them, but by removing some of it from the surface; this braiding is almost imperceptible near the point of the cell; it becomes deeper above, and the workers excavate it still more to the big end of the pyramid. The cell once closed thus becomes thinner, so much so that, in the last hours that precede the metamorphosis of the queen into a nymph, one may see its motions through the thin coat of wax upon which this braiding is founded, provided the cells are held between the eye and the sunlight. It is quite remarkable that, in making the cells thinner from the time when they are closed, the bees regulate this labor, so that it terminates only when the nymph is ready to undergo its last metamorphosis: upon the 7th day, the cocoon is almost completely *unwaxed*, if I may use this word; it is at this part that the head and thorax of the queen are located. This leaves to her but the trouble to cut the silk of which it is woven. Very probably this labor is intended to promote the evaporation of the superabundant fluids of the royal nymph, and the bees grade it proportionally with the age and condition of the nymph. I undertook some direct experiments upon this matter but they are not yet completed. On the same 3d of June, our bees closed a third royal cell, 24 hours after closing the second. The following days the same operation was performed on several other cells.

Every moment of the 7th, we expected the queen to leave the royal cell which had been sealed on May 30. On the preceding evening, her period of 7 days had elapsed. The waving upon the cell was so deep that we could perceive in part what passed within; we could discern that the silk of the cocoon was cut circularly, a line and a half from the point, but as the bees were unwilling that she should yet quit the cell, they had sealed the cover to it with some particles of wax. What seemed most singular was that this female in her prison emitted a very distinct sound or clacking: it was still more distinct in the evening and was composed of several notes on the same tone, in rapid succession.

On the 8th, we heard the same sound from the second cell. Several bees kept guard around each royal cell.

On the 9th, the first cell opened. The young queen that emerged was lively, slender, of brown color; we then understood why bees retain the females captive in their cells, beyond the term; it is that they may be able to fly, the instant they are liberated. The new queen occupied all our attention: whenever she approached the royal cells, the bees on guard pulled her, bit her and chased her away; they seemed very irritated against her and she enjoyed tranquillity only when at considerable distance from any royal cell. This performance was frequently repeated during the day; she piped twice: we saw her doing so, standing with her thorax against a comb, her wings crossed on her back, in motion, but without being unfolded or farther opened. Whatever might have caused her to assume this attitude, the bees seemed affected by it and remained motionless.

The hive presented the same appearance on the following day. Twenty-three royal cells still remained assiduously guarded by a great many bees. Whenever the queen approached, the guards became agitated, surrounded her, bit her, mobbed her and usually drove her away; sometimes, in those circumstances, she piped, assuming the attitude already described, and from that moment the bees remained motionless.

The queen confined in cell No. 2, which she had not yet left, was heard piping at different times. We also saw accidentally how the bees fed her. By attentive examination, we noticed a small aperture in the end of the capping which she had cut, and out of which she might have emerged, had not the workers covered it with wax to retain her still longer. She alternately thrust and withdrew her tongue through this slit: the bees at first did not notice it, but at length one of them saw it and applied her own proboscis on that of the captive queen, then gave way to others also approaching her with honey. When she was satiated, she withdrew her trunk and the bees again closed the opening with wax.

This same day, between midday and one o'clock, the queen became extremely agitated. The royal cells had multiplied very much; she could go nowhere without finding one, and as soon as she approached she was ill-treated; she fled elsewhere, but obtained no better reception. Her travels agitated the bees; they remained for a long time in great confusion; then they precipitately rushed to the entrances of the hive, issued and settled upon a tree in the garden. It singularly happened that the queen could not follow them and head the swarm herself. She had attempted to pass between two royal cells before the bees had abandoned them and was so confined and bitten as to be unable to move. We removed her and placed her in a separate hive, prepared for a particular experiment: the bees that had swarmed and that had gathered upon a branch soon perceived that their queen was not with them and returned to the hive of their own accord. Such is an account of the second colony (swarm) of this hive.

We were extremely desirous of ascertaining what would become of the other royal cells: 4 of the sealed ones contained fully developed queens, which might have emerged had not the bees prevented them. They were not opened during the moments previous to the agitation of the swarm nor at the time of issue.

On the 11th, none of these queens was as yet liberated: that of No. 2 must have ended her transformation on the 8th; so she had been a prisoner for 3 days; and her confinement lasted longer than that of No. 1 which had caused the formation of the swarm. We did not divine the cause of this difference in their captivity.

On the 12th, this queen was at length liberated, we found her in the hive; she was treated exactly as her predecessor; the bees left her quiet when away from the royal cells, and tormented her cruelly when she approached them. We watched this queen for a long time, but not foreseeing that she would lead out a colony on the same way, we left the hive for a few hours. Returning at noon, we were very much surprised to find it almost deserted; during our absence it had thrown a prodigious swarm, which was still clustered, in a thick bunch, on the branch of a neighboring pear tree. We also saw, with astonishment, the 3d cell open, its cap still hanging as by a hinge. In all probability the captive queen profited by the disorder that preceded the issue of the swarm, to escape. We had no doubt then that both queens were in the swarm; we found them both and removed them, so that the bees might return to the hive, which they did, immediately.

While we were occupied in this operation, the captive queen No. 4 left her prison, and the bees found her upon their return. They were at first very much agitated, but calmed towards evening and resumed their ordinary labors; they kept strict guard around the royal cells, and took great care to repulse the queen whenever she attempted to approach them; there were still 18 closed cells to guard.

At 10 in the evening, the queen of No. 5 was liberated, so there were two living queens now in the hive; they first tried to fight, but succeeded in disengaging themselves from each other; during the night they fought several times without result: on the following day, the 13th, we witnessed the death of one of them which fell by the wounds of her enemy. The details of this duel were entirely similar to those that I gave elsewhere on the "combats of queens".

The victorious queen now gave us a very singular spectacle. She approached a royal cell and took this moment to pipe and place herself in the posture which strikes the bees motionless. We thought, for a few minutes, that, taking advantage of the dread she caused to the workers on guard, she would succeed in opening it and killing the young female in it; so she prepared to mount on the cell; but in so doing she stopped her piping and abandoned the attitude which paralyzes the bees: instantly the guards of the cell regained courage; and by tormenting and biting the queen, drove her away.

On the 14th, the queen emerged from the cell No. 6; and at 11 o'clock the hive threw a swarm with all the disorder previously described: the agitation was even so considerable that an insufficient number of bees remained to guard the royal cells, and several of the imprisoned queens made their escape. There were 3 of them in the cluster of the swarm, and three others remained in the hive. We removed those that had led the colony, so as to compel the bees to return.

They returned to the hive, resumed their post around the royal cells and maltreated the queens that tried to approach them.

In the night of the 14th to the 15th, there was a duel in which one queen fell; we found her dead next morning before the hive; but there still remained 3, as one had hatched during the night. On the morning of the 15th, we witnessed a duel between 2 of these queens; and only two were left free at one time: they were both exceedingly excited, either with the desire of fighting, or by the treatment of the bees when they came near the royal cells: their agitation quickly communicated to the bees of the hive, and at noon they impetuously departed with the two females. This was the 5th swarm that had left the hive from May 30th to June 15th. It cast still another on the 16th, of which I shall not give account, as it showed nothing new.

Unfortunately we lost this last swarm, which was very strong; the bees flew out of sight and could not be found. The hive remained now very thinly inhabited; only the few bees that had not participated in the agitation at the time of swarming remained, together with those that returned from the field after the departure of the swarm. The royal cells thereafter were slenderly guarded, the queens escaped from them, several fights enused, until the throne remained with the successful one.

In spite of her victories, from the 16th to the 19th she was indifferently treated by the bees for during those 3 days she preserved her virginity. At length she went forth to seek the males, returned with all the external signs of fecundation and was thenceforth treated with every mark of respect: she laid her first eggs 46 hours after fecundation.

Behold, Sir, a simple and faithful account of my observations on the formation of swarms. In order to render this account more clear, I have not interrupted it with the detail of several particular experiments which I made at the same time, with the intention of elucidating several obscure points. If you will permit, this shall be the subject of future letters. Although my statements are lengthy, I still hope to interest you.

Accept, Sir, the assurance of my respect.

P. S. In reading over this letter, Sir, I find that I have failed to anticipate an objection which might embarrass my readers, and to which I must reply. Since I returned the bees to the hive from each of the 5 swarms that had issued, it is not surprising that this hive was continually stocked so sufficiently that each colony was numerous; but in the natural state, things do not happen in this way; the bees composing a swarm do not return to the hive which they have left, and it will be asked what resource of population enables an ordinary hive to cast 3 or 4 swarms without being too much weakened.

I do not wish to lessen the difficulty; I have said that the agitation which precedes swarming is often so considerable, that most of the bees quit the hive; and it is then difficult to comprehend how, in 3 or 4 days afterwards, this hive may be able to send out another fairly strong colony.

But take notice that, when she leaves the hive, the old queen leaves there a prodigious quantity of worker brood. These soon transform into bees and sometimes the population is almost as large after the first swarm has been cast as before it left. Thus the hive is perfectly capable of furnishing another colony without being too much impaired. The 3d and 4th swarms weaken it more sensibly; but the number of remaining inhabitants is nearly always large enough to continue the labors without interruption, and these losses are soon replaced by the great fecundity of the queens. You will remember that they lay above a hundred eggs per day.

If, in some cases, the agitation is so great that all the bees participate in it and leave the hive, the desertion lasts but for an instant: the swarms depart during the finest moments of the day, at the time when the bees are gathering honey through the country; those that are thus busy at the divers harvests take no part in the agitation of the cast; when they return to the hive they quietly resume the labor, and their number is not small, for, when the weather is fine, at least a third of the bees are in the field at one time.

Even in the embarrassing case of so great an agitation that all the bees desert the hive, it does not follow that all those that try to leave become members of the new colony. When this delirious agitation seizes them, they rush and accumulate all at one time towards the entrances and become heated in such a manner that they perspire copiously; the bees nearest the bottom supporting the weight of all the others, seem drenched; their wings become moist; they are incapable of flight; and even when able to escape, they do not go farther than the bottom board, and soon reenter.

The newly hatched bees do not leave with the swarm, still feeble, they could not sustain themselves in flight. Here, then, are many recruits to people this habitation which we thought deserted.

TENTH LETTER

Continuation of the Same Subject.

Pregny, Sept. 8th 1791.

In order to have more regularity in the continuation of the *history of swarms*, I believe, Sir, that it is proper to recapitulate, in a few words, the principal facts of the preceding letter, and to give upon each of them the developments resulting from several new experiments which I have not yet mentioned.

First. *If, on the return of spring, we examine a well peopled hive, governed by a fertile queen, we shall see her lay, in April and May, a prodigious number of the eggs of males; and the workers will choose this time, to build several royal cells of the kind described by Mr. de Réaumur.* Such is the result of several long continued observations, between which there has never been the slightest variation, and I do not hesitate to announce it to you as a demonstrated fact; but I must add a necessary explanation.

Before a queen begins her great laying of male eggs, she must be 11 months old, when younger she lays only worker eggs. A queen hatched in spring will perhaps lay 50 or 60 male eggs, altogether, during the course of the summer, but before she begins her great laying of drone eggs, which should be of one or two thousand, she must have completed her 11th month. In the course of our experiments, which more or less disturbed the natural sequence of things, it often happened that the queen did not attain this age until October; and from that time began laying male eggs; the workers also selected that time to build royal cells, as if they were induced to it by some emanation from them.[14] No swarm resulted, for in the autumn the requisite circumstances are absolutely wanting; but it is no less evident that there is a secret relation between the laying of eggs of males and the construction of royal cells.

This laying usually continues 30 days. On the 20th or 21st day, from its beginning, the bees lay the foundation of several royal cells; they sometimes build 16 or 20, we have seen as many as 27. As soon as they are 2 or 3 lines in depth the queen lays in them eggs of her own sort, but does not lay them all the same day: in order that the hive may throw several swarms, it is important that the young females that are to conduct them be not all born at the same time; it seems as if the queen knew it in advance, for she takes care to allow at least a day between the laying of each egg deposited in these cells. Here is the evidence: the bees know that the cells must be sealed at the time when the worms in them are about to transform into nymphs; they close these cells at different dates; so it is evident that the worms in them are not precisely of the same age.

The queen's belly is extremely distended, before she begins to lay drone eggs, but it decreases sensibly as she advances, in this laying, and when it is terminated, her belly is very slender: she then finds herself in a state to undertake a journey which circumstances may prolong: therefore this condition was necessary; and as everything harmonizes in the laws of nature, the time of birth of the males corresponds with that of the females which they are to fecundate.

Second. *When the larvæ hatched from the eggs laid by the queen in the royal cells are ready to transform to nymphs, this queen leaves the hive leading a swarm with her: it is a constant rule that the first swarm cast by a hive in the spring is always conducted by the old queen.* I think I can divine the reason of it: in order that at no time there be a plurality of

---

14 NOTE of the translator. The laying of drone eggs by a young queen in October is a very unusual incident and we wonder whether Huber noticed such a thing more than once. It appears to us to have been an exception, probably from the failing of this queen.

females in the hive, nature has inspired the queens with a mutual hate for one another: they cannot meet without seeking to fight and destroy each other. When nearly of equal age, the chance of the combat is equal between them, and chance decides to which the throne shall belong; but if one combatant be older than the others, she is stronger, and the advantage will be with her; she will destroy her rivals successively as they are born. Thus, if the old queen did not leave the hive before the young ones emerge from the royal cells, she would destroy them all at the time of their last transformation: the hive could not swarm and the species would perish. In order to preserve the race, it was necessary that the old queen should conduct the first swarm. But what is the secret means employed by nature to induce her to depart? I do not know.

In our country, it is very rare, though not without example, for the swarm led by an old queen to become populous enough, in the space of three weeks, to give a new colony, which this same queen conducts also: and it may happen as follows:

Nature has not willed that she should quit the first hive before completing her laying of male eggs; it was necessary that she should be freed of them that she might become lighter; besides, if her first occupation, when entering a new domicile, was the laying of more males, she might perish by age or accident before laying those of workers; the bees then would have no means of replacing her and the colony would perish.

All these matters have been anticipated with infinite wisdom. The first action of a swarm is to build worker cells: they work upon them with much ardor and as the ovaries of the queen have been disposed with admirable foresight, the first eggs that she lays in her new habitation are worker eggs. This laying ordinarily continues 10 or 11 days; and during that time the bees build some combs with large cells. It appears as if they knew that she will lay drone eggs also: indeed, she again deposits some, though in much smaller number than the first time; yet enough to encourage the bees to construct royal cells. Now, if in these circumstances the weather remains favorable, it is not impossible that a second colony may be formed, which will be led by the old queen, 3 weeks after her having headed the first swarm. But I repeat it, this fact is rare in our climate: I now return to the history of the hive from which the queen has led the first colony.

Third. *As soon as the old queen has conducted the first swarm, the bees remaining in the hive take particular care of the royal cells, guard them severely, and permit the young queens reared in them to emerge only successively, at an interval of several days from each other.* In my previous letter, Sir, I gave you the details and proofs of this fact: I shall add some reflections. During the period of swarming, the instinct of bees seems to receive a particular modification. At any other time, when they have lost their queen, they design several workers' worms to replace her, prolong and enlarge the cells of these worms, give them food more abundant and of a more pungent taste; and by these cares they cause to grow into queens worms that would have been only common bees naturally. We have seen them build at one time 27 royal cells of this sort, but when they are sealed the bees no longer endeavor to preserve the young females in them from the attacks of their enemies. One of them will perhaps leave her cradle first, and will assail all the other royal cells successively, which she will tear open to sting her rivals, without the workers taking any interest in their defense; should several queens hatch at the same time, they will seek each other, will fight, there will be several victims, and the throne will remain with the victorious female. Far from opposing such duels, the bees appear rather to excite the combatants.

It is quite different in the time of swarms. The royal cells then constructed are of a different shape from the former; they are built like stalactites; when just outlined they fairly resemble the cup of an acorn. As soon as the young queens reared in them are ready for their last transformation, the bees assiduously guard them. The female from the first egg laid by the old queen hatches at last; the workers treat her first with indifference; soon she yields to the instinct which urges her to destroy her rivals; she seeks the cells where they are enclosed; but no sooner does she approach, than the bees pinch her, pull her, chase her and compel her to withdraw; and the royal cells being numerous, scarcely can she find in the hive a place of rest. Ceaselessly tormented with the desire of attacking the other queens, and ceaselessly repelled, she becomes agitated, she hastily traverses the different groups of workers to which she communicates her agitation. At this instant we see numbers of bees rush towards the entrances of the hive; they fly out with their young queen and go seek another home elsewhere. After their departure, the remaining workers liberate another queen, which they treat with the same indifference as the first, chasing her away from the royal cells, and which, perpetually harassed in her way, becomes agitated, departs, carrying another swarm along with her. This scene is repeated three or four times during the spring, in a well peopled hive. At last, the number of bees becomes so greatly reduced that they can no longer preserve a strict watch over the royal cells; several young females emerge at the same time from their prison, they seek each other, fight, and the victorious queen of all these duels thereafter reigns peaceably over the republic.

The longest intervals we have observed between the departure of each natural swarm, were between 7 and 9 days. This is the time that usually elapses between the first colony led out by the old queen, and the swarm conducted by the young liberated females; the interval is shorter between the second and the third; and the fourth sometimes departs the day after the third. In hives left to themselves, 15 to 18 days are sufficient for the casting of 4 swarms, if the weather is favorable, as I am about to explain.

We never see a swarm form except on a fine day, or to speak more exactly, at the time of the day when the sun shines and the air is calm. We have observed in a hive all the precursors of swarming, disorder, agitation; but a cloud passed before the sun, and calm was restored in the hive; the bees thought no longer of leaving. An hour afterwards, the sun having again appeared, the tumult was renewed, it grew rapidly and the swarm left.

Bees in general seem much alarmed at the prospect of bad weather. When they range about the fields, the passage of a cloud before the sun induces them to return precipitately, and I am inclined to believe that it is the sudden diminution of the light which disquiets them, for if the sky is uniformly cloudy, and there are no alteration of clearness and obscurity, they go to the field for their ordinary collections and even the first drops of a light rain do not make them return in great precipitation.

I have no doubt that the necessity of a fine day for the casting of a swarm is one of the reasons which induced nature to give the bees the means of protracting the captivity of their young queens in the royal cells. I will not conceal the fact that they sometimes appear to use this privilege in an arbitrary manner; however the confinement of the queens is always longer when bad weather lasts for several days together. Here the final object cannot be mistaken. Were the young females at liberty to leave their cradles, as soon as they completed their last development, there would be a plurality of queens in the hives during the bad days, and consequently combats and victims: the bad weather might continue until all the queens reached the term of their development and attained their liberty. After the fights, one alone, victorious over the others, would remain in possession of the throne, and the hive, which naturally should produce several swarms, could not give a single one: the multiplication of the species would thus be left to the chance of rain or fine weather, instead of which it is rendered independent of either by the wise disposition of nature. By allowing a single female to escape at one time, the formation of swarms is ensured. This explanation appears so simple that I think it superfluous to insist upon it.

But I should mention another important circumstance resulting from the captivity of queens in the royal cells; it is that they are able to fly and leave as soon as the bees free them, and by this means they are capable of profiting of the first moment of sunshine to lead away a colony.

You know, Sir, that none of the bees, whether workers or drones, are able to fly before a day or two after leaving the cell, they are still weak, whitish, their organs are infirm; at least 24 or 30 hours are required before the acquisition of perfect strength, and the development of their faculties. It would be the same with the females, were not their confinement protracted beyond the period of transformation, but we see them emerge strong, brown, full grown and in better condition for flying than they will be at any other time of their life. I have elsewhere mentioned the constraint employed by the bees to retain the females in captivity; with a band of wax they solder the capping of the cells to the sides. I have also explained how they feed them, so will not repeat these details here.

Another remarkable fact is that the females are set at liberty according to their age. We marked all the royal cells with numbers at the time when they were sealed by the workers; and we chose this period because it exactly indicated the age of the queens. We noticed that the oldest one was always liberated first, the one immediately younger was next, and so on; none of the females was freed from prison before the elder ones.

I have asked myself, a hundred times, how do bees distinguish so accurately the age of their captives? I should do better to answer this question, like so many others, by a simple avowal of my ignorance; however, Sir, permit me to offer a conjecture. You know that I have not abused, as some authors do, the right of giving myself up to hypothesis. May not the piping or sound emitted by the young queens, in their cells, be one of the means employed by nature to inform the bees in the age of their queens? It is certain that the femals whose cell was closed first, pipes first also. The queen in the cell closed next pipes sooner than the others, and so on to the end. As their captivity may last 8 or 10 days, it is still possible that the bees may forget which queen piped first, but it is also possible that the queens diversify their song, increasing it as they become older, and the bees may distinguish these variations. We have been able, ourselves, to recognize differences in the piping, either in the succession of notes, or in the intensity of the piping; there are probably still more imperceptible variations, which escape our organs, but which those of the workers may recognize.

That which gives weight to this conjecture is the fact that the queens reared by the method discovered by Schirach are entirely mute; and the workers never form any guard around their cells (supersedure cells. Tr.), nor do they retain them in captivity for a single instant beyond the term of their transformation: when they have undergone it, they permit them to fight to the death until one has been victorious over all the rest. Why? Because then the sole object is to replace the lost queen; so, provided that among the worms reared as queens, a single one succeeds, the fate of the others is uninteresting to the bees; whereas, at the time of swarms, it is necessary to rear a succession of queens, for conducting the divers colonies; and to ensure the safety of these queens, they must be preserved from the consequences of the mutual hate which animates them against each other. That is the evident cause of all the precautions that bees, instructed by nature, take during the period of swarming; that is the explanation of the captivity of females; and in order that the duration of this captivity be measured upon the age of the queens, it was requisite for them to have some means of distinguishing the time when they should be liberated. This means consists in the piping which they emit, and the variations which they are able to give it.

In spite of all my researches, I have been unable to discover the situation of the organ which serves in producing this sound. I have undertaken a new course of experiments upon this subject, but they are still unfinished.

There is still another problem to be solved: why is it that the queens reared by Mr. Schirach's method are mute, while those bred in swarming time have the faculty of emitting a certain sound? What is the physical cause of this difference?

I thought at first that it must be ascribed to the period of their life when the worms that are to become queens receive the royal pap. At the time of swarms, the royal worms receive the royal food, from the moment of leaving the egg: on the contrary, those intended for queens, by Mr. Schirach's method, receive it only on the second or third day of their existence. It appeared to me that this circumstance was quite influential upon the different parts of the organs, and especially on the vocal organs; but experiments have destroyed this conjecture.

I caused to be constructed glass tubes in exact imitation of royal cells, to observe the manner of metamorphosis of those worms into nymphs, and of the nymphs into queens. In my eighth letter, I described the observations which I here recall. We introduced into one of these artificial cells the nymph of a worm reared for a queen according to Mr. Schirach's method. We performed this operation 24 hours before the time when it was to undergo its last transformation, and we replaced the glass cell into the hive, that the nymph might have the necessary degree of heat. On the following day, we had the pleasure of seeing it divest itself of its cast-skin and assume its ultimate form; she could not escape from her prison, but we had contrived a small aperture, so that she might thrust out her trunk, that the bees might feed her. I expected her to be completely mute; but she emitted sounds similar to those described elsewhere; therefore my conjecture was erroneous.

I next supposed that the queen, being restrained in her motions and in her desire for liberty, this constraint induced her to emit these sounds. From this new point of view, the queens, whether reared by the Schirach method or the other, should be equally capable of piping, but to be induced to it, they must be under restraint. But those produced from worker worms are not under restraint in a single moment of their life, in a natural condition; and if they do not pipe, it is not because they are deprived of the voice organ, it is because nothing impels them to pipe: on the other hand, those that are born at the time of swarming are induced to it by the captivity in which the bees keep them. I give little weight to this conjecture, Sir, and though I state it here, it is less to claim merit than to put other observers in the way of discovering a better conjecture.

Neither will I claim the credit of having discovered the piping of the queen. Ancient authors mentioned it; upon this matter, Mr. de Réaumur cites a work published in Latin in 1671, under the title of *Monarchia Feminina*, by Charles Butler.[15]

He gives a short abstract of the observations of this naturalist, who, we can easily see, had embellished or rather disguised the truth, by mixing with it the most absurd fancies; but it is nevertheless evident that Butler had heard the real piping of queens, and did not confound it with the confused hum frequently heard in the hives.

Fourth. *When young queens leave the hive, leading a swarm, they are still in the virgin state.* The day following the settling in their new abode is usually that in which they go in quest of the males; that time is commonly the fifth day of their life as queens; for they spend 2 or 3 days in captivity, one at freedom in the native hive before issuing, and the fifth in their new domicile; the queens reared from worker worms, by the Lusatian method, also spend 5 days in the hive before flying for fecundation. The ones as well as the others, are treated with indifference by the bees, as long as they retain their virginity; but as soon as they return with the external signs of fecundation, they are welcomed by their subjects with most willing respect. However 46 hours elapse after fecundation before they begin to lay. The old queens, that lead the first swarm in spring, do not need farther commerce with the males to preserve their fecundity. A single mating is therefore sufficient to impregnate all the eggs which they will lay for two years at least.

I have the honor of being, &c.

15 See Réaumur, Vol. V, inquarto, pages 232 and 615.

ELEVENTH LETTER

Continuation of the Same Subject.

Pregny, September 10, 1791.

Sir, I have collected, in the two preceding letters, my principal observations upon swarms, those most frequently repeated, and of which the constantly uniform results left to me no apprehension of error. I have drawn what appeared to be the most immediate consequences, and in all the theoretical part, I have carefully avoided advancing beyond facts. What remains to be mentioned to-day is more conjectural, but you will find there the relation of several experiments which I believe interesting.

I have shown that the principal motive of the departure of the young females at the time of swarming is their insuperable antipathy to each other; I have repeatedly stated that they cannot gratify their aversion because the workers, with the utmost care, prevent them from attacking the royal cells. This perpetual contrariness to their actions at length gives them a visible inquietude, a degree of agitation that induces them to depart: all the young females are successively treated in the same way in hives that are to swarm. But the bees behave very differently towards the old queen destined to conduct the first swarm; always accustomed to respect fertile queens, they do not forget what they owe to her; they allow her the greatest liberty in all her motions; they permit her to approach the royal cells, and even if she attempts to destroy them, the bees do not object. She executes her wishes without obstacle, and her flight cannot be ascribed, like that of the young females, to the opposition she meets; therefore, in the preceding letters, I candidly confessed myself ignorant of the motive of her departure.

However, on more mature reflection, it did not appear to me that this fact affords so strong an objection against the general rule as I had at first conceived. It is very certain, at least, that the old queens, as well as the young ones, entertain the greatest aversion towards the individuals of their own sex. I had the proof of it in the great number of royal cells that I saw them destroy. You will remember, Sir, that in the detail of my first observation on the departure of the old queen, I mentioned 7 royal cells opened on the side and destroyed by this queen. When the weather is rainy for several days in succession, they destroy them all, in which case there is no swarm, as too often happens in our country, where the springs are ordinarily rainy. Queens never attack those cells when there is only an egg or a very young worm in them; but they begin to fear them when the worm is about to transform into a nymph or when it has already undergone this transformation.

The presence of royal cells containing nymphs or worms near the change into nymphs, inspires old queens with the utmost horror or aversion, but there remains to be explained why, being free to destroy them, they do not always do so. On this I am limited to conjectures. It may be that the great number of royal cells in a hive at one time, and the labor required to open them all, creates in the old queens an insuperable terror; they commence indeed with attacking their rivals, but incapable of succeeding promptly, their disquiet increases and changes to a terrible agitation. If, at this time, the weather is favorable, they are naturally disposed to depart.

It may be readily understood that the workers, accustomed to their queen, whose presence is for them a real necessity, crowd after her in her departure, and the formation of the first swarm creates no difficulty in this respect.

But undoubtedly you will ask, Sir, what motive can induce the bees to follow the young queens from the hive, when they treat them so badly, and in their most amicable moments testify perfect indifference towards them. It is probably to escape the heat to which the hive is then exposed. The extreme agitation of the young females, before the cast, induces them to run back and forth on the combs; they pass through the groups of bees, shock them, bewilder them, and impart their delirium to them, and this tumultuous disorder raises the temperature to an insupportable degree. We several times proved it by the thermometer. In a populous hive, in the spring, it is usually between the 27° and 29° (90° to 97° F), but during the tumult which precedes swarming, it rises above the 32° (104° F), and this is intolerable to bees; when exposed to it, they rush precipitately towards the entrances and depart. In general, they cannot endure a sudden increase of heat; they leave their domicile when they feel it, neither do those returning from the field enter when the temperature is extraordinary.

Through direct experiments I have ascertained that the impetuous courses of the queen over the combs really excite the bees, and this is how I ascertained it. I desired to avoid a complication of causes; it was especially important to learn whether, outside of the time of swarming, the agitation of a queen would be transmitted to the bees. I took two virgin females, over five days old, and susceptible of fecundation. I put them in separate glass hives, sufficiently populous; after having introduced them, I closed the openings so that the air had free circulation but the bees could not escape. I prepared to observe these hives at every moment of the day when the weather invites both males and queens to take flight for fecundation: the following day the weather was variable, none of the males issued from my apiary, and the bees were tranquil; but the next day, towards 11 o'clock, the sun shining, my two imprisoned queens began to run about, seeking an exit in all parts of their domicile, and finding none, traveled over the combs with most evident symptoms of disquiet and agitation; soon the bees participated in this disorder; I saw them crowd to the bottom of the hives, where the entrances are situated; unable to escape, they ascended with equal rapidity, and ran blindly over the cells until 4 in the afternoon. This is about the hour when the sun, declining on the horizon, recalls the males to their hives: queens requiring fecundation never remain later abroad; so the two females which I observed became calmer and in a short time, tranquillity was restored. This proceeding was repeated several days in succession, with perfectly similar symptoms, and I became convinced that the agitation of bees, at the time of the casting of swarms, has nothing singular, but that the hives are always in great tumult when the queen herself is agitated.

I have but one more fact to mention, Sir; I have already stated that when the bees have lost their female, they give to simple worker worms the royal education, and that, according to the discovery of Mr. Schirach, they usually repair the loss in 10 days. In this case, there is no swarming; all the young females emerge from their cells at about the same time, and after a cruel war, the empire remains to the most fortunate one.

I comprehend well that the principal intention of nature is to replace the lost queen; but since the bees are at liberty, for this operation, to select eggs or worms of workers during the first 3 days of their life, why do they give royal treatment only to worms of equal age, which are to undergo their last metamorphosis at about the same time? Since they are able, at the time of swarming, to retain the young females in captivity within their cells for more or less time, why do they allow the queens, that are reared by the Schirach method, to escape all at once? By prolonging their captivity more or less, they could fulfill two most important objects, in repairing the loss of their females, and securing a succession of queens to conduct several swarms.

I first supposed that this difference in conduct proceeded from the different circumstances in which they find themselves. They are induced to make all dispositions relative to swarming only when in great numbers, and when they have a queen occupied with her great laying of male eggs; whereas, when they have lost their female, they no longer find drone eggs in the combs to influence their instinct; they are in a certain degree disquiet and discouraged.

Therefore, after removing a queen, I contrived to render all the other circumstances as similar as possible to those in which bees find themselves when they prepare to cast a swarm. I increased excessively the population of the hive, by introducing into it a great number of workers; I supplied them with several combs containing male brood in all stages. Their first occupation was to construct royal cells after Schirach's methods, and to rear worker larvæ with royal food: they also began the building of several cells in stalactite shape; as if urged to it by the presence of male brood; but they did not complete them, for there was no queen among them to deposit eggs in them. Lastly I gave them several sealed royal cells, taken indifferently from hives preparing to swarm; but all these precautions were useless. My bees were occupied only with replacing their lost queen, they gave no particular care to the royal cells which I had entrusted to them; the queens in them emerged at the usual time without having been confined a single instant, they fought several combats, and there were no swarms.

Recurring to subtleties, we might perhaps point out the cause or the aim of this apparent oddity; but the more we admire the wise dispositions of the author of nature, in the laws which he has prescribed to the industry of animals, the greater reserve we need in admitting any supposition adverse to this beautiful system, the more we must distrust the facility of imagination with which, by embellishing the facts, we seek to explain them.

In general, the naturalists who have long observed the animals, and those especially who have selected the insects for the favorite object of their studies, have too readily ascribed to them our sentiments, our passions and even our views. Yielding to admiration, disgusted perhaps with the contempt generally shown in speaking of insects, they have conceived themselves obliged to justify the consumption of time which they bestowed upon them, and have embellished the different traits of the industry of these minute animals with all the colors supplied by an exalted imagination. Even our celebrated Réaumur is not altogether exempt from reproach on this score: in depicting the history of bees, he often ascribes to them combined intentions, love, foresight and other faculties of too elevated an order. I think I perceive that, although he formed for himself very correct ideas of their operations, he would have been pleased if his reader admitted that they are sensible of their own interest. He is a painter who, by a happy prejudice, flatters the original whose features he depicts. On the other hand, the illustrious Buffon unjustly considers bees as pure automatons. It was reserved for you, Sir, to restore the theory of animal industry towards more philosophical principles, and to show that those of their actions which have a moral appearance depend on the association of *purely sensible ideas*. It is not my intention, here, to penetrate such depths or insist upon the details.

But as the ensemble of the facts relative to the formation of swarms presents perhaps more subjects of admiration than any other part of the history of bees, I believe it proper to point out in a few words the simplicity of means by which wise nature directs the instinct of these insects. It could not grant to them the least portion of intelligence; it left to them, therefore, no precautions to take, no combination to follow, no foresight to exercise, no knowledge to acquire. But after moulding their *sensorium* in conformity with the diverse operations with which they were charged, it was through the impulse of pleasure that it directed their execution. It therefore preordained all the circumstances relative to the succession of their different labors, and to each of these it united an agreeable sensation.[16] Thus when bees construct their cells, when they care for the worms, when they collect provisions, we must seek there neither method, nor affection, nor foresight; we must consider, as the determining cause, only the pleasure of a sweet sensation, attached to each of these functions. I address a philosopher, and as these are his own opinions applied to new facts, I believe my language will be understood; but I beg my readers to read and meditate upon those of your works which treat of the industry of animals. Let me add but this: that the attraction of pleasure is not the sole impulse that prompts them; there is another principle, the prodigious influence of which, at least in regard to bees, was not yet known; that is the sentiment of aversion which all the females feel against each other, at all times, a sentiment whose existence is so well demonstrated by my observations, and which explains a multitude of important facts in the theory of swarms.

[16] It has since been ascertained that it is most probably the "agreeable sensation" here mentioned which impels the queen to lay mostly the eggs of workers, which are fecundated as they pass by the spermatheca. It is only when she is fatigued by the continuous recurrence of this agreeable sensation that she rests herself by laying unfertilized or drone eggs which evidently pass out without effort on her part. It is to be regretted that Huber did not know of parthenogenesis when he wrote the above.—(Translator.)

TWELFTH LETTER

*New Details Upon the Queens Laying Only the Eggs of Drones, and on Those
Deprived of Their Antennæ.*

Pregny, September 12, 1791.

Sir, in relating to you, in the third letter, my first observations upon
queens that lay only the eggs of drones, I have shown that they deposit
these eggs indifferently, in cells of all dimensions, and even in royal cells:
I said also that the common bees give, to the worms from the drone eggs
laid in royal cells, the same care as if they were actually to be transformed
into queens; and I added that, in this instance, the instinct of the workers
appeared to be at fault.[17] Indeed, it is very singular that the bees, knowing
the worms of males so well, when the eggs from which they are produced

---

[17] I have ascertained through new observations, that bees recognize the
larvæ of drones, as well when the eggs producing them have been laid in
royal cells, by queens whose fecundations has been retarded, as when they
have been deposited in common cells.

It has not been forgotten that the royal cells are shaped like a pear, the
large end of which is at the top; or in the shape of an inverted pyramid, the
axis of which is about vertical, and the length of 15 or 16 lines. It is known
also that the queens lay in those cells when they are but outlined, when they
fairly resemble the cup of an acorn.

The bees give the same shape and dimensions, at first, to the cells which
serve as cradles for males; but when their larvæ are about to be transformed,
it is easy to perceive that they have not taken them for royal worms; for
instead of closing their cells in pointed form, as they invariably do when
containing the larvæ of the latter sort, they widen them at the end, and after
adding a cylindrical tube, they close them with a convex capping, differing in
nothing from those which they are accustomed to put on the cells of males;
but as this tube is of the same capacity as the hexagon cells of the smallest
diameter, the larvæ which the bees thus cause to descend into this part of
the cell, and which are to undergo there their last metamorphosis, become
drones of the smaller size. The total length of these extraordinary cells is 20
to 22 lines (1 2/3 to 1 5/6 in. Tr.).

Yet, the bees do not always add a cylinder to a pyramidal cell; they are
then content with enlarging a little their lower part, and the larvæ which
make their growth there may become large drones. I am ignorant of the
cause of the differences sometimes observed in the shape of these cells; but
it appears very certain to me that the bees never are deceived in them, giving
us in this occasion a great proof of the instinct with which they are endowed.
Nature, which has intrusted the bees with the rearing of their young, and with
the care of providing them with aliments proper to their age, or even to their
sex, must have taught them how to recognize them. There is so little resemblance between adult males and workers, that some difference must also exist
between the larvæ of both kinds; doubtless the workers distinguish it, though
it has escaped our notice.

are laid in small cells, and never failing to give them a convex capping at
the time of their transformation into nymphs, should no longer recognize the
worms of this sort, when the eggs from which they hatch are laid in royal
cells, and treat them as if they were to become queens. This irregularity
depends upon something which I cannot fathom.

In revising what I had the honor to write you upon this subject, I
realized that there was still an interesting experiment wanting to complete
the history of queens that lay only the eggs of drones; it was to investigate
whether those females themselves could distinguish that the eggs which they
lay in royal cells are not of the female sort: I had already observed that they
do not try to destroy these cells when sealed, and I thence concluded that,
in general, the presence of royal cells in their hive does not inspire in them
the same aversion as it does to the females whose fecundation has not been
delayed: but to ascertain the fact more positively, it was necessary to
examine how the presence of a cell containing a royal nymph would affect
a queen that had never laid any other than drone eggs.

This experiment was easy; I made it on the 4th of September of this
year, upon one of my hives which had been deprived of its natural queen,
for some time. The bees of this hive had not failed to construct several
royal cells to replace their female. I chose this moment to give them a
queen whose fecundation had been retarded to the 28th day, and which laid
none but the eggs of males; at the same time, I removed all the royal cells,
except one that had been sealed 5 days: a single cell remaining was sufficient to show the impression it would make on the strange queen just
placed among the bees. If she endeavored to destroy it, it would be, to my
mind, a proof that she foresaw the birth of a dangerous rival. Please, Sir,
to excuse this use of the term *foresee*, which I recognize as improper, but
it avoids a long circumlocution. If, on the contrary, she did not attack it,
I would thence conclude that the delay of fecundation, which deprived her
of the faculty of laying worker eggs, had also impaired her instinct: and
that is what came to pass: this queen passed over the royal cell several
times, that day and the next, without seeming to distinguish it from the
rest; she laid very quietly in the surrounding cells; and notwithstanding
the cares constantly bestowed by the bees upon this cell; she did not appear
for an instant to suspect the peril with which she was threatened by the
royal nymph there included. Besides, the workers treated their new queen
as well as they would have treated any other female: they lavished honey
and *respects* upon her, and formed around her those regular circles which
one would be tempted to consider as the expression of homage.

Thus, independent of the disorder which the delay of fecundation causes
in the sexual organs of queens, it certainly impairs their instinct; they no
longer entertain aversion or jealousy against those of their own sex in the
nymph state; they no longer seek to destroy them in their cradles.

My reader will be surprised that these queens, whose fecundation has
been retarded, and whose fecundity is so useless to the bees, nevertheless
should be so welcome and should become as dear to them as the females
that lay eggs of both kinds; but I remember observing a fact more astonishing still. I saw workers bestow every attention on their queen though
sterile, and after her death treat her dead body as they had treated her when

alive, and long prefer this inanimate body to the most fertile queens that I offered them. This sentiment, which assumes the appearance of so lively an affection, is probably the effect of some agreeable sensation communicated by the queen to the bees, independent of their fertility. The queens which lay only male eggs doubtless excite the same sensation in the workers.

While recalling this last observation, I remembered a statement of Swammerdam: this celebrated author stated, somewhere, that when a queen is blind, sterile, or mutilated, she ceases to lay and the workers of the hive no longer gather any crop or do any work, as if they knew that in such a case, it is useless to labor; but in advancing this fact, he does not cite the experiments which caused him to discover it; those made by myself have given me some very curious results.

I several times amputed the four wings of queens, and after this mutilation, not only did they continue to lay, but the workers showed them no less consideration than before. Swammerdam therefore has no foundation for saying that mutilated queens cease to lay; indeed in his ignorance of the necessity of fecundation outside of the hive, it is possible that he cut the wings off virgin queens, and that they, becoming incapable of flight, remained barren from inability to seek the males in the air. The amputation of their wings does not render them sterile, if they were fecundated before losing them.

We frequently cut off one of the antennæ to recognize a queen more readily, and this was not prejudicial, either to her fecundity or her instinct, nor to the attention paid to her by the bees; it is true that, as one antennæ still remained, the mutilation was imperfect, and this experiment decided nothing.

But the amputation of both antennæ produced most singular results. On the 5th of September of this year, I caused to be cut off both of the antennæ of that same queen which laid only male eggs, and replaced her in the hive immediately after the operation: from that time, there was great alteration in her manner. We saw her travel over the combs with extraordinary vivacity; scarcely had the workers time to separate and recede before her: she dropped her eggs haphazard, without thinking of depositing them in any cells. As the hive was not very populous, a part of it was without combs; it was there that she repaired; she remained long motionless and appeared to avoid the bees; however a few workers followed her in this solitude, and treated her with most evident respect, seldom did she ask for honey; but when she did, she directed her trunk only with an uncertain groping, sometimes upon the legs and sometimes upon the heads of the workers, and when it reached their mouths it was by chance. At other times she returned upon the combs, then quitted them to run upon the glass sides of the hive, and in all her various motions she still dropped her eggs. At other times she appeared tormented with the desire of leaving her habitation, rushing towards the entrance, she entered the glass tube adapted to it, but the external orifice of this tube being too small for her passage, after useless efforts she returned; notwithstanding these symptoms of delirium, the bees did not cease to render her the same attention as they ever pay to their queens, but she received it with indifference. All the symptoms just described appeared to me as the effect of the amputation of the antennæ;

however, her organization having already suffered from retarded fecundation and as I had observed a sort of weakening in her instinct, the two causes might possibly concur in operating the same effect. To distinguish what particularly belonged to the deprivation of the antennæ, it was necessary to repeat the experiment upon a queen otherwise well organized, and capable of laying both kinds of eggs.

This was done on the 6th of September; I amputated the antennæ of a female which I had been observing for several months, and which, gifted with great fecundity, had already laid a great number of eggs of workers and males. I placed her afterwards in the same hive where the queen of the preceding experiment still remained, and she exhibited precisely the same signs of agitation and delirium which I think useless to repeat: I shall only add that, in order to better judge of the effect produced by the privation of the antennæ upon the industry and instinct of queen bees, I observed attentively how these two mutilated queens treated each other: you have not forgotten, Sir, the fierceness in the combat of two queens, when they possess all their organs: so it was very interesting to learn whether they would experience the same reciprocal aversion, after losing their antennæ. We watched these a long time; they met several times in their courses, and did not exhibit the slightest sign of malevolence. This last fact is, in my opinion, the most complete proof of the change operated in their instinct.

Another very remarkable circumstance, which the experiment just related gave me occasion to observe, was the good reception which the bees gave this second stranger queen, while they still preserved the first. After having so often seen the signs of discontent occasioned by a plurality of queens in their hives, after having witnessed the clusters which they form around supernumerary queens to confine them, I could not expect them to render the same care to this second mutilated queen as they had given the first. Was it not that, after the loss of their antennæ, these queens no longer retained any characteristics serving to distinguish the one from the other?

I should be the more inclined to admit this conjecture, that when I introduced into this hive a third fertile queen, who had retained her antennæ, she was exceedingly badly received. The bees seized her, bit her, surrounded her so closely that she could hardly breathe or move. Therefore, if they treat equally well two females, deprived of their antennæ, in the same hive; it is, probably, because they experience the same sensation from both, and have no longer means of distinguishing them from each other.

From all this I conclude that the antennæ are not a frivolous ornament for insects; to all appearances they are the organs of touch or smell; but I cannot decide which of these two senses resides in them; it is not impossible that they be organized in such a manner as to fulfill both functions at once.

As in the course of this experiment, the two mutilated females constantly desired to escape from their hives, I wished to see what either of them would do, if set at liberty and whether the bees would accompany her in her flight: therefore, I removed from the hive the first queen introduced, and also the third, leaving the fertile mutilated one, and I enlarged the glass tube of the entrance, so that she might pass out.

During the same day, this queen left her habitation; at first she took flight, but as her belly was still full of eggs, she seemed too heavy, could not sustain her flight, fell down and did not attempt it again. No workers accompanied her. But why did they abandon her at her departure, after having given her so much attention, while she lived among them? You know, Sir, that queens governing a weak swarm are sometimes discouraged, and leave their hive, leading away all their little population with them. Similarly also, sterile queens, and those whose homes are ravaged by the moths, depart and are followed by all their bees. Why then, in the experiment which I relate here, did the workers allow their mutilated queen to depart alone?

I shall answer this question by only a conjecture. It appears that bees are induced to quit their hive by the increase of heat occasioned by the agitation of their queen and the tumultuous disorder which she communicates to them. But the mutilated queens, notwithstanding their delirium, do not excite the workers because in their travel they seek especially the uninhabited parts and the glass panes of the hive; they strike some groups of bees in passing; but the shock is similar to that of any other body that produces only a local and instantaneous emotion; the agitation resulting from it is not communicated from one to another like that occasioned by the hurry of a queen which, in the natural state, wishes to abandon her hive and lead out a swarm: there is no augmented heat and consequently no cause to render the hive insupportable to the bees.

This conjecture, which fairly explains why bees persist in remaining in the hive, after the departure of their mutilated queen, does not account for the motive inducing the queen herself to depart. Her instinct is changed, this is all that I perceive, I see nothing more. It is very fortunate for the hive, however, that she should leave it promptly; for, since the bees do not cease caring for her, as long as she remained they would not think of securing another; and if she delayed her flight, it would be impossible for them to replace her; since the worms of workers would have passed the term at which they are convertible into royal worms, and the hive would perish. Observe, Sir, that the eggs dropped by this mutilated queen could never serve to replace her, for not being deposited in the cells, they wither and produce nothing.

One more remark upon the females that lay only male eggs. Mr. Schirach thought that one branch of their double ovary suffered some alteration; he appears to have supposed that one of these branches contains only male eggs, while the other has none but worker eggs, and as he ascribed to some disease the incapacity of certain queens to lay worker eggs, his hypothesis was fairly plausible. In fact, if the eggs of males and those of workers are indiscriminately mixed in both branches of the ovary, it appears, at first sight, that any cause acting upon this organ should equally affect the two kinds of eggs. If, on the contrary, one branch is solely occupied with eggs of drones and the other with worker eggs only, we may conceive that one of these branches may be diseased and the other intact. This conjecture, however presumable, is confuted by observation. We lately dissected several queens that laid only drone eggs and we found both branches of their ovaries equally developed, equally *sound*, if I may use this expression. The only difference which we noticed was that, in these ovaries the eggs did not appear as close together as they are in the ovaries of queens which lay eggs of both sorts.

I have the honor to be &c.

THIRTEENTH LETTER

Economical Views on Bees.

Pregny, October 1st, 1791.

Sir, I shall talk to you in this letter upon the advantages presented by hives of new construction which I have used, and which I have called *book hives* or *leaf hives*, for the promotion of the *economical science* of bees.

I will not relate the different methods hithereto employed to compel bees to yield to us a share of their honey and of their wax; they were all cruel and ill-understood.

It appears evident that when we cultivate bees to share the product of their harvests, we must endeavor to multiply them as much as the nature of the country permits, and consequently spare their lives at the time we plunder them. Therefore it is an absurd proceeding to sacrifice whole colonies to take the riches which they contain. The inhabitants of our districts, who follow no other methods, annually lose enormous numbers of hives, and as our springs are generally unfavorable to swarms, the loss is irreparable. I know well that they will not adopt my method at first: they are too much attached to their prejudices and their old customs; but the naturalists and the enlightened cultivators will be sensible of the utility of the process which I indicate, and if they put it to use, I hope their example will contribute to extend and perfect the culture of bees.

It is not more difficult to lodge a natural swarm in a leaf hive than in any other of a different shape. However there is a precaution essential to success which I must not omit. Though bees are indifferent to the position of their combs and their greater or less size, they are obliged to construct them perpendicular to the horizon and parallel. Therefore, if they were left entirely to themselves, in establishing them in one of my new hives, they would often construct several small combs, parallel to each other indeed, but perpendicular to the plane of the frames or *leaves:* at other times they would fasten them on the joint of two of these frames, and by this disposition nullify the advantages that I claim to derive from the shape of my hives, since they could not be opened at will, without cutting the combs. We must therefore lay out the direction upon which they must build them; the cultivator himself must place the foundations of their edifice, and the method is very simple; it is sufficient that a portion of comb be fastened securely in the upper part of a few of the frames of which a hive is composed: you may be assured that the bees will lengthen this comb, and in prosecution of their work will follow precisely the direction indicated. Therefore you will never have any obstacle to overcome in opening the hive; no stings to dread, for that is also one of the singular and valuable properties of such construction, it renders the bees *tractable*. I appeal to you, Sir, in witness of this fact; in your presence I have opened all the frames of one of my most populous hives and you were much surprised at the tranquillity of the bees. I desire no other proof of my assertion; but I must repeat it, for in the last analysis it is in the facility of opening these hives at pleasure that all the advantages depend for the perfecting of the economic science of beekeeping.

It is not necessary to add here that, when I say that I can render the bees *tractable*, I do not claim the silly presence of *domesticating* them, for this causes a vague idea of *charlatanism*, and I do not wish to expose myself to such reproach: I ascribe their tranquillity, when their home is opened, to the manner in which they are affected by the sudden introduction of light; they appear rather to testify fear than anger; we see a great number withdraw, enter the cells head first, as if to conceal themselves; and my conjecture is confirmed by their being less tractable in the night or after sunset than in the day time.

Thus, we must select the time when the sun is still above the horizon, to open the hives, and do it with care. We must avoid opening the hive too brusquely; in separating the combs we must act slowly, taking care to wound none of the bees: when they are too much clustered upon the combs we must brush them softly with a feather (Note), and, above all things, not breathe upon them; the air which we exhale appears to anger them: the nature of this air evidently possesses some irritating quality; for if we use bellows to blow upon them, they are rather inclined to escape than to sting.

(Note. A broom made of vegetable fiber, asparagus tops, grass, &c., is much less apt to anger them than a feather. Tr.)

Let me return to the detail of the advantages of *leaf* hives. I shall remark first that they are very convenient for forming *artificial* swarms. In the history of *natural* swarms, I have shown how many favorable circumstances were requisite for their success. I knew by experience that they very often fail in our climate; and even when a hive is disposed to swarm, it often happens that the swarm is lost, either because the instant of its departure has not been foreseen, because it rose out of sight, or because it settled in inaccessible places. Thus, instructing the cultivators, in the forming of artificial swarms, is doing them a real service, and the shape of my hives renders this operation very easy. This demands some explanations.

Since, according to Schirach's discovery, bees which have lost their queen can procure another, provided there be worker brood in their combs not over 3 days old, it results that we can produce queens at will in a hive, by removing the reigning one. Therefore, if a sufficiently populous hive be divided in two, one half will retain the queen, and the other half will not be long in procuring one; but for the success of this operation we must choose a propitious moment, and this choice is easy and sure only in *leaf* hives: they are the only hives in which we can see whether the population is sufficient to admit of division, whether the brood is of proper age, whether males are born or ready to emerge to impregnate the young queen at her birth, &c.

Supposing the concurrence of all these conditions, the following is the process to be pursued. Separate the leaf hive through the middle, without any jar. Between the two halves insert two empty leaves, fitting exactly against the others, each of them closed with a box partition on the side where they fit against each other. You will then seek which of the two halves contains the reigning queen and mark it, to avoid error. If by chance she remains in the division having the most brood, she is to be transferred into the one having less, in order to give the bees the greater chances of procuring another female. The two halves must now be connected with one another by a small cord tightly drawn around them, and care must be taken that they occupy the same stand in the apiary as before the operation. The opening which served as entrance, up to this time, now becomes useless, it must be closed; but as each half hive must have an entrance, and as they must be as far apart as possible, a new opening must be made at the bottom of each of the outside frames, that is to say, the 1st and the 12th (see Plate I). However these entrances must not be both opened on the same day: the bees that are deprived of queen must be confined in their half for 24 hours, and the door must be opened only enough to admit of the access of air. Without this precaution, they would soon emerge to seek their queen in the apiary and would not fail to find her in the other division, they would enter it in great numbers, until too few remained to perform the necessary labors: while this accident will not ensue, if they be confined for 24 hours, since that interval of time is sufficient to make them forget their queen.

When all the circumstances are favorable, the bees of the division which is deprived of queen will begin on the same day their labor to procure another, and their loss will be repaired 10 or 15 days after the operation. The young female they have reared soon afterwards issues to seek males, returns home fertilized and at the end of two days commences the laying of worker eggs. Nothing more is wanting to the bees of this half-hive and the success of the artificial swarm is assured.

It is to Mr. Schirach that we are indebted for this ingenious method of forming swarms. In the description which he gives, he holds that, by producing young queens, in the early days of spring, precocious swarms might be procured, which certainly would be advantageous in several circumstances: but unfortunately this is impossible: this observer believed that queens were fertile of themselves; consequently he imagined that, after they were artificially produced, they would lay and give birth to a numerous posterity. But this is an error; the females require the concourse of the males to become fertile, and if they do not find any within a few days after their birth, their laying, as I have proved, is completely disarranged. Therefore if we made an artificial swarm before the usual time when the males are born, the young female would discourage the bees through her sterility or, should they remain faithful to her, awaiting the time of her fecundation, as she could not receive the approaches of the male before 3 or 4 weeks, she would lay eggs producing drones only, and the hive would equally perish. Thus the natural order must not be disarranged; but on the contrary, we must wait, to divide the hives, until they contain drones born or near birth.

Besides, if Schirach succeeded in obtaining artificial swarms, notwithstanding the great inconvenience of the hives which he used, it was owing to much skill and continuous assiduity. He had formed some pupils; these in their turn had communicated to others the method of forming swarms. There are people now in Saxony who traverse the country practicing this operation; but those conversant with the matter can alone dare undertake it with common hives, whereas every cultivator can undertake it with leaf hives.

They will find in this construction another very precious advantage; they will thus compel their bees to work in wax.

This leads me to what I believe is a new observation: while directing our admiration to the parallel position of the combs, which the bees build, the naturalists have overlooked another trait in their industry, namely the equal distance they uniformly preserve between them. Measure the interval between them, you will find it usually of 4 lines (one-third inch). One readily perceives that, were they too distant from one another, the bees would be greatly dispersed, unable to communicate their heat reciprocally and the brood could not receive sufficient warmth. If, on the contrary, they were too close, the bees could not travel freely between them, and the work of the hive would suffer. So they must be separated by a certain distance, always uniform, equally adapted to the service of the hive and the care of the worms. Nature, which taught bees so many things, instructed them in the regular preservation of this distance: it sometimes happens, at the approach of winter that our bees lengthen the cells which are to contain honey, and thus contract the intervals between the combs; but this particular labor is in preparation of a season when it is important to have great magazines, and during which, their activity being relaxed, it is no longer necessary for their communications to be so spacious and free. On the return of spring, the bees hasten to shorten the elongated cells, so they may become fit to receive the eggs which the queen must lay in them, and thus they re-establish the suitable distance which nature has ordained.

This being premised, in order to compel the bees to work in wax, or which is the same thing, to build new combs, it is only necessary to spread apart those already built, that they may construct others in the interval. Supposing that an artificial swarm is lodged in a leaf hive, composed of six frames, each of which contains a comb; if the young queen which governs this swarm is as prolific as she should be, her bees will be very active in their labors and disposed to make great collections of wax. To induce them towards it, an empty frame should be placed between two others, each containing a comb: as all these frames are of equal dimensions, and of the necessary width for containing a comb, it is evident that the bees, finding precisely the necessary space for constructing a new one in this empty frame, will not fail to do so, because they are under the obligation of never leaving a space of more than 4 lines between them. Take notice, Sir, that without the need of guide for the direction to be followed, they certainly will build this new comb parallel to those already there, to preserve the law which requires an equal interval between them, throughout their entire surface.

If the hive is strong and the weather good, we may insert 3 empty frames between the old combs, one between the first and the second, one between the third and the fourth, and the last between the fifth and sixth. The bees will need 7 or 8 days to fill them and the hive will then contain 9 combs. Should the weather continue with favorable temperature, one may introduce 3 more new frames, consequently in 2 or 3 weeks the bees will have been forced to construct 6 new combs. The operation might be still further extended in warm climates, where the country presents perpetual bloom; but in our country I have reason to believe that the labor should not be forced farther during the first year.

From these details, you perceive, Sir, how preferable the leaf hives are to hives of any other form, and even to the ingenious ekes (or stories. Tr) of which Mr. Palteau gave a description, for, by means of the latter, the bees cannot be compelled to work more in wax than they would if left to themselves; whereas they are obliged to do it by the alternating of empty frames. Secondly when they have constructed combs in these stories, they cannot be removed without deranging the bees, destroying considerable portions of the brood and in a word, without causing real disorder in the hive.

Besides, mine have this advantage, that one may daily observe what passes, and judge of the most convenient moment to take from them a part of their crop. When we have all the combs before us, we distinguish easily those that contain only brood, which we must preserve. We see how abundant the provisions are and what share of them we may take away.

I should too greatly lengthen this letter, were I to give you an account of all my observations of the time proper for inspecting hives, on the rules to be followed in the different seasons, and on the proportion to be observed in despoiling the bees of their wealth. It would require a separate work to develop the divers details: I may some day engage in it. Meanwhile I shall be always disposed to communicate my method to the cultivators who may wish to follow it, and the directions of which a long practice has shown me the utility.

I shall add only that we run risk of absolute ruin for the hives, when we take from them too great a proportion of honey and wax. In my opinion, the art of cultivating these insects consists in moderately using the right of sharing their crops, but to compensate this moderation every means must be employed to promote the multiplication of bees. Thus, for example, if we wish to procure, each year, a certain quantity of honey and wax, it will be better to seek it in a greater number of hives, managed with discretion, than to plunder a few of a great proportion of their treasures.

It is certain that we injure greatly the multiplication of these industrious insects, when we rob them of several combs in a season unfavorable to the collection of wax (Note), for the time occupied in replacing them is taken from that which should be consecrated to the care of the eggs and worms, and so the brood suffers. Besides, we must always leave them a sufficient provision of honey for winter; for although they consume less

(Note—Evidently Huber had not yet ascertained the origin of beeswax when he wrote this. His experiments upon the production of wax are given farther. Translator.)

during that season, they do consume, because they are not torpid, as some authors have asserted. Therefore, if they have not enough honey, they must be supplied with some; this requires a very exact measure.[18]

I admit that, in determining to what extent hives may be multiplied in a certain district, we should learn first how many this district can support, and this is a problem still unsolved: it depends on another problem the solution of which is not any better known, the determination of the greatest distance that bees ramble from their hives to gather their harvest. Different authors assert that they may wander several leagues from their home; but from the few observations that I have made, I believe this distance much exaggerated. It appeared to me that the radius of the circle they traverse does not exceed half a league (about 1½ miles). Since they return to their hive with the greatest speed, when a cloud passes before the sun, it is probable that they do not go very far. Nature, which has inspired them with such terror for a storm and even for rain, evidently does not permit them to stray at distances which expose them too long to the injuries of the weather. I endeavored to ascertain this more positively,

---

[18] They are so far from being torpid during the winter, that when the thermometer in the open air drops several degrees below zero (Réaumur), it stills stands at 24° to 35° (86° to 88° F.) in hives sufficiently populous. The bees then cluster together and move to preserve their heat.

Swammerdam was of the same oponion, and I will quote him: "The heat of a hive is so considerable, even in the middle of winter, that the honey does not crystallize or assume a granulated consistency, unless the bees be in too small numbers; moreover when their queens are very fertile, they feed their young with honey, even in the middle of winter, caring for them, warming them and warming each other as well. I do not know whether there are any other insects that have this in common with bees, for hornets, wasps and bumble bees, as well as flies and butterflies, remain torpid during the whole winter, without stirring or changing place."

Mr. de Réaumur found brood of all ages, in several hives, in January. The same thing happened to me, when the thermometer in them stood around 27° (93° F.).

Since I am speaking of thermometric observations, made upon the hives, I shall cursorily remark that Mr. Dubost, of Bourg-en-Bresse, in a memoir otherwise worthy, asserts that worms cannot hatch below 32° R (104° F). I have repeatedly made the experiment with very accurate thermometers and obtained a very different result. This degree is so little suitable that when the thermometer points to it, in the hive, the heat becomes intolerable to the bees, and they leave. I presume that Mr. Dubost was deceived by introducing his thermometer too suddenly in a cluster of bees, and the agitation caused among them, by this operation, forced the thermometer higher than it should naturally go. Had he kept it there a few moments, he would have seen it fall back to the 28th or 29th (95° to 97° F), for that is the ordinary temperature of hives in summer. In August this year, we saw the thermometer, in the open air stand at 27½° (94° F) while at the same moment, in the most populous hives, it did not rise above the 30th° (99° F). The bees had little motion and a great number of them rested on the supports of the apiary.

by transporting to various distances from the apiary, and in all sorts of directions, bees with the corslet painted, that we might recognize them on their return. None ever returned which had been carried 25 or 30 minutes from their domicile, while those transported a less distance readily found their way back. I do not report this experiment, Sir, as decisive. Though in ordinary conditions, bees do not fly above half a league, it is quite possible that they go much farther when the vicinity of their homes does not provide them with any flowers. For a conclusive experiment on this subject, it would be necessary to make it in vast arid or sandy plains, separated by a known distance from a blooming country.

Thus, this question appears undecided; but without pronouncing on the number of hives that a district can maintain, I shall remark that certain kinds of vegetable productions are much more favorable than others to bees. For example, more hives may be kept in a country where buckwheat is cultivated, than in a district of vineyards or wheat.

Here, Sir, I terminate the account of my observations on bees. Though I had the good fortune to make some interesting discoveries, I am far from considering my labor finished; there are still several problems to solve on the history of these insects. The experiments which I project may throw some light on them. I shall have much greater hopes of success, if you, Sir, will continue to give me your advice and directions. Accept the homage of my respect and my gratitude.

FRANCIS HUBER.

End of the First Volume.

EXPLANATION OF PLATE II.

Fig. 1 represents the organs of male bees, such as they are after they have been drawn out of their body and stretched, so that no part of them should hide the rest.

a, the posterior part of the body, the top of the last ring.

s, s, the seminal vesicles.

d, d, the deferent vessels (vas deferens).

q, q, constricted passage connecting the vas deferens with the seminal vesicles.

x, x, tortuous vessels, which are longer than they appear here and connect with the testicles.

t, t, testicles.

r, duct into which the seminal vesicles may empty their milky product, and which Swammerdam calls the "root of the penis".

l, junction point of the duct with the body that we call the lentil.

li, the lentil.

ie, ie, two brown, scaly or chitinous plates, which strengthen the lentil at its edges.

n, another chitinous plate.

> On that surface of the lentil which cannot show in this cut, there are also two plates similar to those marked ie, and n; they are similarly located.

k, duct composed of folded membranes, emerging from the posterior part of the lentil.

p, plaited palet.

u, the arch; it shows through the membranes which cover it.

m, membranes forming a fleshy bag, which, when out of the body, forms a sort of woolly mask.

c, c, the two horns, one of which is stretched out, the other folded; they are both ordinarily more folded even than this one is.

Fig. 2 represents that part of the drone organ which remains within the posterior part of the females after mating, and which Mr. de Réaumur has called "the lentil".

li, lenticular body, shown from the edge, from magnifying glass.

r, fragment of the duct which Swammerdam called the "root of the penis" and which breaks at that spot, when the male separates from the female after the mating.

ie, ie, two scaly plates which act as pincers.

n, n, two chitinous plates, shorter than the former and adjoining them.

v, part which I called the **verge or penis.**

VOLUME II.

New Observations Upon Bees.

PREFACE.

Twenty years have elapsed since the publication of the first volume of this work; however, I have not remained idle. But before bringing to light new observations, I wanted time to verify the truths which I believe I established. I had hoped that better trained naturalists would desire to ascertain for themselves the correctness of the results obtained by me, and I thought that, by repeating my experiments, they might ascertain facts which escaped my notice. But no other attempt has since then been made to penetrate farther into the history of those insects, and yet it is far from exhausted.

Although I was deceived in this expectation, I flatter myself with having obtained the confidence of my readers, my observations appear to have given light on several phenomena that had not yet been explained; the authors of several works upon the economy of bees have commented upon them; most of the cultivators have adopted entirely, as the basis of their practice, the principles which I discovered; and the naturalists themselves have taken interest in my efforts to pierce the double veil which shrouds, for me (Huber here alludes evidently to the fact that he was blind. Tr.), the natural sciences. Their assent should have emboldened me sooner to edit the facts contained in this second volume, had not the loss of several persons dear to me disturbed the quietude which such occupations require.

The profound, indulgent and amiable philosopher, whose benevolence encouraged me to come forward, in spite of the disadvantages of my position, Mr. Charles Bonnet, died, and discouragement took possession of me. Sciences lost, in losing him, one of the genii sent from heaven to make science lovable; who, by linking them with the most natural sentiments of man, and by giving to each the rank and degree of interest due to it, bound the heart as well as the mind, and charmed our imagination without misleading it through delusions.

I found, in the friendship and the enlightenment of Mr. Senebier, some relief for the privations imposed upon me. A continued correspondence with this great physiologist, while enlightening me upon the course to follow, revived my existence in some manner; but his death surrendered me to fresh sorrows. Lastly, I was also to be deprived of the use of those eyes which had taken the place of my own, of the skill and devotedness which I had had at my bidding during 15 years. Burnens, the faithful observer, whose services I will always gladly recall, was called back into the bosom of his own people and, being appreciated as he deserved to be, he became one of the first magistrates of a considerable district.

This last separation which was not the least painful one, since it deprived me of the means of diverting my mind from those which I had already suffered, was nevertheless softened by the satisfaction which I found in observing nature through the organs of the being who is the dearest to me, and with whom I could enter into more elevated considerations. (Huber's wife. Translator.)

But that which most especially connected me again with natural history, was the taste that my son manifested for this study. I communicated my observations to him: he expressed sorrow in leaving, buried in a notebook, work that would seem likely to interest naturalists: he noticed the concealed reluctance which I felt in classifying the materials gathered, and offered to edit them himself. I accepted his offer; the reader will not be astonished therefore, if this work is found to differ in its two component parts. The first volume contains my correspondence with Mr. Bonnet; the second presents a set of Memoirs: in the one, we had limited ourselves to the simple expose of facts; in the other the point was to describe difficult matters, and in order to diminish the dullness, we have sometimes freely made such comments as the subject suggested. Moreover, when giving my notes to my son, I also transmitted my ideas to him; we have blended our thoughts and our opinions; I felt the need of giving him' possession of a subject in which I had acquired some experience.

This new book treats of the work, properly speaking, of the bees, or of their architecture, their respiration and their senses. The Memoirs which I caused to be inserted in periodical magazines, such as that on the origin of the wax and on the sphinx atropos, have been established in their proper place; they both have undergone a few changes and the latter has been enriched with additional experiments. Lastly I am publishing upon the sex of worker-bees (a long debated question) a Memoir which, I trust, will no longer leave any doubt concerning Schirach's discovery.

I might have added several observations to those which I now give to the public; but they do not present a sufficient ensemble, and I prefer to wait until they may be accompanied with facts concerning them.

FOREWORD OF THE PUBLISHER.

The Observations which I publish in the name of my father long exercised his patience and that of Burnens. It was not sufficient to follow with exactness the maneuvers of the bees, it was also requisite to perceive their connection, and understand the aim to which they pointed.

Another and perhaps a greater difficulty was to clearly see complicated forms and secure a distinct idea of their combination. Models of clay, made with great skill, supplied that which speech could not explain.

In this way, my father secured, from the accounts given by Burnens, a fairly complete theory of the architecture of bees.

He conceived no doubts of the correctness of his observations, but in order to obtain new ideas, or the confirmation of facts already understood, he desired that I should revise them myself before they were published.

Therefore I procured hives similar to those that he had used, and it was with great enjoyment that I witnessed, in my turn, all the points of this astonishing industry; it was with equal pleasure that I was enabled to agree with the conscientious exactness of the observer in whom my father had placed his confidence, and I can add only a small number of details to those already recorded.

INTRODUCTION.

No people, perhaps no nation has had as many historians as these republics of laborious insects, whose industry seems to be intended for us. There are periodical works solely relative to the culture of bees; associations have been founded, the object of which is to discuss the advantages of such or such method; the centuries have accumulated observations; but in spite of the progress of sciences, we are still ignorant concerning the constituents of beeswax; it is true that most of the authors to whom we are indebted for those numerous writings, gave us their uncertain opinions as precepts, sometimes their dreams as theories based upon experience; and, piling up the quotations, citing one another, they have contributed to the perpetuation of errors instead of dispelling them. But there are, fortunately, a few respectable authors as to talent and truthfulness, who, overstepping the common limits, sought, like true naturalists, to ascertain the laws which govern those colonies.

The bees have even attracted the attention of geometricians; those of antiquity already understand the purpose of the hexagon prisms of which they build their combs; but it was reserved for modern theories to appreciate the extent of the geometrical problem which those insects solve in the construction of the base of their cells. These bases, built in pyramids, offered, for speculation, one of the greatest philosophical subjects, to those who do not believe that everything may be explained by the supposition of blind necessity. Skilled mathematicians have found that, between all the forms that bees might select in an endless list of pyramids, they preferred that which offered the greatest advantages; for it is not to them, says Réaumur (the writer who knew nature best) "it is not to them that the honor is due, it was ordained by an intelligence which sees the immensity of infinite things, and all their combinations, more clearly and more distinctly than it can be perceived by our modern Archimedes."

But without attributing to the workman the glory of the invention, it must be granted, at least, that the execution of so complicated a plan could not be entrusted to stupid creatures, to gross animal machines. If we can prove, in what follows, that bees may, in certain cases, depart from their routine, that this regularity in their work is subject to exceptions, and that they are able to counterbalance their errors by additions or partial reductions, so that no inconvenience results for the whole: if we prove that there is no irregularity in their work without a purpose, we will appreciate the greatness of their task and the delicacy of their organization.

In order to give a proper idea of the work of bees, let us assume an isolated cell placed with its opening downwards upon a horizontal plane; it thus represents a small six-sided prismatic column, surmounted with a capital in pyramid shape, depressed and obtuse, Plate I, fig. I.

The six faces of the hexagon, which appear at first sight as so many plates of wax, of rectangular shape, are cut at right angles at the orifice; but at the opposite extremity they are cut obliquely; so that their greater edges are not of equal length. Each plane is united to its neighbor by a similar edge, the long edge of the one to the long edge of the other, and its short edge to the short edge of a third; the result is that, if we were to remove the capital, we would notice that the edge of the hexagon tube forms projections and recesses alternately, that is to say, three projecting angles (h, a, r) and three recessive angles (c, i, s) fig. 2.

From the top of the three projecting angles, three edges proceed which meet opposite the center of the cell (am, hm, rm, fig. 1); these divide the base into three parts, and the spaces between them being filled to the edge of the recessive angles, they assume the shape of losanges, or rhombs (achm, fig 1). Small scales of wax fill these spaces, so that each cell is composed of six panes in trapeze shape and three rhombs.

The combs of the bees, as we know, are composed of two rows of cells back to back, not singly however, but in part: each cell resting against three cells of the opposite side (figs. 3 and 4).

To fulfill these conditions, the bees need only to erect, upon the three edges which divide the base of each cell, similar panes to those of the cell itself, and which, joining other plates of similar shape, produce hexagon prisms. This is what we almost always see in the combs of bees: one may test it by piercing with a pin the three rhombs which form the base of a cell. When examing the opposite side of the comb we find that we have pierced the bottom of each of three cells.

In addition to the economy of material which appears to ensue from this position of the cells, we notice a still more positive advantage, that of contributing to the strength of the whole.

We wonder how such small insects have been led to follow so regular a plan; how the multitude of them can concur in such an arrangement, what means nature uses to direct them? Let us transcribe a few quotations that will make known to us the opinions of various naturalists upon this matter.

A celebrated author, a painter rather than a faithful observer of nature, was not perplexed in the explanation of these marvels. "We must acknowledge," he wrote, "that taking the bees singly, they have less genius than the dog, the monkey or the greater number of animals: we must acknowledge that they have less docility, less fondness, less feeling, in fact less qualities relatively to our own; then we must acknowledge that their apparent intelligence is due to the union of their multitude; however this union itself does not presuppose any intelligence, for it is not with moral views that they unite, it is without their consent that they find themselves together: this association is only a physical union, ordained by nature, independent of any views, or any reasoning. The mother-bee produces ten thousand individuals at one time; if these ten thousand individuals were still more stupid than I believe them to be, they would still be compelled to organize themselves in some fashion, in order to continue their existence; as they work with equal ability, if they began by harming each other, they would at length be compelled to harm each other as little as possible; that is, to help each other, so they appear to have an understanding and to have similar aims; the observer will soon ascribe to them the intellect which they lack, he will try to explain each action; each motion will soon be given a motive, and from this will follow numberless reasoning marvels or monsters; for those ten thousand individuals which have been produced together, live together and have undergone their metamorphoses in similar time, cannot fail to do exactly the same thing, and with the least feeling will adopt the same mode of living, of arrangement, of agreeing with each other, of occupying their home, coming back to it after having left it, &c., hence architecture, geometry, order, foresight, love of country or of the republic, all based upon the admiration of the observer.

"Society in animals that appear to gather together freely and for convenience implies the experience of feeling, but the association of beasts which, like the bees, are together without having planned it, does not imply anything; whatever may be the results, it is evident that they have not been anticipated, nor ordained, nor conceived by those that execute them, and that they proceed only from the universal mechanism and laws of motion established by the Creator. Place together, in the same room, ten thousand automatons animated with a living force, and all induced, through the perfect resemblance of their outer and inner being and by the conformity of their life, to do exactly the same thing in the same place, and a regular work will necessarily result: the relations of harmony, similitude, position, will be there, since they will depend upon the conformity of life: the relations of contiguity, of extent, of shape will be present also, since the space is limited and circumscribed; and if we admit the least degree of feeling in these automatons, even only such as is necessary for them to be conscious of their own existence, seek their own conservation, avoid noxious things, prepare useful things, &c., their work will not only be regular, well proportioned, similar, equal, but it will also have symmetry, strength, convenience to the highest point of perfection, because, in making it, each of those ten thousand individual has tried to place itself in the most commodious way, and because it has been compelled also to act and to place itself in the position least uncomfortable to others.

"Moreover, those cells of bees, those vaunted and admired hexagons furnish me one more arm against enthusiasm and admiration; that figure, though geometrical and regular as it appears, and is, in hypothesis, is but a mechanical and rather imperfect result often found in nature, noticeable even in its most crude productions; crystals and several other stones, several salts, &c., often assume this shape in their formation. We see the same hexagons in the second stomach of ruminants; we find them in seeds, in seed-capsules, in certain flowers, &c. Fill a vessel with peas or with some other cylindrical seed, and close it hermetically, after having filled with water all the spaces between those seeds; then boil the water, and all those seeds will assume the six-sided shape. The reason of this is purely mechanical; each cylindrical seed, in swelling, occupies a greater space in the space allowed; they necessarily become hexagonal by reciprocal compression; each bee seeks to occupy also a sufficient space, it is therefore necessary also, since their body is round, that their cells be hexagonal through the same cause of reciprocal obstacles.

"We admit in the bees more intelligence, because their work is more regular: we say that they are more ingenious than wasps, hornets, &c., that are architects also, but whose structures are coarser and more irregular than those of bees; we blind ourselves to the fact, or perhaps we do not know, that the greater or less regularity depends solely upon the number and the shape, and not in the least upon the intelligence of those little beasts; the more numerous they are, the more forces act in like manner or in opposition to each other, and therefore the more mechanical constraint, the more forced regularity and apparent perfection will there be in their productions."

One can readily recognize the author of this discourse through the arguments and the style which embellishes them; we shall leave to some more eloquent writer the task of refuting Mr. Buffon. The two passages which we will now quote, taken from the "Contemplation de la Nature." (part XI, notes 9 and 11 of the XXVII° chapter, last edition), while answering in a direct manner the hypotheses of this author, will give a correct idea of the progress in the history of bees, through Maraldi and Réaumur, relative to the building of combs; it will serve at the same time to indicate their opinion on the origin of beeswax.[1]

"The jaws, the trunk and the six legs are the main instruments which have been given the bees to execute their different labors. The teeth are two little sharp scales, working horizontally, and not up and down like our own: the trunk, which the bee unfolds and stretches out at will does not act in the manner of a pump; I mean that the bee does not use it to suck; it is a sort of long tongue covered with hairs, and it is by licking in the flowers that it loads itself with a liquid which is passed to the mouth to descend through the esophagus into a first stomach, which is its receptacle. One perceives that this liquid is honey; the bees are familiar with the little nectariferous glands, situated at the base of the calyx of flowers and containing this honey; after filling their honey sac with it, they go and disgorge it into the cells; they fill them and thus store it away, closing the cells with a capping of wax. But there are other honey cells which they do not seal, because they are store cells for the daily needs of the community.

"It is also upon the flowers that the bees gather the wax-producing material or raw wax; the dust of the stamens composes this material. The industrious bee dips into the interior of flowers that have the greatest abundance of this dust; the little hairs with which her body is covered become loaded with this dust; the worker plucks it off with brushes existing on her legs for this purpose, and forms with it two pellets that the legs of the second pair place in basket-like cavities existing on the third pair of legs. Loaded with those two pellets of wax-forming material, the diligent bee returns to the hive, and deposits them in cells provided for that purpose. These cells thus become wax-magazines and remain open; but the bee is

---

[1] Mr. Bonnet having written nothing in the text of the manner in which bees gather honey and wax, nor of their art in the construction of their beautiful works, this omission is supplemented in a note transcribed here.

not satisfied with thus unloading her burden: she enters into the cell, head
first, spreads the two pellets, kneads them, and deposits upon them a little
saccharine matter. If the labor which she has executed in gathering this
harvest has fatigued her too much, another bee comes along and kneads
the pellets and spreads them; for all the Helots of this little Sparta are
equally aware of all that needs to be done in each particular case, and acquit
themselves equally well of it. But it does not always happen that the bee
has only to dip into the blossoms to gather this dust with her fleece; there
are circumstances when the harvest is not so easy, and requires some dexterity on the part of the worker. Before its full ripeness, the dust is enclosed in capsules which botanists have named "the apex of the stamen."
The worker which seeks pollen, from still closed capsules, is compelled to
open those capsules and she does so with her mandibles, then she seizes
the pollen grains with her first pair of legs: the articulations of the end of
these legs act like hands; the grains are then passed to the second pair
of legs which, after depositing them within the baskets of the third pair,
tamp them down by striking them several times; the slight moisture of
the grains helps to hold them there also and to pack them together; the
worker repeats the same maneuvers, completing the filling of the two baskets, and hastens to the hive with her plunder.

"This dust which the bees gather from the flowers, is not the same as
the wax which they mold with so much industry, it is only the raw material, and this material requires a preparation and digestion in a particular
stomach, in a second stomach. It is there that it becomes true beeswax;
the bees then disgorge it through their mouth, in the shape of a pap or
white foam, which hardens quickly in the air: while this dough is yet
ductile, it assumes easily any shape which the bee may desire to give it, it is
for her the same as clay for the potter.

"A great physicist, who studied deeply the geometric work of bees,
thought that he could reduce it to its actual value by considering it as the
simple result of a coarse mechanism; he thought that bees, crowded against
one another, naturally gave wax a hexagonal figure, and that it was with
the bees' cells as with any balls of soft material which, pressed against
each other, would assume the shape of dice. I am thankful to this physicist
for his aloofness from the allurements of the marvelous; I should like to
praise him upon the correctness of his comparison, but we will show that
the work of bees is far from the simplicity of mechanism that he was
pleased to imagine.

"The reader has not forgotten that the cells of bees are not simple
hexagon tubes, these tubes have a pyramidal base, formed of 3 pieces in
losanges, or 3 rhombs, and it is with these that they form the foundation
of the cells: on two outside faces of this rhomb they erect two of the walls
of the cell; then they shape a second rhomb which they fasten to the first,
giving them the proper slope; on those exterior walls they erect two new
walls of the hexagon; lastly they build the third rhomb and the two last
walls: all this work is at first rather massive but must not remain thus.
The skilled workers perfect it, thin it down, polish it, straighten it; their
jaws serve them as planes and files. A really fleshy tongue, fastened at
the base of the jaws, also helps the work of the teeth. Many workers suc-

ceed each other in this labor; that which one has only sketched another finishes a little farther, a third perfects it, &c., and although it has thus gone through so many hands, it appears as if made in a mold.

"We have just shown, (in note 9), that each cell's base is pyramidal, and that the pyramid is formed of 3 equal and similar rhombs; the angles of these rhombs might vary infinitely; that is, the pyramid might be more or less pointed, more or less flat: the savant Maraldi, who measured the angles of the rhombs with extreme precision, found that the large angles generally measured 109 degrees and 28 minutes, while the small angles measured 70 degrees and 32 minutes. Mr. de Réaumur, who meditated upon the processes of insects, ingeniously surmised that the choice of these angles, between so many others, was based upon the possible saving of wax, and that, of all the cells of equal capacity with pyramidal base, those that could be built with the least quantity of material were those whose dimensions corresponded with these actual measurements. So, he requested a skilled geometrician, Mr. Koenig, who knew nothing of these measurements, to determine by reckoning what should be the angles of a hexagon cell with pyramidal base, in order to require the least possible material in its construction; for the solution of this fine problem, this geometrician resorted to a minute analysis, and found that the angles of the large rhombs should be of 109 degrees and 26 minutes, and the small ones 70 degrees and 24 minutes; a surprising agreement between his solution and the actual measurements. Mr. Koenig demonstrated also that, in preferring a pyramidal base to a flat base, the bees save the amount of wax which would be needed to build a flat base.[2]

[2] Mr. Koenig thought that bees should make the rhombs of the cells 109° 16′ and 70° 34′ in order to use the least possible quantity of wax (Réaumur Vol. V, Memoir VIII).

Mr. Cramer, formerly professor in Geneva, to whom Koenig had suggested the same problem, found that these angles should be 109° 28½′ and 70° 31½′. This result is the same as that secured by Father Boscovisch, who notes that Maraldi had superficially given the angles as 110° and 70°, and that those which he gave 109° 28′ and 70° 32′ were of the dimensions necessary, in order that the angles of the trapezium be equal, near the base (Mem. of the Royal Academy 1712). In addition, Father Boscovisch indicates that all the angles which form the plane of the cell are equal, and of 120°, and he assumes that this equality of obliquity facilitates the building of the cell, which might be a motive of preference, as well as the economy of it. He demonstrates that bees do not by any means save the quantity of wax that would be used in a flat base for the construction of each cell, as Messrs. Koenig and Réaumur had believed.

Maclaurin writes that the difference between a cell with pyramidal base and a cell with flat base, that is to say, the economy that bees secure, is equal to one-fourth of the six triangles, which would have to be added to the trapeziums or faces of the cells, so they should become rectangles.

Mr. Lhuillier, a professor in Geneva, estimates that the bees save 1/51 of the total expense and demonstrates that it might be as much as 1/5 if the bees had no other requirements to fulfill; but he concludes that it is not

"While following the reasoning of the historian of insects upon the geometric shape of the cells of bees and wasps, the illustrious Mairan expressed himself as follows: 'whether beasts think or not, it is positive that 'they conduct themselves in thousands of occasions as if they did think; the 'illusion in this matter, if it be an illusion, was well arranged for us. But 'without intending to touch upon this great question, and whatever be the 'cause, let us for a moment surrender ourselves to appearances and use 'every day language.

'Geometricians, among whom we must number Mr. de Réaumur, have 'endeavored to make us appreciate all the art contained with the wax 'combs, and the paper wasps nests, so ingeniously laid out in tiers, sus-'tained with columns, and these tiers or stories built in an infinity of sex-'angular cells. It was not without cause that the statement was made that 'this figure was the most convenient, if not the only convenient one, among 'all possible polygons, to fulfill the intentions that we must attribute to the 'bees and wasps that construct them. It is true that the regular hexagon 'is the necessary outcome of the apposition of round, soft and flexible bodies, 'when pressed against each other, and that it is apparently for that reason 'that we see it so often in nature, as for instance in the capsules of the 'seeds of certain plants, in the scales of several animals, and sometimes 'in the particles of snow, on account of the small spherical or circular 'bubbles of water which have flattened against each other in freezing; but 'there are so many other requirements to fulfill in the building of the hex-'agonal cells of bees and wasps, and which are so beautifully fulfilled, that 'even if we should deny them a part of the honor to which they are entitled 'on this, it is hardly possible to deny that they have added much by choice, 'and that they have skilfully taken advantage of this necessity imposed 'upon them by nature.' "

The writings of the naturalists, in whom I have the greatest confidence, are therefore not favorable to the opinion expressed by Mr. de Buffon, who attributes one of the marvels of nature to entirely mechanical combinations. Experience had already taught us that we cannot explain the work of bees through such gross means, and I soon became convinced, through my own observations, of the correctness of Mr. Bonnet in this regard.

My researches will doubtless bring numerous modifications to the ideas

greatly perceptible on each cell, although it might prove more perceptible on the entire comb, because of the mutual fitting in of the cells on the opposite sides of the comb (Memoir of the Royal Academy of Sciences of Berlin, 1781).

Lastly, Mr. Le Sage demonstrates that, whatever be the obliquity of the rhombs, the capacity of the cell remains the same. The combs, he says, are two cells deep, disposed in such a way that whatever we may take away or give to the front ones must be given or taken away from the rear ones, so that :1° the entire comb would neither lose nor gain anything and also that 2° the front ones would still be equal to the rear ones, owing to the symmetry with which they are reciprocally incased within each other.

held in his time upon the art with which these insects construct their combs; but I hope they may contribute to the support of a very different theory from that of the eloquent historian of animals.

N. B. Skilled, modern mathematicians have also exerted themselves upon the problem of the minimum amount of wax in the cells; but their conclusions are quite different from those of their predecessors. The note just quoted, taken from the papers of Mr. G. L. Le Sage, of Geneva, indicates the progress made in this research.

New Observations Upon Bees.

CHAPTER I.

My Opinions Upon Beeswax.

Since the time of Réaumur and de Geer, whose works have inspired a general taste for entomology, observing minds have caused great steps to be made in science; all its branches are extended, and the history of bees, more than any other, has been enriched, in this interval.

Schirach and Riem opened a new road, and perhaps we ourselves have contributed to clear it of the prejudice which clogged its progress, by establishing the facts announced, in a more rigorous manner.

Since then, some observations were published in different countries, but with so little development and in so inaccurate a manner as compared with what is now required of natural sciences, that they would sink in oblivion did we not endeavor to support them by facts that may strengthen them.

Naturalists have principally directed their attention to wax: several chemists have also attempted to analyse it, but there is so little accord in the results of these labors, as to prove the insufficient discussion of this subject, which requires new examination.

One opinion appeared well established, among those which we have quoted from the contemplation of nature, when Mr. Bonnet wrote that which he had accepted, after the best writers of his time, concerning the conversion of the dust of the stamens into beeswax. The reader must have perused with interest the details which he gave of the manner in which the bees harvest this substance, load themselves with it, store it and preserve it; all of these facts had been scrupulously observed by Réaumur, Maraldi and several other savants, so that no doubts may be raised upon this point; it is also evident that this dust, taken by the bees from the flowers, is of real use to them, since they bring home such great quantities of it, but is this truly the elementary principle of beeswax?

Appearances favored this hypothesis; the bees supplying the cultivator with two precious substances, honey and beeswax, and each day gathering, under his very eyes, the nectar of flowers and their fecundating dust, one might readily believe the latter substance to be crude wax.

Réaumur entertained some doubt, not upon the actual conversion, but upon the manner in which it took place; was wax formed from this dust itself or was the latter only one of the principal ingredients of it? After

109

several experiments, quite simple but inconclusive, he inclined to the latter opinion, but he always expressed it with the reserve which is noticeable in friends of the truth; he thought to have made sure that the bees submitted pollen to a special elaboration, that it was converted into real beeswax in their stomach, and that this was disgorged from their mouth in the shape of a sort of pap. He had noticed, however, the very great difference existing between the fecundating dust and beeswax itself, and several observations made by him should have caused him to dismiss this idea, had he drawn correct consequences from them.

Science had stopped at this point, when a Lusatian cultivator, whose name has not reached us, made a most important discovery. Mr. Willelmi, a relative of Schirach, who caused such great progress to be made in the history of bees, wrote to Mr. Bonnet, August 22d, 1768: "Allow me, Sir, to write here an abridged account of some new discoveries that the Society (of Lusace) has made. We believed until the present that bees discharge wax through their mouth, but it has been noticed that they exude it through the rings which form the posterior part of their body. In order to ascertain it, one must draw the bee, with the point of a needle, from the cell in which she works, one will then notice, by stretching her body slightly, that the wax with which she is loaded is to be found under her rings, in the shape of scales, &c. (Histoire de la Mère Abeille, by Blassière.)

The author of this letter did not name the naturalist who made this beautiful observation; whoever he be, he deserved to be better known. However, this did not appear to Mr. Bonnet as established upon sufficient proof to make him relinquish the already accepted ideas, and, persuaded by his influence, we did not investigate the basis of his opinion.

But, several years afterwards, however, in 1793, we were greatly astonished to find small scales of a material resembling beeswax, under the rings of some bees.

This discovery was of greatest interest, in every respect; we displayed these scales of wax to several of our friends, and, having exposed them to the flame of a candle, we found in them the characters of true beeswax.

However, John Hunter, an Englishman of high repute, observing bees at the time when I did so myself, conceived some doubts which brought him the same results. He discovered the true wax receptacle under the belly of these insects, and gave the detail of his observations in a memoir inserted in the philosophical transactions, in 1792.

By raising the lower segments of the abdomen of bees, he found scales of a fusible material which he recognized as beeswax. He ascertained the difference existing between the pollen of the stamens and the material of which combs are built, and he attributed a new property to those pellets which bees bring home on their legs. This was a notable step forward, but Hunter was unable to witness the use made of these scales of wax which he assumed to be produced within the body of the bee, he could offer only conjectures upon the use of pollen. We carried our own observations farther, and were able, not only to confirm his experiments, but also to give them greater development; thus those facts, announced in Germany, in England and in France, could not fail to secure the confidence of all naturalists.

It was under the inferior rings of the belly of the bees that we found the scales of wax; they were arranged in pairs under each segment, in small pockets of peculiar shape, and located on the right and left of the angular edge of the abdomen; none was found under the rings of the drones or of the queens, the structure of these parts being very different in these two classes; the workers alone, therefore, possess the faculty of secreting wax, to employ the expression of John Hunter (See note at end of volume).

The form of these pockets or reservoirs, which was not noted by this author and which Swammerdam and so many other naturalists who studied the bee overlooked, yet deserves the greatest study, since it belongs to a newly found organ.

The underside of the belly of the bee (Plate II, fig. 2) presents nothing on the outside which is not common with the abdomen of wasps and several other hymenopters, they are demi-segments partly overlapping one another, but they are not flat, as are those of most insects of the same family; they are arched; for the abdomen of the bees is noticeable in an angular prominence which exists from one end to the other (a, b, fig. 2). The edge of these segments is scaly, but if they are lifted, or if we stretch the abdomen of the bee by drawing it gently at one of its extremities, we disclose the part which was concealed, in ordinary conditions, by the upper edge of the other segments (figs. 1 & 4).

This part (c, d, e, g, fig. 5) which must be considered as the base of each ring, since it adheres to the body of the insect, is a membranous, soft, transparent and yellowish white substance; it occupies at least two-thirds of each segment; it is divided in two by a small horny ridge (a, b,) which corresponds exactly with the angular projection of the abdomen. This ridge, starting from the center of the scaly edge (d, g, r, s) going towards the head, crosses the membranous part, bifurcates at its extremity and divides into a bow shape right and left, supplying a solid edge to both sides of the membrane (n, c, b, e, m, g, fig. 5): the scales of wax are found in nature upon these two small areas (fig. 7). Their outline, formed of both straight and curved lines joined together, exhibit at first sight the appearance of two ovals; but when we analyze their composition, we recognize that they are of irregular pentagonal shape. The membranous areas are sloping, like the sides of the body itself; they are entirely covered by the edge of the preceding segment and form, with the latter, small pockets open only on the lower side. The segments, or the two plates which form the wax cavity, are united together by a sort of membrane, like the two parts of a portfolio.

The scales of wax are exactly of the same shape as the membranous areas upon which they are found. There are only 8 in each individual bee; for the first and the last ring, being of a different shape from the rest, do not have any. The size of the scales decreases with the diameter of the rings whereon they are molded; the largest are under the third and the smallest under the fifth.

We noticed that the wax scales were not alike in every bee; a difference was perceptible in their shape, their thickness and their consistency.

Upon some of the bees, they were so thin and so transparent that a magnifying glass was necessary to perceive them; upon others we could discover only crystals in needle shape such as are seen upon freezing water.

These spiculæ, or scales, did not rest immediately upon the membrane; they were separated from it by a slight coat of a liquid substance, perhaps serving to lubricate the junctures of the rings, or to render the extraction of the scales easier, as otherwise they might adhere too firmly to the walls of the cells.

Finally, some other bees had scales so large that they projected beyond the rings, their form more irregular than that of the previous ones; their thickness, altering the transparency of the wax, made them appear of a whitish yellow color; one could perceive them without raising the segments which usually cover them entirely.

These shades of difference in the scales of different bees, this progression in their shape and thickness, the fluid interposed between them and the walls of their cells, the relation between their size and shape, all those circumstances together appeared to indicate the transudation of this material through the membrane which moulds it.

We were confirmed in this opinion by a singular fact. On piercing the membrane, whose internal surface seemed to be applied to the soft parts of the belly, we caused the escape of a transparent fluid which coagulated in cooling; in this condition it resembled beeswax: when submitted to the influence of heat, it liquified again.

The same experiment, made upon the wax scales, had similar result; they became liquid and coagulated again according to the temperature, exactly as does beeswax.

We carried our researches farther upon the analogy of this substance with finished beeswax; for this purpose we selected the whitest fragments of wax that we could find, taking them from newly built comb, to make the same test; for wax from old combs is always more or less colored.

FIRST EXPERIMENT.

We dropped into spirits of turpentine a few scales taken from under the rings of workers; they were dissolved and disappeared before reaching the bottom of the vessel, without rendering the fluid turbid; but an equal amount of the spirit could not dissolve, either as completely or as quickly, the white fragments of worked wax, many particles remaining suspended in the liquid.

SECOND EXPERIMENT.

We filled with sulphuric ether two vessels of equal size, the one was appropriated for wax from the rings of bees, the other for fragments of beeswax of equivalent weight. Scarcely had the fragments of wax from combs touched the ether when they divided and fell in powder to the bottom of the vase; but the scales taken from the bees themselves were not disintegrated; they preserved their shape and only lost their transparency, becoming of a dull white color. No change took place in either of the vessels in the space of several days. On evaporating separately the ether from each, a thin coat of wax was found on the glass; we repeated this experiment frequently, the fragments of combs were always reduced to powder; the scales, on the contrary, were never dissolved by the liquid; after several months the ether had dissolved but a very small proportion of them.

From this experiment the evidence was that the wax of the bees' rings was less compounded than that which had been built into cells, since the latter was dissolved by the ether while the former remained whole; the one was dissolved by turpentine only in part, while the other was completely dissolved by it.

If the substance taken from the rings of the bees is crude wax, it must undergo some preparation after leaving its cells and the bees must be capable of impregnating it with a substance giving it the ductility and whiteness of true wax. Hitherto, we knew only of its fusibility, but such being the chief property of the combs, we could not doubt that the scales enter in their composition.

In the hope ascertaining the primary source of the waxy matter, we had recourse to the dissection of the wax organs, but though undertaken by a skillful hand, it did not fulfill our expectations. (For the details, see the letter of Miss Jurine at the end of this volume).

No direct communication could be found between these organs and the interior of the abdomen; no vessels were found appearing to connect them, with the exception of a few tracheæ, doubtless intended to admit the air into these parts. But the membrane of the wax-producing organs is covered with a net-work of hexagonal meshes (Plate II, figs. 8 & 9) to which we must perhaps attribute some function connected with the secretion of wax. This net-work is not found in the males, but it exists in queens with modifications which alter its texture, and occupying in them two-thirds of each segment.

(At this point is a paragraph which is not intelligible, probably owing to some error in the publication, for it appears to be self-contradictory. We omit it. Translator).

The net-work in question is separated from the other internal parts by a grayish membrane which lines the entire abdominal cavity; when the stomach is full of the juices elaborated by it, it may allow them to transude through its very thin walls; and these juices, traversing the grayish membrane which is not thickly woven, may come in contact with the net-work of hexagon meshes. It is not impossible that, by a sort of digestion through this net-work, these juices be resorbed, producing the secretion of wax.

Although it is as yet impossible to decide upon anything on this point, it seems admissible, without breaking physiological laws, to consider this matter as produced by a particular organ after the manner of other secretions.[3]

[3] Plate III is intended to represent the lower segments of the abdomen of the three sorts of bee: fig. 1, segment of the worker; fig. 2, segment of the queen; fig. 3, segment of the male.

Figs. 4, 5 and 6 are the same, viewed in profile, to show the inclination of the pieces of which the segments are composed.

The discovery of wax scales, of the wax-producing areas, of their trans-udation, by overthrowing ancient theories, opens a new epoch in the history of bees. It raises doubts upon several points which were considered as solved and which may not be any longer explained without the acquisition of additional information. It brings up a host of questions and offers a wider field to the researches of physiologists and amateurs of natural history; it opens new vistas to chemists, by exhibiting to them, as an animal secretion, a substance which appeared to belong to the vegetable kingdom. In a word, it is the corner stone of a new edifice.

CHAPTER II.

On the Origin of Wax.

When nature exhibits a peculiar organization in one of its productions, one may be certain that it is with a useful purpose, an aim which will sooner or later be evidenced to us.

The existence of the wax organs under the rings of the bees, the shape and structure of the membranes upon which the wax scales appear to be molded; the hexagonal net-work, immediately below, its absence in insects that do not produce any wax, its presence in bumble bees with a marked modification; lastly the graduations observed in the plates of wax, from their appearance in the shape of crystals to their projecting outside of the rings, the fusibility of this material, which however differs in some regard from beeswax itself, everything indicates organs devised for an important function and we believe they are endowed with the faculty of producing wax.

However we had not discovered the channels which should bring this substance into its reservoirs; its elaboration might be produced by the action of the net-work of hexagon meshes; but we had no means of ascertaining it: the art assumed in animal and vegetable secretions will perhaps always escape our analysis, for the metamorphoses of the liquids in organized beings, when secreted by the glands and viscera in which they are elaborated appear to be carefully veiled by nature.

The means of simple observation thus being obstructed for us in this research, we felt it necessary to employ other methods for ascertaining whether wax is actually a secretion, or whether it resulted from the collection of a particular substance.

Providing it were a secretion, we had first to verify the opinion of Réaumur, who conjectured that it came from the elaboration of pollen in the stomach of bees, though we did not believe, as he did, that it was disgorged through the mouth. Neither were we disposed to adopt his views regarding its origin; for we had been struck, as was Hunter, with the fact that swarms newly gathered in empty hives do not bring home any pollen and yet construct combs; while the bees of old hives, having no new cells to build, gathered it abundantly.

It is singular that Réaumur, who had made this observation, had yet failed to realize how unfavorable it was to the common view; however well he was, more than any one, free from accepted prejudice.

We decided to make extensive experiments, to learn definitely whether bees deprived of pollen, for a series of days, would still produce wax; this was important, for we remembered that Mr. de Réaumur, in order to explain his suppositions, had assumed that it took a certain time for the elaboration of pollen within the body of bees. The indicated experiment was to retain the bees within the hive and to thus prevent them from gath-

115

ering or eating fecundating dust. It was on the 24th of May that we made this experiment upon a swarm which had just left the mother hive.

We placed this swarm in a straw hive with sufficient water and honey for the consumption of the bees; we carefully closed the entrances, so as to prevent all possibility of escape, leaving free access for the air needed by the captive bees.

The bees were greatly agitated at first; we succeeded in quieting them by placing the hive in a cool and dark place; their captivity lasted five days; at the end of that time we allowed them to take flight in a room, the windows of which were carefully shut; we were then able to examine their hive conveniently; they had consumed their provision of honey; but the hive, which did not contain an atom of wax when we placed them in it, had acquired five combs of the finest wax, during those five days; they were suspended from the arch of the skep; the substance of them was of pure white color and of great fragility.

This result, from which we did not as yet draw any consequences, was very remarkable; we had not expected so prompt and complete a solution of the problem. However, before concluding that the bees had been enabled to produce wax from the honey with which they were fed, it was necessary to make sure, through other experiments, that no other explanation was possible.

The workers, though held captive, might have gathered the pollen at the time when they were at liberty, on the eve or on the day of their imprisonment and have enough of it in their stomach or in their pollen baskets to extract from it all the wax that we had found in the hive.

But if such was the case, this source was not inexhaustible, and the bees being unable to procure more, would soon cease to build combs, they would fall into absolute inaction; so it was necessary to prolong the test in order to make it decisive.

Before proceeding to this second experiment, we deprived the bees of all the combs which they had built during their captivity. Burnens, with his usual skill, made them return to the hive and closed them in, as before, with a new ration of honey. This test was short; on the following day we perceived, in the evening, that the bees were working with new wax; on the third day we visited the hive and actually found five new combs, as regular as those that they had built during their first imprisonment.

The combs were removed five times successively, always under the precaution of preventing the bees from escaping outside. The same insects were preserved, and were fed exclusively with honey, during this long captivity that we might have prolonged with equal success, had we thought it necessary. On each occasion that we supplied them with honey they produced new combs; so it is beyond doubt that this substance effects the secretion of wax without the help of fecundating dust.

Since it was possible that the pollen might have similar properties, we did not delay in making the matter clear by another experiment which was only the reverse of the preceding one.

This time, instead of giving honey to the bees, we gave them nothing but fruits and pollen for food; we enclosed them under a glass bell, with a comb the cells of which contained only accumulated pollen: their captivity lasted eight days, during which time they did not produce any wax, nor were scales seen under the rings: could any doubt then exist upon the real origin of beeswax? We entertained none.

Could it be argued that wax is contained in the honey itself and that the bees preserve it out of this liquid in order to use it when needed? This last objection had some likelihood, for honey nearly always contains parcels of wax; one may see it rise to the surface when the honey is diluted in water; but the microscope, by exhibiting to us the fact that these patricles belonged to previously built cells, that they were of the same shape and thickness as the broken walls of cells, gave us an indication of the lack of weight of this argument which had stopped us for a moment.

In order to formally obviate this objection, and to enlighten ourselves on a particular opinion of our own, thât is: that the sweet principle was the true cause of the wax secretion; we took a pound of white sugar reduced to syrup and gave it to a swarm confined in a glass hive.

We made this experiment still more positive by establishing for a comparison, two other hives, in which two swarms were hived, one fed with very dark brown sugar and the other with honey. The result of this triple test was as satisfactory as it was possible to wish it.

The bees of all three hives produced beeswax; those that had been fed with sugar of the different grades gave more of it and in greater abundance than those that were fed with honey only.

A pound of white sugar, reduced to syrup, and clarified with the white of an egg, produced 10 gros 52 grains of beeswax darker than that which bees extract from honey. An equal weight of dark brown sugar yielded 22 gros of very white wax; a similar amount was obtained from maple sugar.

We repeated these experiments seven times in succession, with the same bees and we always obtained wax in nearly the same proportions as above. It therefore appears demonstrated that sugar and the saccharine part of honey enable the bees that feed upon it to produce wax, a property entirely denied to the fecundating dust.

The facts which these experiments gave us were soon confirmed in a more general way. Although there was no uncertainty upon these questions, it was well to ascertain whether the bees, in the natural state, would follow the same course as those which we had held captive: a long course of observations, of which we will give but a sketch, proved to us that when the fields offer to the bees a great crop of honey, those of the old hives store it eagerly, while those of the new swarms convert it into wax.

I did not then own a large number of colonies, but those of my village neighbors served for a comparison, even though they were constructed of straw and did not offer the same conveniences as my own. Certain remarks which we made upon the appearance of the combs and of the bees themselves when working in wax enabled us to avail ourselves of those hives so unfavorable for observation.

Beeswax is originally white, soon afterwards the cells become yellow, and brown with time; when the combs are very old their color is of a blackish hue. It is therefore very easy to distinguish the new combs from those which were built previously, and therefore to know whether the bees are building combs or whether the work is suspended, merely by raising up the hives and glancing at the edges of the combs.

The following observations may also furnish indications of the presence of honey in flowers. They are based upon a remarkable fact which was unknown to my precursors; it is that there are two kinds of workers in the hive; the ones which may attain a considerable size when they have filled themselves with all the honey that their stomach may contain, are in general destined to the elaboration of wax; the others, whose abdomen does not perceptibly change in appearance, retain only the quantity of honey which is necessary for their sustenance and immediately hand out to the others that which they have harvested; they are not in charge of the provisioning of the hive, their particular function being to care for the young: we will call them nurse bees, or small bees, in opposition to those whose abdomen may be dilated and which deserve the name of wax-workers.

Although the external difference by which the two sorts may be recognized be inconsiderable, this distinction is not imaginary. Anatomical observations have taught us that there is a real difference in the capacity of their stomach. We have also ascertained that the bees of one sort cannot fulfill all the functions shared among the workers of a hive. In one of these tests we painted with different colors the bees of each class, to observe their behavior, and we did not see any interchange. In another test, we gave the bees of a queenless colony both brood and pollen, and we at once saw the small bees busy themselves with the food of the larvæ, while those of the wax-working class paid no attention to them.[4]

When the hives are full of combs, the wax-working bees disgorge their honey into the usual magazines and make no wax; but if they have no reservoir in which to deposit it, and if their queen does not find already built cells to deposit her eggs, they retain in their stomach the honey which they have gathered, and at the end of twenty-four hours wax exudes through the rings; then the labor of comb construction begins.

One might believe that, when the country does not furnish honey, wax builders may encroach upon the provisions stored up in the hive; but they are not permitted to do it; a part of the honey is carefully put away; the cells in which it is deposited are protected with a wax covering which is removed only in case of extreme need and when there is no other way to procure it elsewhere; they are never opened during the good season; other reservoirs, always open, supply the daily needs of the community; but each bee takes only that which is absolutely necessary for present requirements.

The wax-workers appear with large bellies at the entrance of the hive only when the country supplies an abundant crop of honey; they produce wax only when the hive is not full of combs. It may be conceived, from what we have said, that the production of the waxy matter depends upon a concourse of circumstances that do not always appear.

The small bees may also produce wax, but in very inferior quantity to that produced by the real wax workers.

----

4 Huber did not then know what we learned later, by the introduction of Italian bees, that the difference in functions is due to the difference in age, of the bees of the colony. (Translator.)

Another characteristic, whereby an attentive observer cannot fail to recognize the time when bees collect sufficient honey to produce wax, is the strong odor of both these substances which is produced from the hives at that time and which does not exist with such intensity at any other time.

From such data it was easy for us to recognize whether the bees worked upon their combs in our hives and in those of the cultivators of the same district.

In 1793, the inclemency of the season had retarded the departure of swarms; there were none in the country before the 24th of May; most of the hives swarmed in the middle of June. The country was then covered with flowers, the bees collected much honey, and the new swarms worked in wax with activity.

On the 18th, Burnens visited 65 hives and saw wax workers before the entrances of all; those that entered into the old hives speedily stored their harvest, and did not build any combs; but those of the swarms converted their honey into wax and hastened to prepare lodgings for the eggs of their queen.

The 19th was showery, the bees went out, but we did not see any wax workers; they brought in only pollen. The weather was cold and rainy until the 27th; we became anxious to learn what had resulted from this atmospheric condition.

On the 28th we raised all the hives. Burnens then saw that the work had been interrupted; the combs which he had measured on the 9th had not received the least accession, they were of citron yellow, there were no longer any white cells in any of the hives.

On the 1st of July, the weather being warmer, and the chestnut and linden trees in bloom, we again saw the wax workers; they brought in much honey; the swarms lengthened the combs; we saw everywhere the greatest activity: the gathering of honey and the work in wax continued until the middle of the month.

But on the 16th of July, the heat having risen above 77° (F), the country felt the drouth; the flowers of the meadows and those of the trees just mentioned were entirely faded, they no longer yielded honey; their pollen alone attracted the bees, they gathered abundantly of it, and there was no wax produced. The combs were not lengthened, those of the swarms made no progress.

It had not rained for six weeks; the heat was great; neither did any dew temper it during the night, and the buckwheat which had bloomed for several days gave no honey to the bees, they found only pollen in it; but on the 10th of August, it rained for several hours; the following day they exhaled the odor of honey and we saw it actually glitter in the open blossoms. The bees found enough for their food, but too little to be induced to work in wax.

The drouth returned on the 14th and lasted till the end of the month; we then examined the 65 hives for the last time, and saw that the bees had not worked in wax since the middle of July; that they had stored much pollen, that the provision of honey had diminished considerably in the old hives and that there was scarcely any in the new swarms.

The year was therefore very unfavorable to the labor of bees; I attribute it mainly to the condition of the atmosphere which was not charged with electricity; a circumstance which has great influence on the secretion of honey in the nectaries of flowers. I have noticed that the harvest of the bees is never more abundant nor the work in wax more active than when a storm is preparing and the wind is in the south, the air moist and warm; but heat too long protracted and the drouth ensuing, cold rains and north wind entirely suspend the elaboration of honey in plants, and consequently the operations of bees.

When we confined the bees, for the purpose of discovering whether honey was sufficient for the production of wax, they supported their captivity patiently; they showed astonishing perseverance in rebuilding their combs, as fast as they were removed by us: had we left a part of those combs to them, their queen would have laid eggs in the cells, we would have seen in what manner the workers conducted themselves towards their young, and what would have been the effect upon the latter of the deprivation of the fecundating pollen; but since we were occupied solely with the question relating to the origin of wax we preferred to make a separate treatment of that which concerns the feeding of the young.

The experiment to be made required the presence of larvæ in the hive; honey and water were needed; the bees must have combs containing brood and must be carefully confined, so that they might not go to the field after pollen; we chanced to have a colony which had become useless from sterility of the queen; we sacrificed it for this experiment; it was in one of my leaf hives, both ends of which were glazed: we removed the queen and substituted, for the first and last combs, some combs filled with brood, eggs and young larvæ, but no cells with fecundating dust; we removed every parcel of this matter which John Hunter conjectured to be the basis of the food of the young.

The behavior of the bees in these circumstances is worthy of some attention. On the first and second day of the experiment nothing extraordinary happened; the bees brooded over their young and appeared to care for them.

But on the third day, after sunset, we heard a great noise in this hive; impatient to discover its cause, we opened a shutter and saw all in confusion; the brood was abandoned, the workers ran in disorder over the combs; we saw thousands rush towards the lower part of the hive; those about the entrance gnawed fiercely at its grating; their intention was not equivocal, they wished to emerge from their prison.

Some imperious necessity obliged them to seek elsewhere what they could not find in their home: I feared to see them perish if we restrained them longer from their instinct; we set them at liberty. The entire swarm escaped, but the hour was not favorable for the harvest; so the bees did not depart from the hive, they flew about it. The increasing darkness and the coolness of the air soon compelled them to re-enter. Probably the same cause calmed their agitation, for we saw them remounting peaceably upon their combs; order seemed re-established, and we profited of this moment to close the hive.

The next day, July 19th, we saw the rudiments of two royal cells that some bees had outlined upon one of the brood combs. In the evening, at the same hour as the preceding day, we again heard a loud buzzing in the enclosed hive, the agitation and disorder being manifested at the highest degree; we were again obliged to let the swarm escape; but it was not out long; the quieted bees returned as before.

On the 20th, we noticed that the royal cells had not been continued as they would have been in ordinary conditions. A great tumult took place in the evening, the bees appeared in delirium; we set them at liberty and order was restored on their return.

The captivity of these bees having endured five days, we thought it useless to protract it farther; besides we wished to know whether the brood was in good condition, whether it had made the usual progress, and try to discover what might be the cause of the periodical agitation of the bees. Burnens having exposed to the light of day the two combs of brood which he had given them, he first noticed the royal cells, but did not find them enlarged; indeed why should they be, since they contained neither eggs nor worms, nor that peculiar kind of jelly given to the individuals of their class? The other cells were vacant also; no brood, no pap; the worms must have died of hunger. By removing all the fecundating dust, had we taken away from the bees all means of nourishing them? To decide this question it was necessary to confide other brood to the same bees to care for, while giving them abundance of pollen. They had not been able to make any harvest while we examined their combs; for on this occasion they had been set at liberty in a room all the windows of which were closed; after having substituted young worms for those which they had allowed to perish, we returned them to their prison.

The next day, the 22d, we noticed that they had resumed courage; they had strengthened the combs which we had given them and were clustered upon the brood. We then provided them with fragments of combs into which other bees had stored up fecundating dust; but in order to observe what they would do with it, we took some of the pollen out of a few cells and spread it upon the hive stand.

The bees immediately discovered both the pollen in the combs and that which we had exposed; they crowded upon the cells and also upon the bottom of the hive, took the pollen, grain by grain, in their mandibles and conveyed it to their mouths: those that had eaten of it the most greedily climbed upon the combs before the rest, stopped upon the cells containing the young worms, inserted their heads in them and remained there for a certain time.

Burnens opened gently one of the windows of the hive and powdered the workers which were eating pollen, for the purpose of recognizing them when they would ascend upon the combs. He observed them during several hours and by this means ascertained that they took so great a quantity of pollen only to impart it to their pupils.

On the 23d we saw royal cells outlined; on the 24th we removed the bees which concealed the brood and found that all the young worms had jelly as in the ordinary hives, that they had grown and had advanced in their cells; that others had been lately closed up because they were nearing their metamorphosis; finally we had no longer any doubt of order being restored, when we saw the royal cells lengthened.

Out of curiosity, we removed the parcels of comb which we had laid upon the stand of the hive and saw that the quantity of pollen in them had been sensibly diminished; we returned them to the bees, increasing their provision still farther, so as to prolong the actions which we witnessed. We soon saw the royal cells sealed as well as several of the common cells; we again opened the hive, everywhere the worms had prospered; some had their food still before them; others had spun and their cells were sealed with a wax covering.

This result was already very striking, but what excited our astonishment above all was, that in spite of their captivity so long protracted, the bees seemed no longer anxious to go out; we could not see the agitation, the increasing and periodical trouble, the general impatience which they had manifested in the first part of the experiment; several bees, indeed, attempted to escape in the course of the day; but when they found it impossible they returned peaceably to their young.

This trait, which we have witnessed several times, always with the same interest, proves so undoubtedly the affection of bees for the larvæ whose education is entrusted to them, that we shall not seek for any other explanation of their conduct.

Another fact, no less extraordinary, and the cause of which is more difficult to discern, was that exhibited by bees which were constrained to work in wax, several times successively, by giving them sugar syrup. During the first part of the tests they gave their young the usual care; but at the last they ceased to feed them, they even frequently dragged them from their cells and carried them out of the hive.

Not knowing what this disposition should be ascribed to, I endeavored to revive the instinct of these bees by giving them other brood to care for; but this attempt was unsuccessful; the bees did not feed the new larvæ, although they had pollen in store. We offered them honey, hoping to supply thus a more natural method of alimenting their young; but it was useless; all the brood perished; perhaps the bees could no longer produce the jelly which is the food of the larvæ; except in this particular they appeared to have lost none of their faculties, they were equally active and laborious. At last, from motives unknown to us, all deserted their hive together one day and did not return to the hive.

Whatever be the cause of the alteration which we noticed in the instinct of bees which have been fed too long with sugar, one may not see without admiration that this substance is modified in the flowers so as to be used by bees without inconvenience; but everything in nature is adapted for long continued use, and the elements are combined with so much foresight that they never act in isolation but with all the energy proper to them.

CHAPTER III.

On the Architecture of Bees.

The great problem that bees present to us by their astonishing industry does not exclusively belong to the exact sciences: physics, chemistry, anatomy even would find applications in it; but their efforts would be insufficient without the help of natural history, which observes the habits of animals and studies all the circumstances of their active life. It is natural history which, by raising the veil, uncovers facts to us under their divers disguises; and leads the other sciences upon the way of other researches to which they are adapted.

Thus when we demonstrate that wax is an animal secretion, and that it proceeds from the sweet part of honey, we leave it for the chemists to decide in what manner this secretion operates, whether sugar or one of its constituents changes to wax, or whether it is only the stimulating cause of a particular action, and we also invite the anatomists to seek for the organs which have escaped our attention.

It is time to examine how bees use the substance exuding from their rings, and to discover how they prepare it to convert it into true beeswax, for this substance does not leave the lodges where it is moulded in a perfect state, it differs in several respects from what it is after having been carved; it has only the fusibility of wax, it is friable and brittle, it does not have the ductibility which it will acquire later; it is still as transparent as plates of talc, whereas that which constitutes the cells is opaque and of a yellowish white color.

We must also watch the bees when they are busy removing the scales of wax from under their wings, we must learn how they trim the bottoms of their cells, the prisms composed of trapezes; observe the manner in which they join the bottom of each cell with that of three other cells, how they give to their design the proper slope, &c., &c.

We might form ingenious suppositions upon all these marvels but we cannot divine the processes of insects; we must observe them. The most simple methods may not present themselves to our mind; we usually seek to explain the behavior of animals after our own faculties, according to our lights and our means; but the being which directs their instinct takes his views outside of the limits assigned to us and in a sphere of ideas in which our most learned designs, our most specious reasoning betoken the limits of our nature.

We have been able to ascertain, through the hypotheses of a celebrated writer, how insufficient are the most extensive knowledge and the brighest conceptions without the concourse of observation, to explain, in a plausible manner, the art displayed by the bees in constructing their cells. Consummate naturalists failed when they attempted to penetrate this mys-

123

tery: Réaumur, who had come nearest to the discovery of the truth, had passed judgment in too fleeting a manner to satisfy our curiosity and his own, so he candidly acknowledges that he gives only conjectures upon this point. Hunter, the most enlightened of modern observers, did not succeed in following the bees as to the use they make of the scales of wax which he had discovered under their rings; could I hope to be more fortunate than savants who were provided with such perfect organs and were so well drilled in the art of nature study?

Perhaps the new methods which I employed, by helping our efforts have contributed in throwing some light upon a subject which excited a keen interest in my mind.

One may suppose that bees are provided with instruments similar to the angles of their cells; for one must explain their geometry in some way; but those instruments can only be their teeth, their claws and their antennæ. Now there is no more similarity between the shape of the teeth of the bees and the angles of their cells than there is between the sculptor's chisel and the work which emerges from his hands. Their teeth (Pl. IV, figs. 1, 2, 3) are in effect hollow chisels, cut obliquely in gouge-shape, born upon a short pedicle and divided into two longitudinal cavities by a scaly projection, their edges meet above and rest against each other (fig. 1); the underside shows a sort of throat divided by the projection and bordered with long and strong hairs which are probably intended to hold the particles of wax during the work in the combs (figs. 2, 3). When the teeth are brought together they form an acute curvilineal angle, and the inner angle which they form when working apart is still less open. There are none of the angles of rhombs and trapezes of the cells.

The triangular shape of their head, which presents only three sharp angles, explains no better the choice of these figures; for even if we suppose that one of them be analogous to the acute angle of the lozanges, where would we find the measure of their obtuse angles?

Shall we seek in the legs of the bees some connection with the regular work which these insects execute? They are composed, as those of most other insects, of the haunch (a), the thigh (b), the leg (c), and of the foot or tarsus (Pl. 4, fig. 4, de).

The first three parts have nothing in them distinguishable from those of most other hymenopters, with the exception of the leg proper of the third pair; it is this limb in shape of basket which Réaumur calls the "palet" and upon which the bees carry the fecundating dusts (c, figs. 4 & 5): it is triangular, smooth, with a row of hairs, lengthwise along its exterior edge, those of the base arise, he says, and curve up towards the upper part of the leg, so that all these hairs form the edge of a sort of basket, the outside face of which would be the bottom.

Aside of the triangular palet, the most remarkable thing about the legs of bees is the tarsus, of which the first articulation is much larger than the rest and in all three pairs is of a very different form from those of other insects of the same genus (d, figs. 4 & 5).

This first articulation of the tarsus is called the brush, from the well-known use of this part, which is employed in gathering the pollen grains scattered over the body of the bee, as she collects them. In the legs of the first pair, it is lengthened, rounded and entirely hairy, all the hairs being turned towards the extremity of the tarsus. In the legs of the second pair, the brush is oblong, of irregular shape, flattened, smooth on the outer side, much covered with hairs on the opposite side; these are all turned downwards: it is joined exactly to the middle of the other piece, into which it fits.

The brush of the third pair offers some very remarkable peculiarities which will appear the more so when we make their use known; this piece is shaped very differently from that of the second pair of legs; the only resemblance they have to each other is to be both flat, smooth on the outside and hairy on the other side; but the brush of the third pair (d, figs. 4 & 5) is larger than that of the second and of a peculiar shape. It appears at first sight as a rectangular parallelogram: it was first designated as "square piece" to distinguish it from the palet, the edges of which are triangular, but when examining it carefully we notice that it diverges from the shape described. The rising edges of it cease to appear parallel, when we notice that they are not exactly in straight line and that they tend to come together at one of their extremities; the underside is slightly notched, the upper side is more so and is prolonged in the shape of a very sharp and projecting tooth, while at the other end it rises in the shape of an arc to supply a joint with the leg; but this movable piece is not joined into the middle of the base of the other as in the other pairs; it is on the forward angle of the triangular piece that we find the joint which unites them, and the inferior face of the palet being about straight, it forms a real claw with the upper edge of the brush.

Réaumur who gave the description of these two pieces had not noticed that they could spread apart and make an angle the upper edge of which is represented by their joint: he had not noticed that the edge (ab) of this angle was smooth on its outside and that the hairs which form the edge of the basket at that spot come from the sides of the pallet; that these hairs, of great length, curve towards the base and form a sort of arch by coming together; but if the outside of the palet is smooth at that spot, it is not the same on the opposite side (Pl. IV, fig. 6): we see there a row of scaly teeth, similar to those of a comb, almost straight, parallel to each other; of equal length, very acute and slightly sloping towards the opening of the pincers: corresponding with bundles of very strong hairs with which the neighboring portion of the brush is provided.

The scaly projection supplied by the brush at its extremity is slightly turned outwards, and when the two parts of the pincers meet, their ends do not correspond exactly with the edge of the palet, so that the teeth of the one cross with the hairs of the other.

This organization is too obvious not to have a particular aim; indeed nothing similar appears on the legs of either males or queens; but is seen only in bumblebees (bremus) a race very near to the honeybee and whose habits have some analogy with hers. We will soon show its usage among the bees; but it is evident that it cannot in any way serve as a model for the angles by which the different sections of cells are joined.

The tarsus is composed also of three conical articulations very small and elongated and terminating in two pairs of claws. Réaumur may be correct in considering this as two articulations, one of which is conical and elongated, the other a fleshy part, with claws arming the foot.

Do the antennæ possess these direct patterns for the geometrical forms of the pyramidal bases of which we have as yet found no pattern on the body of the insect? They are bent and composed of twelve articulations; the first two form a peculiar section, which moves in every direction on its base and serves to support the next section composed of the other ten. The first articulation of the antennæ is globular, the second cylindrical and much elongated; the third, which is the first of the second section, is conical and very short, the second very long and conical, the remainder are all cylindrical and the last is terminated in a soft point. This organization enables the antenna to make all sorts of motions, and it can, through its flexibility, follow the outline of every object; through its position it may encircle a body of small diameter, and extend in every direction.

Thus, neither the antennæ, the teeth, nor the legs of bees are able to serve as patterns for the structure of cells; but the chisel, pincers and compass which they represent are proper instruments for the building of all the parts of a cell; the result which they produce depends entirely upon the aim of the insect.

If the workman is not supplied with a model for his work, if the pattern upon which he cuts each piece is not outside of himself and in his sight, we must admit that some intellect directs his operations.

It is true that we might suppose that the scales of wax, when they emerge from under the rings, have already a shape similar to that which is intended; but we know that the shape of these scales is an irregular pentagon, which resembles neither the trapezes nor the lozenges of which the cells are composed.

Hunter having noticed that the thickness of the bases was about that of one of the scales, inferred that the bees used them as produced and accumulated them upon each other to form the sides which appeared of heavier thickness. We should then take it for granted that the bees were taught to trim these scales and arrange them in regular order; but these are only conjectures and facts are necessary to solve as complicated a question as this.

Réaumur, even with glass hives, had not solved the mystery of comb building; he thought that one could gain a correct idea of their operations without witnessing their work; this mistake deprived him of the pleasure of seeing in action the most singular work of all those that insects display. I thought that it was indispensable to witness it, in order to understand the process of building and I sought more proper methods for this than any of my predecessors had used.

One may imagine that glass hives of four sides are sufficient to see the bees construct their combs and that the only other requirement is assiduity and attention; but their architecture is always concealed from our view by clusters of bees several inches in thickness. It is in this cluster, and in darkness, that the combs are built; they are fastened, at their inception, to the ceiling of the hives; they are prolonged downwards, more or less, according to the time of building, and their diameter is increased in proportion to their length.

I saw the necessity of witnessing their initial work; but how is one to see in the midst of such a host of insects, how could we hope to reach the center of a sanctuary guarded by so great a number of stings and such courageous guards? For this purpose it was indispensable to lighten the upper part of the hive; for *there* was the work which I was anxious to witness. I hoped to succeed with the following apparatus; but experience showed me that it had to be modified. It was a large bell-shaped receiver; which I hoped to use in place of an ordinary hive; there was nothing in its curves very different from the shape of the skeps in which we hive bees; but I had not foreseen the inability of the bees to hang in clusters under this slippery arch. A few bees managed to hang to it, but were unable to sustain the weight of those that hung to their legs: so I was compelled to abandon this scheme, but I retained this plan as closely as I could. Understanding that the bees needed supports I attempted to satisfy them by gluing thin wooden slips at certain intervals to the arch. I thought that they would work between these slips and that I would be enabled to watch them; but they did not consult my convenience and fastened their cells to the wooden slips; I was, however able to take some advantage of this arrangement.

We introduced into this hive a swarm of a few thousand workers, a few hundred drones and a fertile queen. They at once ascended to the highest point of their home, and those first reaching the slips, fixed themselves to them with the claws of their forefeet; others scrambling up the sides, joined them, by hanging to their third pair of legs with their own first pair. Thus, they made chains fastened by their two ends to the upper parts of the receiver which served as bridge or ladders for the workers joining their gathering; this formed a cluster with its extremities hanging clear to the bottom of the hive, like an inverted pyramid or cone, the base of which was at the top of the hive.

The country then afforded but little honey; but it was important that the object of our researches be not too much delayed, for we could not leave the hive a single instant without running the risk of losing the opportunity of witnessing the beginning of the combs. Had we left the bees to their natural state, we should have had to watch them for several days before seeing them occupied with building; so we fed them with sugar syrup, in order to hasten their work.

They crowded to the edge of the manger containing it, then returned to the pyramidal cluster. Soon we were struck with the appearance of this hive, through the contrast of the usual agitation of the bees with their present inaction. All the external layers of the cluster constituted a kind of curtain formed exclusively of wax workers; hanging together they displayed a series of festoons crossing each other in every direction, and in which the back of most of the bees was turned towards the observer: this festoon had no other motion than that which was communicated to it from the inner layers, whose fluctuations were displayed in it.

However, the small bees appeared to have retained all their activity, they alone went to the fields, brought back pollen, kept guard at the entrance of the hive, cleansed it and stopped up its edges with odoriferous resin, known as propolis; the wax workers remained motionless above fifteen hours; the curtain consisted of the same individuals and we made sure that none replaced them. Some hours later, we noticed that almost all the wax workers had scales under their rings. The next day, this phenomenon was still more general; the bees on the outside of the cluster had slightly changed their position; one could see the under part of their abdomen distinctly. By the projection of the scales, their rings seemed edged with white; the curtain was rent in several places; less tranquility reigned in the hive.

Convinced that the combs would first appear in the center of the swarm, and that they would soon be noticeable, we concentrated our attention upon the vault of the receiver. The area of the base was in a good light, we could distinctly see the first links of all the festoons of bees which hung from the top of the vault. The concentrical layers which the bees formed, equally crowded together, left no intervals; but the scene was about to be shifted and we witnessed it.

A worker at this time detached herself from one of the central festoons of the cluster, we saw her spread her companions apart, driving away with her head the leaders fastened at the middle of the arch, and by turning around form a space in which she could freely move. She then suspended herself in the center of the field which she had just cleared, the diameter of which was 12 or 13 lines.

We saw her at once seize one of the scales which projected from her rings (Pl. IV, fig. 8); for this purpose she brought towards her abdomen one of the legs of the third pair, rested it against her body, opened the pincers which we have described, inserted skillfully the edge of her brush under the scale that she wished to remove, closed up this instrument, pulled the scale of wax from its ring and took it with the claws of her anterior legs, to bring it up to her mouth (figs. 7 & 8).

The bee then held this scale in a vertical position: we noticed that she turned it between her jaws with the help of the claws of her front legs, which held it by its opposite edge and could give it a suitable direction. The tongue, folded on itself, served as a support; by raising and lowering it she could pass every part of the circumference under the edge of the jaws and the edge of the scale was soon broken to pieces. The parcels of wax that fell from it stopped in the hairy cavity which we described when we spoke of bees' teeth. These fragments, having accumulated with others freshly cut, were crowded towards the mouth and issued from it as from a drawing-plate in the shape of a very narrow ribbon.

They next passed through by the tongue which impregnated them with a frothy liquid, similar to a pap. The tongue in this operation made most varied maneuvers; it assumed most varied shapes, now flattening like a spatula, now acting like a trowel applied upon the ribbon of wax; at other times it appeared like a pointed brush.

After having imbued the entire substance of the ribbon with the liquid that loaded it, the tongue forced this ribbon forward and passed it again through the same drawing-plate, but in the opposite direction; this motion brought it towards the sharp edge of the jaws, where it was again chopped up under their carver.

At length, the bee applied these particles of wax to the vault of the hive. The gluten which impregnated them promoted their adhesion; she separated them with a cut of her jaw, from the portion not yet to be used; then with the same instruments she gave them the direction which she intended for them.

The liquid which she mixed with the wax gave it a whiteness and opacity which were wanting when the scales left the rings; doubtless the purpose of this process was to give the wax that ductility and tenacity which it possesses when perfect.

The founding bee (this denomination is well deserved) continued this maneuver until all the fragments, which had been worked up and impregnated with this whitish fluid, were attached to the vault; she then manipulated between her teeth the remainder of the scale which she had kept apart during the working of the ribbon. All the portion which had been thus kept intact during the first operation was employed then, and in the same manner. The worker applied to the underside of the vault all the material prepared, fastened additional material under and on the side of it, and continued until she had entirely exhausted the material supplied.

Second and third scales were treated thus by the same bee, yet the work was only sketched, for it was only material ready to assume any shape wanted; the worker did not attempt to shape the molecules of wax which she assembled; she was satisfied to accumulate them together, this required no effort.

However, the founding bee quit the spot and disappeared among her companions, another with wax under her rings succeeded her; she suspended herself at the same spot, seized with the pincers of the posterior legs one of the scales of wax, and passing it up to her teeth, proceeded with the work.

She did not deposit haphazard the fragments which she manipulated; for the little pile which her companion had built directed her and she put her own in the same alignment, uniting the two at their extremities. A third worker, detaching herself from the interior of the cluster, suspended herself to the ceiling, reduced some of her scales to paste and put them near the materials accumulated by her companions, but not in the same manner, they were placed at an angle with the others: another worker appeared to notice it, and removed the misplaced wax before our eyes, carrying it to the former heap; she deposited it in the same order, following exactly the indicated direction. From all these operations was produced a block of rugged surface, hanging perpendicularly from the vault. One could not perceive any angle, any trace of the figure of cells in this initial work of the bees; it was a simple partition, in a straight line, and without the least inflexion; six or eight lines in length; about two-thirds of the diameter of a cell in height and declining towards its extremities: we have seen other blocks from an inch to an inch and a half long, the form was always the same, but none were of greater height.

The empty space in the center of the cluster permitted us to see the first maneuvers of the bees and to discover the art with which they lay the foundations of their edifice, but this space was filled too promptly for our wishes, too many bees collected on both sides of the block, obstructing the view, so that it was no longer possible to follow their work.

But if we were unable, with this apparatus, to see as much as we should have wished to learn, we considered ourselves very fortunate in doing justice to Réaumur, who thought he observed the wax discharged from the mouth of the bees in the shape of a pap; doubtless it was this whitish and frothy liquid with which they moisten the waxy substance to give it properties which it does not possess in the origin, and which he mistook for the wax; this observation, by indicating the cause of the opinion of this naturalist; solved one of the greatest difficulties of the subject of which we are speaking; for one cannot reject a fact advanced by so judicious a writer without explaining the cause of his error.

CHAPTER IV.

Continuation of the Architecture of Bees.

Natural history does not present any phenomenon whose final causes are more tempting to seek than bee architecture. The order and symmetry which reign in their combs invite us to these researches, which please both the heart and the mind at the same time.

I shall not investigate as to whether some error has been made in the attribution of these causes and whether nature has not been credited with narrow aims in planning such strict economy among the bees. I shall not decide whether the fine problem solved by Koenig, Cramer, Maraldi, is rigorously applicable to the work of these insects, or whether we should not, in the actions of insects, admit of a certain freedom of action which is not needed in purely physical matters; the reckoning of the modern geometers appear to be better in harmony with the liberal views of the Author of nature, when they figure upon intended economy as only a secondary object in the plan followed by the bees.

There is, indeed, a more important requirement for these insects, which could not have been fulfilled, if their art was confined to this sole meritorious purpose.

When I undertook the researches which I am about to relate, I was far from foreseeing that they were to lead me to new conclusions on the structure of combs.

Distinguished observers had made this a subject of meditation, and appeared to have fully developed a theory on the pyramidal bases of combs; even their names appeared to confirm the accepted ideas concerning this matter, and I did not expect to discover important facts, unknown till then, through instructions given by me to a simple villager.

But the most interesting discoveries are not always those that require the most time and effort. A glance, to the base of newly built combs, suggested to us that the details of their construction had not yet been sufficiently studied. The anomalies which they presented appeared to us to be of the greatest importance; I will recall in a few words the usual shape of the cells, in order to describe the traits which seem to furnish a key to the architecture of bees.

The cells which any one may examine are composed of two parts, a prismatic hexagonal tube, and a pyramidal base (Pl. 5, fig. 1). The latter (bcdg), which must be considered the most delicate and essential part of the entire work, is formed of three rhomboids or lozenges, equal and similar, united together in a common center and inclined in a determined angle so as to produce a slight cavity.

While these three pieces produce a depression on one of the sides of the comb, they produce a projection (fig. 2) on the other side: and here each

corresponds to two other pieces which, through their inclination, help to
form similar pyramidal bases; that is why each cell is fastened to three other
cells by a common base.

On the edge of each pyramidal base (fig. 1) the prismatic hexagonal tube
rises, the six sides of which are cut at right angles at the orifice of the cell,
and are shaped at their lower extremity so as to fit the angular contour of
the pyramidal base.

These cells, by their shape and combination, fulfill probably all the conditions that we might expect from the work of the bees; but are they capable
of becoming fastened with sufficient strength to the part of the hive which
is to sustain them?   This is a very important point which seems to have
been overlooked.

A very simple figure (fig. 3) is sufficient to show us that hexagonal
prisms, placed side by side can be fastened by only one of their angles to
the surface of the ceiling and would leave large vacuities between these
angles.   And yet the combs need to be solidly fixed.

This condition is so important that it is taken in consideration by nature, at two different times, if we may so express it. First, when the combs
are built; secondly when those have become too heavy to be trusted with
so frail a support.

The following observations showed us by what precautions the bees provide for the stability of their constructions.

Having directed our attention upon the base of the combs in a newly
stocked hive, we were impressed by the appearance of the first row of cells,
through which the comb is fastened to the ceiling of the hive.   It was
different from the rows below it, in such remarkable peculiarities, that we
saw fit to examine a number of others for comparison. We found, indeed,
that even those of most recent building presented a similar contrast between
the fundamental cells and those of which the comb is composed; so that what
had first impressed us as an anomaly was really a rule (fig. 11).

The upper part of the combs being always partly hidden rrom view by
the edge of the supports, I realized that they would not promote our observations; that it was necessary to take possession of the work and remove
from it the workers whose vigilance would incommode us: but it was important not to alter their masonry, and especially to preserve intact the cells
of the first row, which attracted our curiosity.   So I had such combs removed from my leaf hives as I wished to examine; we left them for this purpose in the frames in which they had been built; without such precaution
we should have failed in our purpose: it was then only that we were able to
examine the shape and arrangement of the cells of the first row.

Their orifice, instead of a hexagon, presents the shape of an irregular
pentagon (fig. 4): a horizontal line which is that of the hive ceiling, two
vertical and perpendicular lines and two oblique lines united at the bottom
in an obtuse angle, formed the contour of the cell; so the wax tube was composed of only four pieces, two vertical and two oblique, the ceiling forming
a fifth side.

These are not the classical shapes to which we were accustomed.   We
desired to know whether the bottom of the cells correspond with the shape
of their edges; in order to see this more distinctly we cut the tubes away

from their bearings; we saw then that their bases were very different from those of the ordinary cells.

We retained only the wall which separates the cells on both sides (fig. 4 and 5). It displayed angular projections and recesses; but as it was throughout of about even thickness, that which was a projection on one side proved to be a recess on the opposite side.

However, on one side the base of each cell was composed of three pieces while on the other it had but two, because these cells, alternately opposite, were unequal: this requires a greater explanation.

Of the three pieces which compose the base of the cells of the first row, on one side which we shall call the *anterior* side, only one of them was in the shape of a rhomb; the other two were irregular quadrilaterals, or trapezes. These, hanging (a, b, fig. 6) from the ceiling by their short side, descended perpendicularly; their vertical edges were parallel; but one was shorter than the other; it is by this one that the two quadrangles were joined together in an obtuse angle; the fourth edge, the lower one of these pieces, was oblique; and it was between the oblique edges of these trapezes that the rhomb was fastened which forms the bottom of the cavity. It is easy to understand the cause of its inclination, since the top of one of its obtuse angles was below the joint of the two trapezes; and its sharp angles at the lower extremity of the large edges of these trapezes, and consequently a little lower. Thus the rhomb is slanting or inclined as are the lower edges of the trapezes (fig. 8).

On the opposite side of the comb, the bases of the cells of the same row are composed of only two trapezes (fig. 9) similar to those that form a part of the base of the cells just described, only they appear turned differently, for they are joined to the base of the cell by their greater sides: they make, with each other, an angle exactly equal to that which unites the trapezes of the anterior face; but these two pieces do not belong to a single cell of the anterior face, they form the back of two neighboring cells: so the cells of this face can only correspond in their base to two opposite cells. On the contrary, those of the anterior face having one more piece, must correspond with three cells (fig. 14 and 15); the rhomb c which they show fills the space between two cells of the posterior face, and is the first piece of the cells of the second row, which are themselves composed of three rhombs.

Through these simple arrangements the stability of the comb is assured, for it reaches the ceiling of the hive in the greatest possible number of points.

We see another aim in this arrangement through the influence of the composition of the first row upon the formation of cells with pyramidal bases; but we will mention it in a few words only, referring those who desire to exhaust the subject to the notes which follow this chapter.

The rhomb situated at the base of the cells of the first row, on the anterior face, having a determined inclination because of its position at the base of the trapezes whose obliquity it follows, and this rhomb belonging on the opposite face to the pyramidal base, its inclination is partly indicated, for if we add two similar pieces below the rhomb, when joined together they will have a similar inclination and will form a pyramidal base on the posterior face.

Regarding the pyramidal bases of the anterior face, they will have their origin in the same pieces on the opposite side, of which they are the reverse; thus all the properties of the pyramidal bases appear to be derived from the structure of the cells of the first row.

EXPLANATION OF THE FIGURES, PLATE V

Figure 1 is that of an ordinary cell, resting upon its base and seen in perspective. Its tube (ae) rises above the pyramidal base bcd; one must notice the angular edges of the base and realize why the tube is composed of irregular quadrangles.

In figure 2, we see the bottom of a cell, front view. It is backed by three other cells, a, b, c, whose bases are seen from the rear.

Figure 3 is that of two pyramidal bases; (ab) is a line which they touch in only one spot.

Figure 4 is a piece of new comb, fixed to the ceiling of the hive.

Figure 5 represents the same comb shown from the opposite side; in each of them the tubes of the cells have been removed, with only a small edge left to distinguish their contour. The bases of the first cells, immediately below the ceiling are those which I call cells of the first row.

Figure 4 represents the edge or orifice of a cell of the first row.

Figure 6 shows the base of an anterior cell of the first row, detached from the comb; (ab) its trapezes (c) the rhomb which terminates it. In figure 9 we see the base of the posterior cell of the first row, formed of only two trapezes. In Figure 9 we see the same pieces, but on their opposite face and in the same position as they are in figure 13 (ab). As these are drawn in perspective, which alters the appearance of their pieces to a certain extent, owing to the recess of the cells, they are shown flat and separate in figures 7 and 10, under braces which indicate their union; we thus see their geometric shape.

Figure 8 is intended to exhibit the projection of the rhomb, projecting beyond a line (a, b) drawn from one of its acute angles to another; the part (acb) projects beyond the cavity, while the part (adb) is within it: so the rhomb projects in exactly half of its length; it slopes in the direction of its short diagonal, but is horizontal in its long diagonal.

Figure 11 gives a front view of the cells of the first row with their enlarged tube in perspective, abc being the base.

Figures 12 and 13 show the bases of three cells which would be back to back; figure 13 showing two anterior cells and figure 12 a posterior cell fitted between these two, b being the back of b, and a the back of a. See fig. 9°.

Figures 14 and 15 are the inverse of one another; the first shows a base of the first row; with the back of three cells that meet it on the opposite side; two of the first row (f, a and g, b) and one of the second row (c, e, d); we make sure of this by looking at figure 15, in which the three posterior cells (g, b) (f, a) and (c, d, e) shown facing, are backed to the anterior cell of the first row (b, a, c), shown here from the rear, the piece (c), which is opposite the rhomb (c) of the anterior cell, becomes here the upper piece of the pyramidal base (d, c, e), formed below the cells (g, b) and (a, f) figure 15.

Figures 16 and 17 are also the opposite of each other placed on the same line so that we may understand the manner in which the cells are joined. The first represents a small piece of the comb composed of two anterior cells of the first row and one anterior cell of the second row.

The second shows one posterior cell of the first row and two posterior cells of the second row.

We notice here that the pyramidal base of the anterior face, figure 16, is composed of two rhombs situated in the interval between the cells of the first row, but the two pieces (eo) are the same as (eo) figure 17, which belong to two cells of the posterior face; lastly, the rhomb (a) completing the cell of figure 16, belongs on the opposite side to the space between two cells, or to a cell of the third row.

Figures 18 and 19, which represent two small pieces of comb without any shading, give us opportunity to compare each piece of the bases of the cells on both sides.

EXPLANATION OF THE FIGURES OF PLATE VI.

The figures of this plate are on a larger scale than on the previous one. The first represents a very small portion of comb, shown as if the prisms were transparent, so as to exhibit the connecting wall in which the bases of both sides are built. These prisms are delineated only in their edges and their orifices. As they are shown here in their entire length, the midribs of the bases appear a little short: the eye is supposed to be in a position to see both the bases and the orifices.

As figure 1, we see two cell bases of the first row, beneath which a pyramidal base is displayed. The adjacent pieces to this cell have been retained, so that those of the posterior plan may be full; thus we see in this figure the back of four posterior cells, one in the first row, two in the second, and one in the third: this figure corresponds with figure 16 of Plate V, where the bases of these cells are seen in front view.

Horizontal lines have been drawn from all the angles of the contour of these bases; by their union they represent the prismatic tubes the openings of which are seen at the other extremity; the lines emerging from the posterior angles represent those of the cells on that side.

Figure 2 represents the same piece of comb inverted so that we may see obliquely the bases of the cells of the posterior side; it corresponds to figure 17 of Plate V, which shows the bases of similar cells in front view. We see here, facing us, the bases of the cells which we saw in the rear in figure 1; the bases of the cells on the anterior side show only their back. Glancing at the orifices of those cells, we are impressed by the difference between those of the first row and those of the lower rows; by following the lines from the mouth of the cells inward, we reach the angles of the bases which belong to those same cells.

Figure 3 represents in profile the intermediary wall; it is shown here on its interior face, we may notice the angular shape of the contours of all the bases of which it is formed.

The side walls are lengthened to the orifice; four cells are represented, two of the first row and two of the second row, so that their position be better grasped.

We see, by this figure, that the walls situated on the vertical edges of the trapezes are rectangular quadrangles, and that all the other walls are shaped obliquely near the bottom, and at right angles at their other extremity.

Figure 4 is that of an anterior cell of the first row, detached from the group of figure 3.

Figure 5 is an isolated posterior cell of the same row.

SECTION II.

Work of the Bees in Shaping the Cells of the First Row.

The details which we have just presented, upon the composition of the cells of the first row, appeared to us to indicate a progressive march in the work of the bees; but we could form only conjectures upon their method of action.

In order to secure a more complete idea, it was necessary to see these insects build the foundations of their combs and construct these cells in such different shape from what had been recognized till then; it was important to follow the building of these pyramidal bases which display at the same time the skill of the worker and the talent of the architect. We could there catch nature in action and observe instinct in one of its finest developments.

Since we had discovered new facts which could lighten our way, a still more active curiosity possessed us, and in spite of the difficulties of all kinds which opposed our efforts, we did not lose our courage.

As I have already stated, it was impossible to follow the work of these insects within the cluster which surrounds the workers in charge of the architecture. I had vainly thrown daylight upon the base of the cluster hanging to the dome of the hive; I had been able to see only the preparations for their masonry. I did not attempt to isolate a handful of them, for I knew that they work only when they are gathered in great numbers. To drive them away while the work progressed would not have fulfilled the purpose any better: I did not desire to see only the progress of their work, I wanted to witness their actual work.

After mature reflection upon the means which might be provided through the habits of the bees, and having found nothing which fully answered my purpose, or that did not prove more or less inconvenient; I attempted to thwart their habits in some particulars, hoping thereby that when they were compelled to act under new conditions, they might allow us to perceive some traces of the art which had been taught them. But the choice of methods was difficult; it was desirable to keep away all the workers that were not indispensable in the construction of the combs, without discouraging those from which we expected to secure some information; it was especially indispensable not to drive them from their natural conditions.

As the bees always begin the foundations of their combs at the ceiling of their hive, at the exact spot where the cluster hangs which is formed from the gathering together of the swarm, it seemed that the only way to isolate the wax workers was to induce them to change the direction of their masonry; but I did not foresee how I could compel independent beings to do this.

I finally decided to make an attempt which would not compel them in any way, but would even permit them to follow their usual routine, and even to dispense with building any combs at all if the work devised by me should be too much against their usages.

I wished to compel these bees to construct their combs upwards; that is to say, the reverse way from their daily custom, which however is not without examples among them: so I devised the following apparatus:

I had a box made, eight or nine inches high and twelve inches wide, at the bottom of which we cut an entrance; the upper side or lid could be removed at will, and was made of a single piece of glass, in a movable frame. I selected combs full of brood, honey and pollen, from one of my leaf hives, so that they would contain all that the bees could wish. I cut them in strips a foot long and four inches high and adjusted them vertically lengthwise, in the bottom of the box, leaving between them such spaces as the bees usually arrange themselves. (Plate I, figure 5).

We then covered the upper edge of each of these combs with a slat or lath, which did not project beyond it and allowed free communication between all the parts of the hive. These laths, resting upon combs four inches high, gave the bees opportunity of building above them in the remaining space five inches deep by twelve inches long; it was not likely that those bees should attempt to build combs upon the underside of the horizontal glass ceiling, since they cannot hang in clusters on the slippery surface of glass; it was then necessary for them to build the combs upwards from the laths, and I felt certain that I would have better success by this process than before.

But it was only a small step to have invented an apparatus which could better serve our purpose; I must repeat here with a feeling of gratitude and with the satisfaction felt when we acknowledge modest merit; if I have made a few steps forward in this career, I owe it to the assiduity, the courage, and the correct eye of the indefatigable man who assisted my efforts; I owe it to Burnens. These difficult observations required minute precautions; a sudden unexpected light, a neglected opportunity, an instant of suspended attention, could lead us away from the facts into some erroneous system.

Having noticed that the horizontal glass plate, interposed between his eyes and the objects to be studied, altered their perspective or their appearance in some respects, Burnens decided to set aside this chance of error; in spite of my protests and with the chances of danger that he incurred, he watched unprotected all the details relating to the architecture of the bees; the gentleness of his motions and the habit of repressing his respiration when near the bees, could alone preserve him from the anger of these formidable insects; so that I did not have the regret of paying too dearly for his devotion. This action, worthy of the most passionate lover of natural history, shows what may be achieved through the desire for knowledge and must certainly increase the confidence of my readers in the observations that resulted.

After Burnens stocked this hive, the swarm established itself, as we had foreseen, among the combs in the lower part of the box, and we then observed the small-bellied bees displaying their natural activity; they dispersed throughout the hive to feed the young larvæ, to clear their lodgement and adapt it for their convenience. Evidently the combs which had been given them and which had been roughly cut to fit the bottom of the box, and damaged in several places, appeared to them shapeless and ill-conditioned; for they commenced their repair at once; we saw them cut up the old wax, knead it between their teeth and form bindings to consolidate the combs. We were astonished beyond expression to see this multitude of workers, employed together in a work for which it did not appear they should have been called, such agreement, zeal and prudence, in *beings that have no right to thoughts.*

But it was still more surprising to see about half of this numerous population taking no part in the labor and remaining motionless while others fulfilled the functions which appeared to be required of them.

You will understand that the wax workers, in a state of absolute repose, recalled our former observations. Gorged with the honey that we had put within their reach, at the end of 24 hours of complete inaction they secreted this substance so long believed to have been gathered upon the anthers of flowers. The wax, wholly formed under their rings was ready to be put to use, and with great satisfaction we saw a little block rising upon one of the laths that we had prepared to serve as base for their new constructions. In this regard, those insects fulfilled our anticipations and as the cluster was established between the combs and below the laths, there was no obstacle through its bulk to the progress of our observations.

Upon this occasion we witnessed for the second time the work of the founding bee and the successive labors of several wax workers to erect the block upon which we were building our hopes.

When the material was thus prepared, these architects gave us the most complete display of the art with which nature has endowed them. Would that my readers could share the interest which this sight inspired; but it is difficult to form a correct idea of it, unless one follows step by step the work of the bees while comparing with the greatest care the text and the figures.

Although I aimed to simplify this part of the work as much as possible, I realize that it may be unintelligible to a great many readers; but I feel certain that the true lovers of natural history will not allow the difficulty of the subject to discourage them and will find compensations in the novelty of the observations. But in order to help relieve from mind fatigue those who do not care to deeply study the matter I will prelude with a slight sketch. (See the figures of natural size Plate VIIA. We should bear in mind that the block rises perpendicularly above the lath, and that it is thus in the position in which we see it when we hold the book vertically).

It was in this block (of wax), at first very small, but successively enlarged, as the work of the bees progressed, that the bases of the first cells were carved.

We understood from the first moment why they were entertwined; the bees built, before our eyes, this first row, which gives the key to all their architecture.

They imperfectly carved a small cavity of the width of an ordinary cell, on one side of the block (Pl. VII A, fig. 1); it formed a sort of fluting the edges of which were made to project by the accumulation of wax. On the reverse side of this cavity, opposite, two others, contiguous and equal, (fig. 2) were made, similar to the first but a little shorter. These three cavities, of like diameter, were partly backed against each other, since the center of the one was opposite the edge between the other two.

The first of these cavities, being longer, corresponded on the other side with a still uncut portion of the block, above the cavities of the first row, and it was in this spot that the outline of the first pyramidal base was begun (fig. 2).

Thus a single fluting, on the anterior face, corresponded with three cavities on the opposite side, two of them on the first row and one on the second.

The raised edge of these flutings having been converted by the bees into two rectilinear prominences, which together formed an obtuse angle, each of the cavities of the first row became pentagonal, if we consider the lath as one side (fig. 3 and 4). But the fluting of the second row, the base of which was situated between the oblique faces of the bases of the first row, became hexagonal, two sides being in its base, two parallel and lateral, and two oblique formed upon the raised edges (fig. 4).

The interior conformation of the cavities appeared to be derived naturally from the respective position of their outlines. It seemed that the bees, gifted with an admirable delicacy of feeling, applied their teeth principally where the wax was thickest, that is, in the parts where other workers had accumulated it, while working on the opposite side, which explains why the bottom of the cells is excavated in an angular shape behind the projections upon which the walls of the other corresponding cells are to be erected.

The bases of the cavities were thus divided into several parts which formed an angle, and the number and the shape of these parts depended upon the erection of the bases on the opposite side of the block, dividing the space; so that the largest fluting, opposite three others, was divided in three parts, while on the other side, those of the first row, opposite, were composed of two pieces only.

In consequence of the manner in which the flutings were opposed to each other, those of the second row and all the subsequent ones, partially applied to three cavities, were composed of three equal pieces in rhomboid form. A glance at the figures makes it clear. I may here properly remark that each portion of the work of the bees appeared as a natural consequence of the preceding work, so that chance had no part in the admirable results which we witnessed.

I will now return to the thread of these operations, with all the details which were noticed.

DETAILED DESCRIPTION OF THE WORK OF THE BEES.

(See the enlarged figures, beginning at the bottom, Plate VII, B).

We had reached the long desired moment; at last the bees were about to carve, under our eyes, and it was with some emotion that we saw them give the first chisel strokes upon the block which had just been erected on the lath.

It rose perpendicularly above it and differed only by its position from those that we had seen before. It was a minute, straight and vertical wall, five or six lines in length, two lines in height and half a line thick (Pl. VII

B, fig. 1 & 2). Its edge was arched and its surface rough; it appeared much too light to suppose that bees should carve entire cells out of it; but it seemed sufficiently thick to form the wall out of which the cell bases are carved and which separates the two sides of the comb.

(This wall is shown by the zigzag lines in figure 3. Let us note that the work of bees is the reverse of what Mr. Buffon had imagined: he thought the bees built a big lump of wax in which they dug cavities by the pressure of their bodies. They build a lump, but it is so thin that it would hardly make the twenty-fourth part of the thickness of a comb: it is in this block, which is very small at first, that they build their cells as in relief, and upon its edges they attach tubes five or six lines deep. We have used the word "block" for this first outline, although it gives the idea of a massive body, but as the cell bases are carved out of this wall of wax, we cannot give it another name yet).

We saw a little bee leave the cluster hanging between the combs, climb on the lath upon which the wax workers had laid the material which they had removed from under their rings, turn around the block, and after having examined both sides, begin work on our side of it. We will call this face of the block the anterior face, and we will consider the opposite side as the posterior face, no matter how we may view it later. The worker, placed on the anterior face, fixed her position horizontally so that her head faced the middle of the block (fig. 4) and moved it briskly; her teeth worked in the wax but removed fragments of it only in a very narrow space, about equal to the diameter of an ordinary cell (abgf). So there remained, at the right and the left of the cavity which she made, a certain space in which the block was still in the rough.

After having chewed and moistened the particles of wax, she deposited them in the edges of the cavity: after working a few instants, she walked away from the block: another bee took her place in the same attitude, and continued the work which had just been sketched by her, a third bee soon took the place of the second, deepened the cavity, accumulated wax to the right and left, raised the already sharp lateral edges of the cavity, and gave them a straighter shape (ab, gf). It was with her teeth and her anterior legs that she compressed and fixed the particles of wax in the required position.

More than twenty different bees took part in this same work: the cavity then had more depth at the base of the block than at its upper edge (adg, fig. 4): the depth of the cavity diminished from the lath up to the letter c: it resembled a fluting wider than long; its superior contour was less marked than its vertical edges. The horizontal diameter of the cavity was equal to that of an ordinary cell, but its length, in a vertical direction, was only a line and three-fifths, or about two-thirds of its diameter. I will designate this cavity as N° 1.

When the work reached this point, we saw a bee, leaving the cluster formed by the workers, walk around the block and select its posterior face as her labor aim; but a remarkable fact was that she did not begin at the center of the block as the others had done on the anterior face, she placed herself so that her teeth acted only upon one-half of this face (cdih, fig. 5), so that the middle (ab) of the cavity which she laid out, was opposite one of the edges which lined cavity N° 1. At about the same time another bee began work to the right of this one, in that part of the block which she had left untouched, and which was the right side of this posterior face (cdkl, fig. 5). So these bees carved two cavities, side by side, and we will call these N° 2 and 3; after they had worked for some time, their places were taken by other workers which contributed in turn and separately in giving them the proper depth and shape. These two adjacent cavities were separated only by a common edge, formed from the gathering together of the wax particles drawn from their interior, and this edge (dc, fig. 7) was in the center of this face and corresponded with the center of the cavity made on the opposite side by other workers (dc, fig. 6). Thus a part of each of the two cavities on the posterior side was opposite the anterior cavity; this could be verified by piercing both faces with pins (fig. 6 & 7).

These cavities were of the same diameter and were limited at right and left as with those of the anterior face, by small projecting borders which I call vertical arris, and which will serve as base for the vertical walls of the cells after the bases are carved.

The three outlined cavities did not have the full dimensions in every direction that they were to secure when completed; I have already said that they did not have the length of an ordinary cell; I mean the veritical diameter of those cavities (cd, fig. 6); but the block itself was not of a sufficient length to complete the diameter of the cell. So the bees continued to increase its size.

While they were still at work upon the excavations begun by their companions, we saw some wax workers remove scales of wax from their rings and apply them upon the edges so as to lengthen them; they increased its size nearly two lines in every direction (fig. 8).

The small bees which appeared more especially charged with sculpturing the cells were able to continue their outlines; they prolonged the cavities upon the newly added material and lengthened also the edges which bordered them (fig. 9 & 10); but the raised edges were prolonged only at the right and left of the cavities and not at their upper extremity: they were also less prominent as they reached from the base, and we noticed that cavity N° 1 was much more prolonged than cavities Nos. 2 & 3; otherwise their shape was similar; they were semi-elliptic, slightly lengthened, rounded at the top, arched inside, and had no angular shape; the first was a little longer than the diameter of an ordinary cell; but the others were shorter than this diameter in perceptible amount.

This difference, the aim of which we already perceived, after our observations upon the formation of the cells of the first row, was not an imperfection.

I have said that each of these cavities was round at its upper extremity; the bees soon put edges upon them in this part as they had done on the vertical sides, but they did not purpose to give them an arched edge.

The arch on the border of each of these cavities was divided into two equal ribs, and it was in this direction that the bees erected projecting ridges (fig. 11 & 12); we noticed that they formed an obtuse angle and this appeared equal to those of the rhombs of pyramidal cell bases; we could then conjecture that this angle would be part of a rhomb.

We noticed that the bees accumulated much wax on the upper edge of cavity N° 1, and it was at the top of this accumulation that the two oblique edges joined. But, on the contrary, the two ridges which terminated the posterior cells at the top were not raised on a projection, but they followed the concavity of the fluting.

(See these bases, facing, in figures 11 and 12, and sidewise in figures 15 and 16; figures 13 and 14 represent the cavities before their upper edge was changed to angular edges, as in figures 9 and 10: figures 15 and 16 show the block at the time when the upper edge is changed into a ridge. In these figures, the rough portion of the block should extend as far as in the others.

At this time, each of the cavities was bordered by four ridges, two of them lateral, perpendicular to the lath, and two shorter ones oblique, joined to the former by one of their extremities and united together at the other extremities: the lath itself bordering them at their base (fig. 11 and 12, 15 and 16).

Now it became more difficult to follow the operations of the bees, because they often interposed their head between the eye of the observer and the bottom of the cell; but we noticed that the partition upon which their teeth worked had become transparent enough to enable us to see through it what passed on the other face; we could thus see very distinctly the end of the teeth of the bee working at carving on the opposite face and follow all her movements. We made this still more perceptible, by placing the hive so that the light would strike more fully upon the cavities which we desired to see outlined.

We saw, as a shadow, the contour of the cells on the opposite face, as the thick ridge did not permit the free passage of daylight and we recognized clearly that the height of the cell bases, N° 2 and 3 was less than that of cell N° 1, and that their vertical ridges were shorter (Plate VIII, fig. 17 and 18). The dotted lines here design the shadows of the arris on the opposite face. See the denoting letters.

One perceived, through cavity N° 1, (cd, fig. 17), the shadow of the vertical ridge which separated cavities N° 2 and 3, but as the ridge forming this division was between the two shorter cells its shadow did not appear in the full length of cell N° 1.

This shadow terminated at two-thirds of the length of the anterior cell, starting from the base of the block (c, fig. 17); there it appeared to divide into two branches (cbcf) which extended obliquely, one to the right, the other to the left of the center and appeared to terminate immediately behind the upper extremity of the vertical ridges (ab gf) of cavity N° 1.

These oblique branches of the vertical shadow were none other than those of the oblique ridges (cb cf, fig. 18), making the edges of cavities N° 2 and 3, in their highest part; the one belonged to the first and the other to the second of these cavities.

Through the portion still in the rough of the mass, one could also see, but less distinctly, the rest of the contours of these same cavities extending to the right and left of the anterior base, designated by N° 1 (ab, ih: gf, kl, fig. 17).

It is quite evident that the bases of cells 2 and 3 were partly backed against that of cell N° 1. They terminated in an obtuse point opposite the upper extremity of the vertical ridges of this isolated cavity (b, f, fig. 17); from this the result was that the anterior cavity was longer than the other two, with the same proportionate difference that existed between its total length and that of its vertical ridges.

When one examined the block from the opposite side (fig. 18) one could see the shadow of the edges of cavity N° 1, and this appeared to reach at the top beyond the contour of the cavities N° 2 and 3.

One perceived at the base of each of the latter cavities the shadow of one of the vertical ridges (ab, gf) which bordered the cavity of the anterior face, shadows which ran from the top to the bottom of the twin cavities of the posterior face, and appeared to divide them into two equal parts. But this was only the result caused by the reciprocal position of the ridges of the two faces.

While following the work of the bees that were busy deepening the cavities which they had outlined, we perceived that the dark lines were gradually replaced by cavities or angular furrows, and that the entire effort of the workers was directed opposite those ridges which we could see as shadows through the thinned block; the bees were digging on both faces behind the ridges of the opposite face.

Thus, those which were working on the anterior face carved in the direction of the shadow of the posterior ridges which exhibited the figure of a Y, the branches of which were directed forward from the main stem (fig. 17). The intermediate ridge formed the stem of the Y, and the two oblique ridges (bc, cf) belonging to the posterior cells, represented the two branches of that letter.

The bees were not only working to thin out the back of these projecting ridges, they also scraped and smoothed the space between the shadow of these ridges and the ridges of the cavities upon which they were working.

Their work was directed along the shadow of the vertical ridge (cd) and afterwards in the direction of the oblique shadows (bc, cf) made by the oblique ridges of the opposite cells; when each space was smoothed between the ridges on their side, (ab, be: ef, fg) and the ridges of the posterior face (cb, cd, cf), it produced a cell base such as we have mentioned above, for the first row; it was composed of two trapezes and one rhomb (fig. 19).

This cavity, first shown in a semi-elliptic form (fig. 9, Plate VII) and later bordered with four ridges (fig. 11), being divided in two-thirds of its length by a furrow (dc, fig. 17), which occupied its center, and the two surfaces (abcd: cdfg) adjacent to the furrow having been flattened and thinned down to the depth of the furrow itself, they furnished two planes inclined towards each other; but as this furrow did not reach the full length of the cavity, these planes were limited only by the vertical ridges (ab, gf) of this face and by the supporting lath itself. Their upper extremity, (cf, cb) was not yet finished, or at least it was in the part of the cell not yet smoothed; but the bees, working to shape the furrows (bc, cf, fig. 19), corresponding to the oblique ridges bearing the same letters on the posterior face, gave these inclined planes an oblique termination; and as they were joined on the other three sides with parallel ridges and with the lath, these planes became equal trapezes (ab, cd: cd, fg) and were situated to the right and left of the principal furrow.

But the space remaining between the two oblique furrows and the upper extremity of the cavity (bef), being limited on one side by the sides of the obtuse angle (bcf) formed by these oblique furrows, and on the other by the sides of the obtuse angle (bef), formed by the upper edges of the cavity, and these sides and angles being equal, it produced a rhomboid (bcef) similar to those of which the pyramidal bases are composed.

This piece, by its inclination, formed an angle with each of the trapezes, and consequently also, with the two trapezes united, a solid angle (fig. 19) the summit of which was placed at the junction of the three furrows, or similarly, behind the bifurcation of the opposite ridges (c, fig. 19 and 20¾); but this solid angle was not a pyramidal base, it was a base composed of two trapezes and one rhomb.

This is the manner in which the bees work to form the base of the first anterior cell of the first row.

We have shown that they carved behind the projecting ridges, on the posterior face, two adjacent cavities separated only by a ridge (fig. 10); that they had determined the length and shape of these cavities by establishing two oblique ridges on their upper edge (fig. 12), and carved a furrow of the whole length of these cavities (fig. 18).

Thus they had divided them into two equal parts, and when the pieces to the right and left of the furrow were smoothed by their labor, these two pieces together made an angular plane (fig. 20).

They were of equal size, and as one of them was backed by one of the trapezes of the anterior cell, and as it was limited by the ridges, the shadow of which might have served as pattern for the bees working on the opposite side, it resulted that these two pieces, similar and equal to those of the anterior face, were themselves equal and similar to each other. The bases of the cells of the posterior face, in the first row, were then composed of two trapezes, such as we had already described, and this composition was a natural consequence of the method of the bees at the beginning of their work.

The three bases of cells which I have just described were the first built; but while they carved the furrows which separated them, others having lengthened the block in every direction, they were enabled to carve other cavities. They began their carving behind the vertical ridges of cells 2 and 3, and to the side of cavity N° 1, then on the posterior face, behind the opposite ridges: so that the trapezes were backed by other trapezes of similar shape and size (fig. 21 and 22). Usually, they dug out a face while others were making ridges on the opposite. So they formed cavities behind the lateral edges of the last built cells. Thus several bases, alternating on the two faces of the block, presented a first row of contiguous cells the tubes of which were not yet lengthened.

While these bees were polishing and perfecting these bases, other workers began the outlines of a second row of cells above the first, and partly behind the rhomb of the anterior cells; for their work follows a combined progress. We cannot say: *"When the bees had finished this cell they began new ones"*; but we can say: *"While some workers advance a certain piece, others outline adjacent cells."* Moreover, the work made upon one face of the comb is a part of what is needed on the opposite face: it is a reciprocal relation, a mutual connection of the parts rendering them subservient to one another. It is therefore undoubted that a slight irregularity of their work on one side will affect the shape of the cells on the other side in a similar way.

SECTION III

Construction of the cells of the second row.

The bottoms of the anterior cells of the first row, composed of two trapezes and one rhomb, were larger, as we noted, than those of the cells opposite or back of them, since the latter were composed of only two trapezes; so there was more space between the upper edge of the posterior cells and the edge of the block, than there was above the anterior cavities; this space was great enough for the base of an ordinary cell (fig. 20 and 22); but there was not room for a complete bottom above the anterior cells (fig. 19). The rough space between and above the posterior cavities in the opening of the angle of their oblique edges, extended much beyond their points (from bc up to n, fig. 20: or bc up to r, fig. 22). It was in that spot that several bees began the sketch of a new cell (fig. 22).

The first bee excavated a vertical fluting (fm, bp) in the space between the oblique edges (fc cb) of two neighboring cells and made edges for this new cavity, by accumulating the wax from this cavity to the right and to the left. In figures 23 and 27 the cell in question has been isolated so that we may better follow its development. The letters are the same as on figure 22. The contour (fmbp, fig. 23) shows the beginning of its outline. Its vertical ridges (fmbp) were exactly above the points of the two inferior cells N° 2 and 3. These ridges started from these points and ascended vertically along the cavity up to a short distance from the edge of the block, which did not extend any farther than needed for the building of the entire base of the cell: the fluting was still terminated by a curved outline (prm, fig. 23). But other bees established two rectilinear margins on its curvature, which, united as two chords in the center of the arch, formed the obtuse angle (mrp, fig. 22). This cavity was then bordered by six ridges; the two lower ones (fc cb) belonging to the cells of the first row, N° 2 and 3, between which the lower edge of this cell was placed; the lateral ridges (fm bp) parallel to each other ascending vertically, lastly the two upper ridges (rm pr) terminated the contour, joining one another and also joining the others at their lower extremity. These six ridges, equal in length, formed the hexagonal contour of the cell; but this contour was not uniform in its projection; it was higher at the angles (cpm) and depressed at the points (bfr) as may be seen more plainly in fig. 28, which displays the same cell at an angle.

The lower part, still unfinished (fcbe, fig. 23) of the space comprised between the six ridges was backed by the rhomb of cell N° 1, since cells 2 and 3, above which the hexagon was formed, were themselves backed partly by this cell. The rhomb, inclined from the horizontal, but whose main diagonal was horizontal shown on the side of cell N° 1 (c, fig. 21), exhibited its lower side. After the bees had outlined and made edges on the bottom of the hexagonal cell, they busied themselves in smoothing down the other **face** of this rhomboidal piece, and lined it with the furrows (fe and eb) which corresponded to the ridges of the same name on the anterior face.

This piece was then a rhomb, and this rhomb (fcbe, fig. 22) seen from above, was the first and upper piece of a pyramidal base.

It occupied one-third of the surface of the cavity, for the obtuse angle (feb) being in the center, and its edges resting upon the two edges (fc and cb), which formed one-third of the circumference, it is easily conceived that the entire bottom of the cell was to be three times that of this rhomb. In fact there was above the rhomb, inside of the hexagon, enough space to admit of two rhombs similar to this one, but turned differently.

This part of the base of the cell remained in the same condition until the work upon the opposite face was far enough advanced to allow the bees to build a ridge on the reverse face of the cell in a vertical direction (er, fig. 21): (which could take place only after they had outlined the two cavities opposite the hexagonal cell). But after this ridge was established on the anterior face, behind the piece to be divided, one bee busied herself in making the base of the hexagonal cavity in that direction and made a furrow in the still unfinished space (er, fig. 22), from the upper edge of the rhomb, to the upper edge of the hexagon; when the two parts of this were finished, we saw that she had perfected two additional rhombs (ferm and erbp) equal to the rhomb (fcbe). Thus the six edges of the hexagonal contour enclosed three rhombs of equal size; or a pyramidal base complete: the first of them having been built on the lower edge of the block. It is easy to understand that, during this operation, other cells were outlined to the right and left, upon the adjacent cells of the first row, and there is no need of any further explanation in this regard since the work is similar to that which we have just described.

The block was still further enlarged by the wax producers and there was still more space above the cells of the first row for the construction of new cells (fig. 21). The space between the cells and the drawn line shows, on fig. 22, that this space was not yet filled during the building of the posterior cell of the second row, but it was filled when they built the anterior hexagonal cell.

A bee placed herself on the anterior face, so as to work in the unfinished space between the points of two cells of the first row, designated by numbers 1 and 4, between their oblique edges (fe fv). This bee immediately carved a furrow above the vertical edge that separated them, in a space equal to the diameter of an ordinary cell, but this space was already limited below by the cells of the first row. The bee gave to this cavity a fluting shape, its edges were made by two vertical ridges (er vn), and its upper edge, first made in a circle (fig. 25) was later changed by two other workers into straight ridges (on ov, fig. 21); making an obtuse angle; thus the cavity became hexagonal as with the opposite side, which was backed by it.

The dividing of this cell, (fig. 21 and 25) did not appear to cause the bees any trouble: the pieces which composed it were already partly shaped on the posterior face; on that side, two contiguous cells had between them a ridge (fm, fig. 22), which was to serve as guide: its shadow divided into two equal parts the inferior portion of the hexagon cavity. One could also see the shadow of the oblique ridges of those two posterior cells, from the center m of the cell, one to the right and the other to the left, running towards vertical ridges at r and n (fig. 21).

This cavity appeared to be divided into three equal parts by the shadow of the posterior ridges. What we discerned in shadows was soon made real by the work of the bees; the shadows were converted into furrows opposite the ridges; the interval and the edge of the cell were smoothed until they showed distinct rhombs; but the bees, while shaping the vertical furrow divided the inferior part of the cavity, and the two first rhombs of the pyramidal base were formed to the right and left; then by following the oblique ridges of the posterior cells, they formed a third rhomb situated in the upper part of the cavity, and inclined similarly to the one of cavity N° 1.

This rhomb (onrm, fig. 21) was not opposite any outlined cell on the posterior face; it was backed by still crude material, comprised between the upper sides (rm mn) of two cells of the second row; so this space was to be later a part of the posterior face of a cell of the third row.

The result of the work of the bees, within the hexagonal cavity, was another pyramidal base; it differed in no way from the bases of the same row on the posterior face, which backed it, except in the position of its rhombs.

From this it is easy to conceive the manner of building of additional cells; they are always located between the upper oblique sides of the neighboring cells; above their points the bees will build vertical ridges which will be the right and left borders of the new cavity; then the contour will be made by erecting two other ridges horizontally, on the upper edge of the fluting, which will produce an hexagonal contour.

The inferior part of these cavities will always correspond with the walls of the opposite cells, that is why all the cells of that side will be divided by two rhombs in the lower part and one rhomb in the upper. (Of course it is the reverse in combs built downwards; so we must invert the figures in order to follow the natural order, as the work must be the same and the result similar: the building of pyramidal bases).

The posterior cells are all formed on the model of those which we have described; one rhomb in the lower part and two rhombs in the upper. The anterior hexagonal cells are all situated a little higher than the posterior ones, for their lower part corresponds with the upper rhombs of the opposite cells.

We still have to make a few remarks concerning the difference between the pyramidal bases and the bases of the first row: the latter are composed, as we have shown, of two trapezes and a rhomb, or two trapezes only, which ascend perpendicularly from the lath, so the position differs from those of the pieces of pyramidal bases; as the three pieces of a pyramidal base start from the top of the pyramid towards the edge which outlines the contour of its base, they are all three inclined forward in the same proportion. We have taken for granted, in our former explanations, that the furrow at the base of a cell was vertical. It was simply to show that it appeared to ascend vertically, when seen from its face. But when we cut the block vertically, we see that the furrow is oblique, since it starts from the base of the cavity to reach its edge; fig. 24, 28 represent a posterior and an anterior pyramidal base; none of their edges or furrows are vertical. It is not the same with the trapezes of the base of the first row, they are actually vertical no matter on which side we view them.

The result is that the union of the latter with the oblique rhomb of the cells of the anterior face must be in a slightly different angle from those of a pyramidal base.

Each of the six ridges which form the edges of a pyramidal base is to serve as basis for one of the six sides of a cell. The four sides of those of the first row (fig. 31) are also fixed in the same way around their base. The prisms which are a result of the union of the sides are fastened to the edges of the cavities made in the block.

At first sight, it would seem that there is nothing plainer than the adding of wax upon the edges of the contour of a cell base, but owing to the unevenness of this rim, which we have noticed, and which produces three projections and three recesses for the pyramidal bases, a projection for each of the bases of the anterior cells of the first row, and a recess for the posterior ones; on account of this unevenness the bees must begin by filling out what is lacking, by adding more wax on the shallower edges than they put on the projecting ones; in this way all the edges of the cells offer a uniform surface from the beginning and before the cells have acquired their proper dimensions. But the surface of a new comb is not entirely plane, for there is a progressive decrease in the work of the bees. The walls of the cells are prolonged in an order corresponding with the completion of the bases to which the cells belong (fig. 30), and the length of the tubes is so regulated that there is no gap or conspicuous irregularity among them. Thus the surface of a new comb is lenticular (fig. 29, 30, 31); the thickness of it decreasing to the edges, because the lately outlined cells are shorter than the older ones. This progression continues in the comb while it is increased in size; but as soon as the bees lack space for its prolongation, it loses this lenticular shape and becomes parallel. The bees form all the cells of the same depth by bringing the newest to the depth of the first built; the comb has then reached the shape that it is to preserve; but it is not yet fully completed; we will show later the termination of the work.

How can we explain the combination of their operations; why does instinct lead them to give a different form and different dimensions to the bottom of the first rows of either side, which have so great an influence on the remainder of the comb? How can the bees working on one face of a comb determine the space to be excavated for the invariable mutual relation of the bases? We should clear up this question, as the remainder of the problem depends upon it.

We do not see the bees visiting the two surfaces alternately, to compare the respective position of the cavities which they outline; nature did not instruct them to take measurements which would appear to us indispensable for the construction of symmetrical work: these insects content themselves with feeling the part to be hollowed out with their antennæ, and appear by this means sufficiently apprised, to execute a very complicated work, in which all seems to be combined with great exactness.

Not a parcel of wax is removed before their antennæ have felt (palped) the surface to be sculptured. Bees do not trust to their eyes for any of their operations; but with the help of their antennæ, they can build, in darkness, those combs which are deservedly regarded as the most admirable production of insects. This organ is so flexible an instrument that it lends itself to the examination of the most delicate parts of the most distorted pieces; it may be used by them as compasses in the measurement of the smallest objects, such as the edge of a cell.

Bees, therefore, appear to be regulated in their work by some local circumstance; we noticed that, while sketching the bottoms of the first cells, before there was any ridge on the reverse, they sometimes caused such a ridge to appear on the opposite surface, by the simple pressure of their legs upon the wax still soft and flexible, or by the efforts made with their teeth to excavate the interior of the block. Sometimes it occasioned a breach of the partition, which was soon repaired, but a slight protuberance always remains on the opposite surface, which may serve as guide for the bees working upon that side. They place themselves to the right and left of this ridge to begin a new excavation, and heap up a part of the materials between the two flutings resulting from their work.

This ridge, converted into a real rectilinear rib, becomes a guide for the bees to recognize the direction to be followed in making the vertical furrow of the anterior cell.

We have often conceived, when seeing these insects follow so accurately the reverse of the ridges to excavate the corresponding furrows, that they perceive the greater or less thickness of the partition, from its flexibility, elasticity, or from some other physical property of beeswax: whatever may be the case, it is certain that they give the bases of the cells a uniform thickness, without having any mechanical means of measuring them; for the same reason, they may perceive very distinctly whether there is a ridge behind the partition, and excavate into it until they have reached the point which must not be exceeded.

I do not wish to present these explanations with more positiveness than as simple hypotheses. I desired to show the linking of the operations of the bees, but I have not undertaken to discover the secret causes of their actions.

I believe however that they may be explained without resorting to extraordinary causes. The length of the cavities, their respective position and the thickness of the block once determined, the inclination of the oblique sides of the trapezes of the first row, to which that of the lozenges of the second is subordinate, is established of itself, without any need of instruments for measuring angles or without calculation on the part of the bees.

What we need to understand is the manner in which they establish the relation between the unequal cells of the first row. One of the contributing causes for securing these dimensions, upon which so many important conditions depend, is the manner in which the block is enlarged.

Its original height determines about the vertical diameter of the posterior cavities, which is equal to two-thirds that of a common cell. But they cannot complete the bottom of the anterior cell until the block is enlarged, which on that account is extended more than necessary for finishing the cell, but just enough to give sufficient space for the entire base of a posterior cell of the second row; for the rhomb making part of it is already comprised in the interval of the cells formed of trapezes. The bees, adding to the block two-thirds of the diameter of a cell, are enabled to construct, on the anterior face, the bottoms of cells of the second row, a part of which is already intercepted between the upper edges of the first cells; but there will not be room yet for the construction of a third row, until the block shall be enlarged anew.

The bees cannot deviate from the prescribed rule, unless particular circumstances alter the bases of their work, for the block is always lengthened in uniform quantity; and what is admirable, this is done by the wax producers, the depositories of its first elements, who do not have the faculty of sculpturing the cells.

Thus in dividing the functions between the wax producers and the small bees, the author of nature appears to have distrusted the exclusive lights of instinct.

What simplicity and depth in the means, what linking of causes and effects! It is a diminutive image of this harmony which strikes us in the great works of creation.

Such processes could not be foreseen. One does not divine the ways of nature, it lays out methods that confound our science, and it is only by studying it carefully that we may succeed in unveiling some of its mysteries.

From the facts just described, should we not draw the conclusion that the geometry which shines in the work of the bees is rather the result of their operations than the principle that causes them?

———

Our readers will doubtless share the pleasure which we experienced when we received the following communication, in which one perceives a singular connection between the geometrical solution supplied by a skilful mathematician, and the work of the bees, such as we have exhibited from our observations.

The bases of the cells of the first row, which determine the inclination of the rhombs of the entire comb, represent two sides of a prism cut so as to form three angles equal to the rhomboidal plane which they intercept. One might believe that the bees succeed in constructing their cells by the sole knowledge that they have of the required section of the prism, and the solution supplied by Mr. Le Sage shows it to be more simple than one had thought.

We find great satisfaction in recalling here the labors which are too little known, of a savant who is beloved of his countrymen, and we are authorized to state that the project of publishing his principal works has not been overlooked by Professor Prevost, of Geneva, who mentioned it in the preface of his "Notice upon the life and writings of Le Sage, 1 vol. in-18 at J. J. Paschoud, Paris and Geneva.

ARTICLE COMMUNICATED BY MR. P. PRÉVOST, PROFESSOR
AT GENEVA.

In 1781, Mr. Lhuilier sent to Mr. DeCastillon a memoir upon the "minimum of wax of the bees", which was read at the Academy of Berlin and inserted in his Memoirs for the same year. This learned mathematician gives in it, in a few words, the history of the researches made upon this subject, by Maraldi, Réaumur, Koenig, &c., and treats the subject by a more simple method than had yet been done in previous works, since he reduces the problem to a few elementary propositions.

In this memoir he gives honorable mention to Mr. Le Sage. He mentions him also in a later work and gives more details on the mathematical process through which this philosopher solved the problem relating to the shape of the base of the cells constructed by the bees. He informs us, that Le Sage was, to his knowledge, the first to treat this matter in an elementary way; that he had treated it algebraically; that he had employed, for that purpose, a method easily applicable to all the problems which do not exceed the second degree; a method which had been kindly communicated to Mr. Lhuilier ten years previous to the time when he published his own.

The memoir of Mr. Lhuilier contains not only the solution of the problem relative to the construction of the rhomboidal bases, so as to obtain, for a given cell, the least expense of wax, but also that of the problem relative to the "*minimum minimorum*," or to the shape of the cell of equal capacity that would cost the least, as well as other remarks regarding this subject. It ends with a memorandum from Mr. de Castillon, relative to the actual dimension of the cells of the bees.

This memoir and the latin work following that which I have mentioned, having been published for a long time and being consequently within reach of those who occupy themselves with these matters, it is sufficient to refer to them. But it may give them pleasure to find here an outline of the first elementary work which has been undertaken to solve the problem of the rhomboidal bases of the cells. A paper, written in Mr. Le Sage's own hand, and of very ancient date, presents this work in a very simple form. It was drawn from one of his portfolios in which he had gathered the material for a bulletin which is mentioned in the account of his life. We shall transcribe it here without change, up to the second note which we will replace by an explanation.

Notice of G. Le Sage on the base of the cells:

"Given the mutual inclination of the two planes, for instance 120 degrees; cut into them with a third plane, in such way that the three resulting angles be equal.

"This is a problem which even a very shallow artisan could solve with very simple instruments: for the only thing needed is to find the center of a proposed straight line; which even insects may do with their legs (a). This solves the famous problem of the *minimum*, of which we are astonished to find the solution in the base of the bee's cell, and which consists in using the least possible quantity of wax, without diminishing the size of the cell;

and for which they have needlessly used all the apparatus of the calculation of the infinite (b)."

(a) For the geometrical explanations.

"Problem. Given (Plate XI, fig. 2) the width AB of the face of a regular hexagonal prism; add to one of its edges or withdraw from it, the length AX, equal $\sqrt{\dfrac{AB^2}{8}}$

"Solution. Cut AB in two equal parts at C. Draw AD to equal AC. Draw CD; cut the line in equal parts at E. Draw AE, from A to X, upon AD or its prolongation.

Demonstration: $(AE)^2 = \tfrac{1}{2}(AC)^2 = \tfrac{1}{2}\left(\dfrac{AB}{2}\right)^2 = \tfrac{1}{2} \times \dfrac{(AB)^2}{4} = \dfrac{(AB)^2}{8}$

(b) "For the geometrical explanations."

This is the heading of the second note which we have suppressed. It was intended to demonstrate algebraically that the problem relating to the bases of cells amounts to the geometrical problem solved in the first note. Several reasons have induced us to substitute for this algebraical note a few detailed explanations. One may find, in the above mentioned works of Lhuilier (especially in the Berlin Memoirs for 1781, marginal note page 284), the method of Le Sage and his learned disciple, to determine, with the help of algebra, the minimum of expense in the construction of the bases.

Supposing the hexagonal cell to be a straight prism, the question is to cut the ridge conveniently at the desired spot. For this purpose, the rhomboidal base must be a minimum. A simple equation of the second degree, leads to the following formula: The distance from the intersecting point to the hexagonal base is equal to the half-side of this base, divided by the root of two, or, similarly, to the side divided by the root of eight.

CHAPTER V.

Modifications in the Architecture of Bees.

The researches relative to the organization and development of animal productions, may not be, in spite of their importance, the most interesting in the eyes of the naturalist philosopher. Those which embrace the degrees, the resources and the limits of this faculty which serves as judgment for so numerous a class of beings, offer a still wider and more fertile field for his meditations.

The vulgar commonly believe that sensations and physical needs exercise an absolute empire over animals: unquestionably they have influence upon them in many circumstances; but it would be as difficult to explain the conduct of creatures subjected to instinct by the sole attraction of pleasure or fear of pain as it would be unfair to ascribe the virtues of feeling and reasoning beings to personal views alone, though it has often been asserted that self-interest was the only motive of our actions.

If there is a direct connection between the organization and the habits of living beings, this connection is so enigmatic in its characters that we cannot analyze it. We may notice, in physiology, a few salient points, such as the long beaks and webbed feet of some birds, by which we discern the locations they inhabit and the food which they secure; but there is a long reckoning from this to the cunning of animals, the recesses of their instinct; even if we should reason from their customary behavior, we might be drawn into error, for many of them have ingenious resources in difficult circumstances: they leave their usual routine and appear to act according to the situation in which they find themselves; that is indeed one of the most curious phenomenons of natural history.

Invariable laws, concerning the actions of animals, appear to us a subject of admiration, for the mind becomes easily accustomed to ideas of order, and readily accepts a uniform plan; but in the designs of the author of nature, there is a flexibility, a freedom which bears the imprint of supreme power; the most opposite conditions are united without jar or confusion: can we conceive that beings subject to a common law and gifted with some intellect, should be able to swerve from the letter and act accordingly? That they should be able to change their processes and modify the prescribed rules when necessary? How can we imagine that there may be exceptions to the great laws of nature, and that animals be able to act, in some circumstances as if they understood the intentions of the law-maker? Those are phenomena which no theory can explain; but we must not get false views concerning the nature of animals; do not our prejudices blind us as to the distance from their faculties to ours? This would require profound investigations, and it is in that direction that the ultimate labors of the zoologists should tend. To acquit ourselves in part of our own debt in this regard, we will describe some anomalies which we have noticed in the behavior of the bees.

153

I will not yet develop the consequences which seem to result from these; it will be only after making known the bulk of their operations that I will take the liberty of making a few remarks on the true place which these insects occupy in the order of life.

Everything connected with the fabrication and use of combs has been skilfully combined; cells turned downwards like those of wasps would not have suited bees, since they have to store a fluid: each comb presents innumerable small honey-pots laid horizontally; they are provided on both sides; perhaps their shape, and the affinity between the wax and the honey, prevent the latter from escaping; the combs are on parallel planes and are separated from one another by lanes only a few lines in width. It was after measuring these fairly regular distances and the average thickness of the combs that I conceived the invention of book-hives, which I always used with success.

The parallelism of the combs is not one of the least difficult subjects of explanation, nor would it be explainable, did we conceive that their foundation was laid simultaneously by a number of workers. Experience teaches us, to the contrary, that one cannot see the bees begin different blocks of wax here and there at the same time. A single worker deposits materials in an apparently suitable direction; she departs; another replaces her; the block rises; the bees sculpture its opposite faces alternately; but scarcely are some rows of cells constructed when we perceive two other blocks similar to the first, established parallel to the first, which widen and lengthen on either side. These blocks soon become combs, for bees work with astonishing speed: shortly after, we notice two others still parallel and built in relative progression according to the date of their origin; the first one, being the oldest, exceeds those parallel to its two faces by some rows of cells, and the latter exceeds those following by a similar quantity; thus the two faces of a comb are in great part concealed by those next to it.

I shall not try to explain how bees take such accurate measurements and know the direction parallel to that of the first comb. But one perceives clearly that if they were permitted to place different blocks in the roof of their hive at the same time, these outlines would be neither properly spaced nor built parallel to one another.

We see an example of the same method in the manner of outlining the cells; it is invariably a single bee that selects and determines the place of the first cavity; this one, being established, serves to direct the ulterior labors. Did each of several workers sketch a cell at the same time, the symmetry of the cells resulting from this operation would be left to chance; for these insects have no discipline and know no subordination.

A great number of bees work upon the same comb, indeed, but they are not guided by a simultaneous impulse, as might be conceived if one did not observe their operations from the outset. This impulse is successive; a single bee begins each partial operation, and several others successively join their efforts with hers to the same end; each appears to act individually in a certain direction, directed by the bees which preceded her or by the state in which she finds the work which she is to continue; and the bee that commences a new operation is led to it by the effect of a harmony which rules the progression of the work. But if anything in the conduct of the bees could give the idea of almost unanimous consent (which we present as a doubtful thing) it is the inaction of the rest of the colony while a single bee determines the position of the comb. Immediately, others assist her and add to the height of the block; then they again cease acting and a single individual, of a different profession, if the word may be allowed in speaking of insects, traces the first outline of the base of a cell which, by its peculiar shape prepares a different kind of work; it is a base or a fundamental plan for establishing the entire edifice. A subtle sense of feeling shows to the bees, across the partition, the situation of the margins of the cavity, and it is from this that they direct their efforts for the division of the base of the new cells: but it is not only by the means of the ridges that they discover the direction to be followed; we have ascertained that they profit by divers circumstances to guide themselves in those excavations. The bee which forms the first cell is a remarkable exception; she works in a rough mass, and thus has nothing to point out the way, instinct being her sole conductor.

The workers outlining the cavities of the second row, on the contrary, can take advantage of the edges and angles previously made on the same face, and use them as basis or point of departure for subsequent operations. I shall soon give a singular example of the art with which they take advantage of these when they have no other resource, but I shall speak first of the ordinary labor of the workers: I had seen them sculpt only upwards; I explained all their maneuvers when they are working in that direction, but the explanation of their behavior and the results which they attain then might belong to a special case.

So it was necessary to learn whether they always act in the same manner and pass through the same proceedings: they sculpt upwards with much less speed than downwards; but this circumstance was favorable to the observing of the diverse labors which the formation of the cells requires; otherwise it would have been impossible to follow the detail of their proceedings; yet the tardiness of the bees in this occurrence had its inconveniences; their work was sometimes interrupted for several hours; the wax was wanting when needed or it was not sculpted soon as deposited, or several blocks were deposited on the same lath. Their work was evidently relaxed or impeded, and it was only through the number of small combs which they built that we were enabled to overlook the irregularities of their operations and form an accurate opinion of their architecture; so it was important to learn whether the process which we had seen them follow was the same in ordinary circumstances; it was to clear this doubt that I had a hive constructed of a new shape (Plate I, fig. 6).

In order to fill my requirements, the top of this hive must be composed of several pieces, removable without disturbing the bees; it was also necessary that each part be separable and removable each time that we desired to ascertain the progress of their work. A ceiling, composed of glass and wooden slips placed alternately in a horizontal plane, was used for this purpose. A screw at each end of the slips permitted us to raise the combs above the top of the hive, so that we might examine them and return them conveniently without deranging the bees; in this way we could remove such of them as we wished to preserve and compel the bees to build others.

When they were established in their new home, they built combs along the wooden laths following the direction of the intersecting line between the slips and the laths.

The first block established by them gave us nothing new; we removed it and the bees built another at once; they again established it on the edge of a lath; we gave them time to carve their first cells: then by turning the screws upon which the work rested, the latter was brought up and allowed us to observe the formation of the new outlines; they showed flutings similar to those seen in the combs built upwards; we again lowered the comb and the bees continued their work. A few minutes later, the comb was again observed, the outlines had been advanced, the faces of the cells on both sides were unlike each other; they showed vertical trapezes; but only the anterior cells had a rhomb at their lower extremity; we then saw the bees proceed with the cells of the second row and became convinced that the march of their operations was in every point similar to what we had witnessed in the upward building.

We compelled the bees to begin a great number of small combs, the outlines of which, more or less advanced, showed us that they were built upon the same principles and with the same gradations as those that had been built upwards.

It is clear, in my opinion, therefore, that the particular configuration of the first cells, on both sides, determines invariably the shape of the pyramidal bases of all the subsequent cells.

One could not have foreseen that the bees, in beginning their masonry, could have taken other measurements and a different method from that which they follow for the rest of the comb. This already proves that these insects do not act altogether mechanically; however, as it might be taken for granted that there is a necessity in this order of work, I will cite a frequent example of an altogether different action.

When I compelled the bees to work upwards, they laid blocks and built combs, upon the horizontal part of the laths; but they were not always so docile. I have often seen them use wax from under their rings to stretch and extend some old combs into the space in which I desired them to build new ones (Plate IX, fig. 2 shows the lath with comb above and below).

The manner in which they do this deserves attention. To extend a comb placed under a lath and bring it up into the space above it, they begin by lengthening forward the upper edges of the cells of the first row, perpendicularly to the comb, and so that their extremities will project a little beyond the lath; after they have thus staked the ground, and fixed the points to work from, they pile wax on the vertical edge of the lath and with this wax they shape curves from the two parallel ridges of a cell and transform them into the walls of a cell. Thus they succeed in outlining regular hexagons on the vertical side of the lath, each with six ridges which will serve as bases to the cells which they will erect at that spot; these cells are flat bottomed, since they are built on the edge of the lath (Plate IX, fig. 2), but their diameter is equal to that of cells which are built upon a block of wax; if the lath is thicker than required for a single row of cells, the bees continue with additional ridges above those previously traced, until they reach the upper edge of the lath; when they build upon its surface a block which they sculpt in accord with the hexagons outlined on the wood; they will then give the first row of cells the ordinary shape of cells of the first row, and three rhombs to all subsequently built cells.

We thus perceive that bees may shape cells upon wood and give them hexagon contours without pyramidal bases; thus they deviate from their usual routine, but not in the measurement of the cells and the shape of their walls, which they outline upon the wood with a symmetry that guides them in their ulterior work. But they do this by taking advantage of the previously built cells to form their ridges and give the curves a proper base. These flat bottom cells are less regular than the ordinary cells; we see in them some cells the contours of which are not angular, or the dimensions of which are not exact; but in all of them we notice the hexagons more or less marked.

After seeing the bees build upwards and downwards, it was natural to investigate whether we could compel them to build their combs in some other direction. We tried to confuse them by placing them in a hive with the upper and lower sides entirely glazed, so that they had no place of support except on the side walls of their dwelling.

They clustered in one of the angles of the hive, in an impenetrable mass; we were compelled to disturb them in order to see their work and found that they had built combs perpendicular to one of these walls: they were just as regular as those which they usually build under a horizontal ceiling. This was a remarkable result, since the bees, habitually sculpting downwards, were compelled to place their foundations on a plane which is unusual to them. But the cells of the first row were similar to those which they construct ordinarily, with the only difference that the ridges were built in a different direction: the other cells were none the less fit for the common uses and distributed on both faces, with the bottoms alternately corresponding with the same symmetry.

I put these bees under still greater trial: having observed that they try to build their combs, in the shortest way, towards the opposite side of the hive, I covered the latter with a pane of glass, in order to find whether they would be content with a surface which they do not usually trust, unless their cluster can hang in the close vicinity to a substance less slippery than glass. I knew that they prefer fastening their combs to wood, and that they accept glass only when they have been deprived of any other substance to strengthen their constructions. I had no doubt however that they would fasten the comb to this pane, taking chances to later strengthen it by securing more stable attachments, but I was far from suspecting what they would do.

As soon as the board was covered with this smooth and slippery surface, they deviated from the straight line which they had hitherto followed, and continued their work by bending their comb at right angle and so that the forward edge would reach one of the walls left uncovered.

Varying this experiment in several ways, I saw the bees constantly change the direction of their combs whenever I approximated a surface too smooth to admit of their clustering at the ceiling or on the sides of the hive; they always selected the direction which would bring them to the wooden sides; I thus compelled them to curve their combs in the strangest shapes, by placing a pane at a certain distance in front of their edges.

These results indicate an admirable instinct; they denote even more than instinct; for glass is not a substance against which bees may be warned by nature; there is nothing as polished as glass or resembling glass in their natural abodes, the interior of trees. The most singular part of their work was that they did not wait till they arrived at the surface of the glass to change the direction of the combs, they selected the suitable spot before-hand; did they anticipate the inconvenience that might result from any other mode of construction? The manner in which they made an angle in the combs was no less interesting; they necessarily had to alter the ordinary fashion of their work and the dimensions of the cells; therefore those on the convex side were enlarged to two or three times the diameter of the others on the opposite face. Can we understand how so many insects occupied at once on both sides would concur in giving them the same curvature, from one end to the other; how they could decide to build small cells on one face, while upon the other face they built cells of so exaggerated dimensions; and is it not still more wonderful that they should have the art of making cells of such great discrepancy correspond between them? The bottom of the cells being common to both sides, the tubes alone assumed a taper form. Perhaps no other insect has ever supplied a more decisive proof of the resources of instinct, when compelled to deviate from the ordinary courses.

But let us observe these bees in natural circumstances, for it is not even necessary to test their instinct in order to see them modify the order of their architecture: by comparing what nature has required of them with the means employed by them in unexpected cases, we will better judge of the extent of their faculties.

Since the cells of bees are to serve as cradles to individuals of different sizes, the caliber of those tubes must be proportioned to the intention of their use. Thus the workers which were to build drone cells, were to follow a larger pattern than when they build ordinary worker cells; but they gave them the same shape, their bases are also composed of three rhombs, their prisms of six walls, and their angles are equal to those of the small cells. The diameter of worker cells is 2 2/5 lines, that of drone cells is 3 1/3 lines; those dimensions are so fairly constant that some authors believed that they might be used as invariable patterns of measurement.

The drone cells rarely occupy the higher part of the combs; it is usually in the middle or in the lateral parts that they are found, and they are not isolated; they are built together and correspond with one another on the two faces of the comb.

No observations have been made of the art with which they manage to construct alternately large and small cells without too flagrant inequalities in their work. The manner in which the drone cells are surrounded can alone explain how the transition is effected: when they are to sculpt drone cells below worker cells, they build several rows of intermediate cells, whose diameter augments progressively until gaining that necessary for drone cells; for the same reason when the bees wish to return to worker size they change by progressive gradation down to the size of cells of that class.

We usually see three or four rows of intermediate cells; the first drone cells still participate in the irregularity of the ridges which adjoin them, some bases corresponding to four cells instead of three. Their furrows are always in the line of the ridges, but one of the sides of the base, instead of being immediately opposite to the center of the cell on the reverse, divides it unequally, which alters the shape of the bottom, so that it no longer presents three uniform rhombs, but consists of pieces more or less irregular (See the appendix which follows).

The farther removed from the transition cells, the more regular are found the male cells, so we often see several consecutive rows without defects; the irregularity is resumed on their opposite confines and does not disappear until beyond several rows of ill-fashioned workers cells.

When building drone cells, the bees establish a heavier block of wax defects; the irregularity is resumed on their opposite confines and does not preserve the same order and symmetry while working upon a larger scale.

Irregularities have often been noticed in the cells of the bees. Réaumur, Bonnet and several other naturalists cite examples of this as so many defects. What would have been their astonishment had they observed that some of these anomalies were calculated, that there is, so to speak, a mobile harmony in the structure of the combs: if, through some imperfection of their organs or of their instruments, the bees made some uneven or illshaped cells, they would still show talent in repairing them, in compensating them by other irregularities; it is much more astonishing that they know enough to quit the ordinary route when circumstances demand that they build drone cells, and that they be able to vary the dimensions and the shape of each piece to return to a regular order; that after having built thirty or forty rows of drone cells, they quit the regular order again to return to the starting point by successive reductions.

How can these insects get through such difficult requirements, such complicated structures, change from the small to the large, from the large to the small; from a regular plan to fantastic shapes and from these back again to a symmetrical figure? No known system can explain it.

Since bees are every year obliged to construct cells of different sizes, we can attribute this trait to instinct, but it is an instinct capable of modification. What circumstance is it which prompts them to change the plan of the cells? Is it alteration in their senses, a change in the temperature, more abundant food or more suitable than what they find during the rest of the season? Not by any means; it seems to be the laying of the queen which determines the kind of cells to be built: as long as she lays none but worker eggs, you do not see the bees build drone cells; but if she finds no room available for the latter kind of eggs, the workers seem to be informed of it at once and we see them immediately gradually changing the shape of the cells, and at length producing cells for the masculine cradles.

There is another circumstance under which bees enlarge the dimensions of the cells; it is when a considerable crop of honey presents itself; not only do they give the cells a much larger diameter than common, but they prolong their tubes as far as space admits. In times of great harvest, we see irregular combs, the cells of which are an inch to an inch and a half in depth.

On the other hand, bees are sometimes induced to shorten their cells. When wishing to lengthen an old comb, the cells of which have received their full dimension, they gradually reduce the thickness of its edges, by gnawing down the walls of the cells, until they have restored the original lenticular shape; they then add wax to the edges of the pyramidal bases, as we have seen them doing in ordinary work: it is a certain fact that they never lengthen the cells of a comb in any direction without having first thinned out its rim, which is diminished in a sufficient space to remove any angular projection.

This law which obliges the bees to partly demolish the cells on the edges, before giving them additional length, deserves more profound investigation than we are able to give it; for even if we can conceive the instinct which leads them to a particular industry, how can we account for that which induces them to undo a part of what they have executed with the utmost care? We must acknowledge that such phenomenae will long be a stumbling-block for all hypotheses that try to explain instinct.

When they construct a new comb there is a regular gradation in all the parts next to the edge, to which they appear to be accustomed and which may be necessary in the formation of new cells. But those edge cells are prolonged later like the cells of the rest of the surface, so that they no longer preserve the decreasing gradation observed in new combs. Thus it is evidently for the purpose of restoring the comb to its primitive form that they reduce the depth of the cells proportionally to their distance from the edge.[5]

All the anomalies exhibited in the labor of bees, are so well appropriated to the object proposed, that they seem to be a part of the plan under which they act, concurring to the general order.

The greatness of views and means of the ordaining wisdom is such that it does not reach its aim through minute exactness, it goes from one irregularity to another which compensate each other: the measurements are lofty, the apparent errors are managed by a sublime geometry, and order results from diversity. This is not the only example that science has divulged to us of preordained irregularities which astonish our ignorance and secure admiration from our most enlightened minds; for the more we study the general laws as well as the special laws, the better we see the perfection of this vast system.

---

[5] Huber does not appear to have perceived that the bees always round off the outer edge of each cell, evidently to give it greater strength, as this rim makes the edges of the cell thicker, especially at the points of junction of one cell with another. It is this heavier rounded edge which they remove whenever they wish to add to the length and, as noticed by several writers, the rounded edge is rebuilt whenever they leave work, so that the surface of the cell upon which they travel is constantly braced by a rounded rim. The beekeeper who uses the honey extractor readily perceives the difference; for the combs, after using the honey knife to remove the cappings, show the lack of this rim. However, the bees rebuild the rim, as they repair the combs, when they are returned to them.

APPENDIX TO THE CHAPTERS ON THE ARCHITECTURE OF BEES.
BY P. HUBER, SON OF F. HUBER.

Having been called upon to review the facts which I have described, I have acquired a little information which had not been transmitted to my father by his faithful secretary; among these facts are found a few peculiarities which I now will present upon the method of comb enlargement, upon the principle and cause of their irregularity and upon the shape of the transition cells in drone combs.

It was not possible to give a complete idea of the enlarging of the combs, in the description of the bees' work, cell after cell. When we consider the matter in its ensemble we discover a few modifications which were not perceptible in very small parts of the comb, and upon which we had not arrested our attention, so as not to complicate our statement.

We have stated that the work of bees was ordinarily conducted downwards: one might believe that it is always so, but this fact, which is applicable to a part of the cells, does not extend to the entire surface of the comb, its shape preventing this. Circumstances sometimes permit us to watch the bees while they are building combs, without disturbing the natural order of their work; those circumstances are rare and do not give us all the advantages found in inverting the order of their work, but they give us a more correct idea of the whole.

For this purpose, it is necessary that the bees, hanging in a cluster at one side of the hive, should work upon the edge, or, in a way, outside of this cluster; after having built one comb they establish a second one, then a third, nearer and nearer to the observer who follows their work through the transparent wall of the hive.

The original base, upon which the bees begin, is composed of three or four cells, sometimes more; after being continued of that breadth for two or three inches, it begins to be enlarged at about three-fourths of this length.

Were the bees to work only downwards, it would form but a narrow strip of a uniform diameter, only a few bees could work upon it at the same time; but it is necessary that the work should proceed rapidly, and that they be able to sculpt at the same time in all directions; the preliminary lengthening of this little strip and its widening at its inferior end enable a large number of bees to work upon the edge, and the entire orbit of the comb is extended in every direction under the work of their shears.

The bees at the lower edge of the comb lengthen it downwards, those on the sides widen it to the right and left; those above the main bulging portion extend it upwards; the wider it extends below, the more necessity there is of its rising directly to reach the vault of the hive.

Thence results a fact which we had not yet mentioned; that the cells of the first row are not the first built throughout the hive; so the primitive cells are only those which are constructed at the upper part before the comb is widened. This small base is sufficient to trace out the pyramidal bases of the entire comb; but although the subsequently built cells of the upper line are built either upwards or obliquely they are of about the same shape as the primary cells; they are composed of vertical plates, with or without rhomb, according to the side from which they are viewed. They fit against pyramidal cells as well as against the ceiling of the hive; there is more irregularity and confusion in them than in ordinary primitive cells but the strength and general order lose in no way thereby.

The same thing occurs when the lateral edges of their combs reach the vertical wall; the bees build the bases of the last cells perpendicularly to this surface, so that they are similar to those of the first row, with the only difference that they are situated horizontally instead of vertically; and when the wall is of glass, one sees the base of all those cells in the shape of a zigzag in its center, as with the first cells built.

Thus bees work in all directions, their processes are uniform in every case. But we should be unable to recognize the original small waxen block, did we not take notice that it now appears as a flat ribbon which runs around the edge of the entire comb. It is in this edge that the bees sculpt new cells and deposit scales of wax; its width is of two or three lines and it is apparently of more compact build than the rest of the comb. The bees work at the same time over all parts of this ribbon when they have abundance of wax.

We must notice, however, that even when their work progresses in all parts, it does not advance in the same proportion; they work more quickly downwards than horizontally, and more slowly upwards than in any other direction; thence ensues the ellipse or lense shape which the comb assumes while it is being enlarged; thence also the greater length than breadth. it being more pointed at its inferior extremity and narrower at the top than in the middle. The shape of the combs, therefore, is fairly regular; their outline usually offers no asperity; and there is a singular harmony in the lengthening of all the cells. We have previously stated that the length of their prisms is in proportion to their age; but investigating with more attention, we recognized that, in a new comb, their length is proportioned to their distance from the edge. Thus the first rows are not those of which the cells are deepest, the cells there are shallower than in the middle of the comb; but when the comb acquires a certain weight, the bees hasten to prolong those cells so essential to the solidity of the whole; sometimes they even make them deeper than those that follow.

The prisms are not perfectly horizontal, their orifice being almost always a little higher than the base, which enables us to recognize the original position of a comb, though detached. Hence the axis of a cell is not perpendicular to the wall which separates the two faces of a comb; this rule, hitherto overlooked, is an insuperable bar to geometrical calculations regarding the shape of the cells, for these prisms are more or less inclined upon their bases, sometimes deviating from the horizontal above 20°, ordinarily 4° or 5°.

However, whatever be their irregularities they are less prominent than those of the bases, and frequently where the latter are irregular, the cells preserve the hexagonal form, as we will show.

Bees in general observe a tendency to symmetry, perhaps not so much in the small details as in the totality of their operations; it sometimes happens, however, that the combs assume a singular shape; but if we followed in details the work of these insects, we could nearly always assign reasons for these apparent anomalies; the bees are compelled to adapt them-

selves to localities, one irregularity produces another, and they usually originate in the arrangements which we make them adopt. The inconstancy of
the temperature, by causing frequent interruptions in their operations,
affects the symmetry of the combs; for we have always remarked that interrupted work is less perfect than continuous labor.

We have sometimes accidentally given too little space between the
supports intended to bear the combs, and thus caused the bees to follow a
particular direction. At first they did not seem to notice the incorrectness
of the dimensions and built their combs on those laths placed too closely
together; but they very soon appeared to suspect the error, and gradually
changing the line of their work, they returned to the customary distances;
this operation giving their comb a more or less curved form. New combs,
built parallel to the first, necessarily had the like deformity, which was
imparted to the following combs successively. However the bees seek as
much as possible to bring them back to the regular form; often a comb is
convex above only; lower down the defect is rectified and the surfaces of
the lower part are brought to a straight figure.

We have seen their love for symmetry in other circumstances much
more striking. From a series of previous irregularities, the bees of one of
our hives, instead of establishing one block upon the lath, as usual, built
two, the one opposite the most advanced part of the built comb, the other
opposite the least advanced portion; the two combs built upon the same
lath being of irregular shape, owing to the irregularity of the previous
comb, could neither meet at their ends nor be extended without being in
each other's way; the bees adopted a very effectual plan, they curved the
edges of these two combs and brought their edges together so perfectly that
they could continue them jointly. The part above this junction was irregular
but as the combs were prolonged downwards, their surface became more
and more level, until it became perfectly uniform.

We saw another work exceedingly regular in its whole, although of a
very peculiar shape. The bees had commenced their comb at the lower edge
of a vertical strip of glass; it was lengthened several inches upon a base
of only four or five cells, without any other support than the wax fastened
to the edge of the glass; but as its weight increased, the bees built several
rows of cells upwards upon one of the vertical edges of this glass, and these
cells, which were fastened to those of the comb, increased its solidity: one
might have considered them as a continuation of the same comb, since their
edges were regular; but their walls were fastened upon the glass, which
served as base for them; the bees appeared satisfied with five rows of those
cells upon the glass; then wishing to give it still more strength, they
attempted to fasten it to a wooden lath located at the upper end of the
glass strip; for that purpose it was necessary for them to continue the work
in that direction. But they constructed only two ascending branches, to
the right and left of the flat-base cells (Plate XI, fig. 1), and these, when
reaching their destination, were divided into two branches, in Y shape, along
the junction point of the wood with the glass.

After the comb had acquired a certain extent in its lower part, the bees
prolonged it upwards to the lath; for this purpose they changed the direction of its edges so as to establish it behind the glass strip which they

wished to avoid; they built it far enough away from it to give their cells the proper depth, and after succeeding in this they carried their masonry parallel with the glass. The comb was built up to the ceiling of the hive and filled all the space that it was possible to occupy, with the exception of the interval between the flat-base cells and the ascending branches; but although this comb was not of the ordinary shape, its symmetry was perfect; the braces built for strengthening it were exactly alike and at equal distances from the center; there was not an extra cell on either side and the projection of their lateral sides was uniform in every part.

We may readily judge, by these various works, of the spirit of union which regulates the bees; we will now detail the irregularities found in the building of drone combs.

In the previous chapter we stated that the drone cells are surrounded with several rows of cells of average size. A comb is rarely commenced with drone cells, the first rows being formed of very regular small cells; but the openings soon cease corresponding exactly with one another, and the bases are less symmetrical; it would be impossible for the bees to build irregular cells in regular shapes; that is why we often see between those cells some masses of wax occupying the intervals. By thickening the sides and giving the contours a more nearly circular shape, the bees sometimes succeed in uniting cells of different diameter, for they have more than one method of compensating the irregularities of the cells.

But although the surfaces of the cells always show hexagon outlines with only slight modification, the bases offer much more pronounced irregularities, which announce a determinate plan and explain their progressive enlargement.

Examining a comb through a vertical line in its middle we observe that the cells next to this line are enlarged without much alteration of shape; but the bases of the adjacent cells are no longer composed of three equal rhombs; each instead of corresponding with three others, corresponds with four cells on the opposite face, while their orifices are not less hexagonal; but their base is composed of four pieces, two of which are hexagonal and two rhomboidal (Plate X, fig. 1). The size and shape of these pieces vary; these cells, which are somewhat larger than the third part of three opposite cells, comprehend a portion of the bottom of a fourth cell, in their circumference. Under the last regular pyramidal bottoms are found those having a base in four parts, three large and one small, the latter a rhomb. The two rhombs of the transition cells are separated by a great interval, while the two hexagonal pieces adjoin and are perfectly similar (Plate X, figs. 2 and 4). In a cell farther down, we notice less inequality between the two rhombs of the bottom; the circumference of the cell embraces more of the fourth cell on the opposite surface, finally we find a great number of cells whose bottom consists of four pieces perfectly regular, namely, two elongated hexagons and two rhombs equal, but smaller than those of the pyramidal bases (fig. 3). As we recede from the cells with regular tetrahedral bases, either downwards or to the right and left, we observe the cells recovering their ordinary shape; that is, one of the rhombs contracts and finally disappears, and the pyramidal shape is resumed, but of larger size than it was in the cells of the upper part of the comb; it is preserved with perfect regularity in many rows, afterwards the cells are again altered and we again see the tetrahedral bases until the cells have resumed the worker size.

Thus it is by encroaching slightly upon the cells of the opposite face that the bees succeed in giving their cells the larger dimensions; the graduation of the transition cells being reciprocal on both faces of the comb, it follows that the hexagonal circumference on each cell embraces four cells.

After the bees have reached any degree whatever of this progression, they may stop there and preserve it in several consecutive rows; they seem to continue longest at the medium, when we find a great many cells with the bottom regularly made of four pieces; they could build the entire comb upon this plan, were not their aim to resume the pyramidal form they have left. When they diminish the diameter of their cells, they return by similar gradations, in inverted order.

In order to gain an idea of the modifications that are possible in the cells, we should carry an hexagonal contour over other contours of similar shape, but a little smaller and arranged like those of the bees.

We could secure the same regularity with perfectly equal tetrahedral outlines; but in order that the bees may be able to return to pyramidal cells of a different dimension, it becomes necessary that the diameter of the intermediary corresponding cells be a little larger on each face of the comb alternately.

As to the manner in which the bees construct them, it is easy to understand that they build the vertical ridges of their cells long enough to go beyond the center of the opposite cells, afterwards outlining the hexagon, &c. The lower oblique ridges cross the ridges of the opposite face and form a supernumerary rhomb. The bees smooth down the spaces between the ridges of the two faces, and the base of the cell then has four pieces instead of three. The shape of those pieces varies according to the greater or less analogy of the opposite ridges with those of common cells. It would be very difficult to measure the inclination of the tetrahedral bases; but they appear to me to be a little shallower than the pyramidal bases. It must be so, for the two rhombs being smaller, the intermediary line which forms the bottom of the cell and which begins at their extremities, will be less sunk and so the cell will be shallower.

In general, it appears that the shape of the prisms of the cells is more essential than that of their bases, for we have seen cells with tetrahedral bases more or less regular, the walls of which were hexagonal, and also cells built upon either glass or wood without wax base, but with six-sided walls. These observations concur with the previous ones to show that the shape of the pieces which form the bottom of the cells depends upon the manner in which this is cut by the contours of the cells of both faces; or in other words upon the direction of the ridges upon which the walls are erected.

The shape of the walls of the tetrahedral cells differs according to the bases to which they belong: those that correspond with one of the faces of the rhomb and a part of the hexagonal face are bevel-shaped, so as to fit upon each other (Plate X, ab fig. 7 and 9), while the two walls which correspond with the large side of the hexagon are rectangular parallelograms (c fig. 9).

N. B. The pyramidal bases which are separated from one another by technical base cells, do not have their losenges situated similarly; it is a consequence of what we have stated (fig. 5 and 6).

These observations show us how flexible is the instinct of the bees, how well it yields to the local conditions, to the circumstances and requirements of the family. Necessity, in the work of these insects, as in all that pertains to the habits of animals, must be limited to a small number of essential points, all others being subordinated to the circumstances.

The limits of their industry are assuredly less narrow than at first supposed; and the reader will admit, with us, that the conduct of bees depends also in some measure upon what might be called the judgment of the insect; this judgment, doubtless, is rather a matter of tact than formal reasoning; but its subtleness resembles choice, rather than habit or habitual mechanism independent of the will of the insect.

CHAPTER VI.

The Completion of the Cells.

Certain facts produce no longer upon us the impression of novelty; we see them without observing them, without trying to discover their causes and their aims; but can we forsee what will excite our curiosity? Is anything indifferent to the naturalist? If he avoids the unconcern which is the effect of habit, as well as the belief that all that deserves attention has already been observed, he soon finds interest in subjects that seemed to call for it the least.

In the course of our researches, we have often thought ourselves at the end of our labor; we perceived no more questions to solve, no more doubts to clear; but the bandage over our eyes fell of itself at last. A simple fact, seen every day without attention, would at last strike us, and we wondered why it should be less interesting than other peculiarities upon which we had spent much time. It was a new country open to us, and we were imperceptibly drawn into a new road, the existence of which we had not even suspected.

After several implements had given us the opportunity of studying the shaping of the combs and the modifications of the architecture of bees, we thought that new researches upon this subject would be useless; we were in error: the combs of bees are not completed when the bases and the sides of the cells are built.

In the origin the material of the cells is of dull white color, semi-transparent, soft, smooth without gloss; but it loses most of these qualities in a few days, or rather it acquires new ones; a more or less distinct yellow tint spreads upon the interior of the cells, their edges become much thicker than they were at first and appear less regular, and these shapes which did not appear able to resist the slightest pressure acquire a consistency of which they did not seem susceptible.

We noticed that finished combs were of greater weight, in equal quantity, than those that were unfinished; the latter broke under the least touch; but the perfected combs bent instead of breaking; their orifices appeared sticky; the white cells could be melted in water at a lower temperature than the colored ones. All these observations indicated a noticeable difference in the composition of the combs and it was evident that those which were not new contained a material differing from beeswax.

In examining the orifices of the yellow cells, we perceived that their circumference was coated with a reddish, unctuous, odoriferous varnish, and we recognized, as we thought, the resin called *propolis*. Afterwards it appeared not to be restricted to the orifices, that reddish threads were sometimes found on their inner walls, upon the rhombs or trapezes; this solder, placed at the points of contact of the different pieces, and at the summit of their angles, appeared to help in strengthening the cells; one would sometimes notice one or two reddish zones around the axis of the longest cells:

when the bees are short of wax, they are sometimes compelled to interrupt their work; when a more ample supply enables them to laborate the material, they resume the work; it is probably during this interruption that they varnish the edges of the cell, and when the latter have been lengthened, they retain traces of the material with which they had been coated.

These peculiarities had evidently not struck any of the naturalists who wrote upon the bees; they knew that propolis was used to coat the inside of the hive; but they were not aware of this resin being used in the building of the cells; this was worth verifying, I made sure of it by comparative experiments, using the ordinary reagents.

The propolis taken from the walls of the hive and from the edges of red-colored cells, submitted to the action of ether, alcohol or oil of turpentine, imparted a golden color to these liquids. The brown matter of cells was dissolved by them, even when cold. The orifices of cells, in either alcohol or turpentine, retained the cell shape and their yellow tint after losing the varnish that coated them. Those placed in ether also lost the red varnish, they became bleached shortly after and disappeared when the wax was dissolved.

The coloring matter of the cell orifices, exposed to a mild heat, became soft and could be drawn into threads; the propolis of the walls did likewise. Nitrous acid, at a low heat, poured on both, whitened the yellow wax in a few minutes, but the varnish of the orifices and masses of propolis underwent no alterations.

Other orifices, put into boiling water, displayed a curious peculiarity; after the wax in them was melted, the varnish remained entire above it, on the cake which it formed, without losing its hexagonal contour, while its diameter seemed a little enlarged.

Fixed caustic alkali which changes wax into a kind of soap, has no effect upon propolis; we tried its action upon very old cells which had already served as cradles to a number of larvæ, the cocoons with which they were lined hiding the varnish and the wax upon which they had been moulded. The primary effect of the alkaline wash was to dissolve the wax by combining with it, separating it from the silky cocoons; then it bleached the cocoons, which are naturally of brown color and gave them the appearance of gauze: they retained the shape of the cells; the reddish threads then appeared, for they were not dissolved, and remained upon the outer edges of the cocoons, just in the way that they had been placed by the bees in the furrows formed by the junction of the different pieces which composed the cells. These threads of propolis were finally separated from the cocoons, but they were not altered by remaining several months in the solution.

From these experiments it is evident that the substance which gives a dark red color to the edges of the cells and to the lines of intersection of their walls, has the greater analogy to propolis; it is clear also that the yellow color of the cells has no relation to the varnish covering the joints of their different pieces.

Notwithstanding my confidence in such conclusions, I felt that they would be indisputable only after I had found the bees in the act. It was then necessary to follow them in their harvest of propolis and make sure of their use of it; but these researches were difficult.

Propolis has similar properties to those of gum-resin and it has long been suspected of belonging to the vegetable kingdom. But for many years I fruitlessly endeavored to find the bees on trees producing an analogous substance; but none of my investigations directed me to those upon which the bees gathered this harvest: though we saw multitudes returning laden with it.

Being fatigued with the uselessness of my attempts, I devised a very simple expedient, from which I could obtain some light. The question was to secure such plants as would be likely to supply propolis, and place them within their reach; this plan succeeded; the first plants that I placed near my hives displayed to me in a short time that which I might have never found out, without this scheme.

In the beginning of July, some branches of the wild poplar, which had been cut since spring, before the growth of their leaves, with very large buds, coated both on the outside and inside with a viscous, reddish and odoriferous sap, were brought to me; I planted them in vessels before my hives, in the way of the bees going out to the field, so that they would be sure to notice them. In less than a quarter of an hour a bee took advantage of this chance; she alighted upon one of the branches, on one of the largest buds, separated its involucra with her teeth, pressing out its parts, drew out threads of the viscous matter; then taking with one of the legs of the second pair what she held in her jaws, she brought forward one of the posterior legs and placed into the pollen basket of this leg the little pellet of propolis that she had just gathered; this done, she opened the bud in another spot, removed more threads of the same material, took them with the legs of the second pair and gently laid them in the other basket. She then flew to the hive; in a few minutes a second bee alighted upon these same branches and loaded up propolis in the same manner.

We made the same experiment upon recently cut poplar limbs, the young shoots of which were filled with propolis; they did not appear to attract the bees; but their sap was neither as thick nor as red as that which we had first offered to them, the buds of which had been preserved since spring.

Since the bees harvested this reddish and viscous substance from the buds of the common poplar, all that was needed was to identify this substance with propolis; no doubt of this remained after an experiment which we then made.

We took dry propolis from the walls of an old hive, we broke it up and soaked it in ether; this liquid assumed a yellow tint in each of nine consecutive experiments; but at the last it was very slightly colored; we evaporated it and there remained at the bottom of the vessel a residue of grayish white color. This residue, after having been steeped in distilled water, was examined with a microscope and distinctly showed vegetable debris, such as epidermis, portions of membrane, some opaque, others transparent, but no tracheæ.

Ether gave a similar reaction on poplar buds, it was colored with yellow several times over, and the residues, steeped in distilled water, showed through the microscope similar debris, but less thoroughly dissected than those found in propolis.

Thus the identity of the two substances was no longer in doubt and we had but to discover the manner in which the bees applied it to use; we desired especially to witness the perfecting of the cells, but it was out of the question to see them work without some lucky expedient. We hoped to follow them more easily in a hive where they would build their combs upwards, because in such a case some of the cells rest against the glass and their cavities are open for the eyes of the observer.

So we peopled a hive so prepared as to fulfill our views. The bees, building upwards, soon reached the glass, but unable to quit their habitation on account of supervening rains, they were three weeks without bringing home any propolis. Their combs remained perfectly white until the beginning of July, when the atmosphere became more favorable for our observations. Serene weather and a high temperature engaged them to forage; and they returned from the fields laden with this resinous gum resembling a transparent jelly; with the color and lustre of the garnet: it was easily distinguished from the farinaceous pellets then brought home by other bees. The workers bearing propolis joined the clusters hanging from the ceiling of the hive, we saw them travel through the outside of these clusters; after reaching the supports of the combs, they appeared to rest, sometimes they stopped on the walls, waiting for their companions to relieve them of their burden. We actually saw two or three approach them and carry the propolis away with their teeth. The upper part of the hive exhibited the most animated spectacle, thither a host of bees resorted from all quarters, the distribution and application of the propolis being then their predominant occupation; some conveyed between their teeth the material which they had secured from the purveyors and deposited it upon the frames and the supports of the combs; others hastened to spread it out like a varnish before it hardened, or formed it into strings proportioned to the interstices of the walls of the hives to be puttied up. Nothing could be more diversified than their operations; but we were most interested in the art which they used in applying propolis on the inside of the cells. Those which appeared to be charged with this task were easily distinguished from the multitude of workers because their heads were turned towards the horizontal pane. Upon reaching it, they deposited the propolis in the middle of the interval separating the combs. Then we saw them apply this substance in the real place of its destination; taking advantage of the points of support which its viscosity supplied, they appeared to hang to it with the claws of their posterior legs, seemingly swinging themselves under the pane of glass; the effect of this motion was to carry their body backwards and forward and at each motion we saw the lump of propolis come nearer to the cells; the bees used their anterior legs to sweep together that which had been detached and to unite these fragments upon the surface of the glass; the latter recovered its transparency when all the propolis was brought to the mouth of the cells. A few bees entered the cells located against the glass; it was there that I expected to see them at leisure: they brought no propolis, but they cleaned and polished the cell with their teeth, worked in the angular corners, making them thicker, smoothed the rough edges; while the antennæ appeared to feel the way; these organs located in front of their jaws evidently enable them to notice such projecting molecules as must be removed.

After one of these workers had smoothed down the wax in the angle of a cell, she emerged from the cell backwards and having approached a heap of propolis, she drew out a thread of it with her teeth; this being broken off by a quick motion of the head, it was taken in the claws of the fore feet and the bee re-entered the cell which she had just prepared. She did not hesitate but immediately placed it in the angle of the two parts that she had just smoothed, but she probably found it too long for the space required, for she cut away a piece of it; both of her front feet were used to fit it and stretch it between the two walls; and her teeth worked to imbed it in the angular furrow to be lined. After these divers operations, the thread of propolis evidently appeared too large for her taste; she raked it over with the same instruments and at each time removed a parcel of it: when the work was completed, we admired the accuracy with which it was adjusted between the two walls of the cell. The worker did not stop there, turning to another part of the cell, she worked with her jaws upon the edges of the two other trapezes and we understood that she was preparing a spot to be covered with another thread of propolis. No doubt she was about to help herself out of the heap from which she had taken it previously; but contrary to our expectation she availed herself of the portion of the thread cut off from the first bit, arranged it in the appointed space and gave it all the solidity and finish of which it was susceptible. Other bees finished the work begun by this one, all the cell walls were soon encircled with threads of propolis, while some were also put on the orifices; but we could not seize the moment when they were varnished, though it may be easily conceived how it was done.

While these observations made known to us the art used by the bees in coating the walls of their cells, we had no explanation of the yellow coloring of their interior. In some of the chemical experiments already mentioned, the coloring pigment of the cells had not been acted upon in the same way as the propolis which coated them; since it appeared to have no analogy with it, it was necessary to ascertain the differences by additional experiments.

FIRST EXPERIMENT.

We picked out a few cells of a comb, the walls of which were of jonquil color; their edges were coated with propolis; we removed carefully the latter from each wall and steeped these yellow cell walls in alcohol: it remained thus in a dark place for three weeks. The alcohol was not colored and the walls of the cells retained their yellow tint. Other cells of jonquil color, from which the propolis had not been removed, were treated in the same manner and gave more and more color to the alcohol. This propolis was soon entirely dissolved, but at the end of the experiment the yellow color of the walls had seemingly become more striking.

SECOND EXPERIMENT.

I enclosed some of the yellow colored cell walls between two strips of glass and exposed them to the light of the sun: a few days were sufficient to bleach them entirely; I placed in the same manner some colored cells coated with propolis, and kept them in the sun for two summer months. The wax soon lost its yellow color, but this long test in no way altered the color of the propolis.

THIRD EXPERIMENT.

I took some yellow cells, coated with propolis upon their orifices and around their edges; I steeped them in nitrous acid, and boiled this solvent for a few minutes: when the nitrous gas began to form, I removed the vial and allowed it to cool. I then saw that the yellow color had disappeared, that the wax was bleached, but the propolis had retained its color; a prolonged test of this kind gave no other result.

FOURTH EXPERIMENT.

I steeped cells of yellow wax devoid of propolis in ether; the liquid first acquired a slight yellow tint, then it became darker and the wax was entirely discolored. I allowed the ether to evaporate, expecting the coloring substance to remain at the bottom of the capsule, but after evaporation of the liquid I found only the small quantity of white wax which had been dissolved.

Cells of white wax, the orifices and walls of which were coated with propolis, were steeped in the same solvent. The ether acquired a fine yellow tint which became more and more intense, and no propolis remained upon the different parts of the cells. I uncorked the vial, and after the ether was evaporated, I found at the bottom a reddish propolis varnish upon which one could notice some of the white wax which the ether had dissolved.

These experiments demonstrate that the substance which colors the wax has no analogy with propolis. My observations have indicated that this tint is not a property of wax; the new cells are formed of white wax; this tint becomes altered in a short time, and changes to a yellow tint which becomes darker and darker with time; sometimes two or three days are sufficient to turn white combs into yellow. I knew nothing of the cause of this change, and I thought, as other naturalists did, that this alteration might be effected by the heat of the hives, or by the vapors of their atmosphere, or by the emanations of the honey or of the wax, and the presence of these substances in the hives. However, these ideas could not withstand a thorough examination; I had often seen new combs remaining unaltered for several months, although used by the bees in the ordinary way. By comparing the combs of several swarms newly hived, we found some of which one side was white while the other face was of a jonquil color: we could sometimes find, on the same side of a comb, a space in which the cells were of a lively yellow, while those adjacent had lost none of their whiteness. We could even ascertain the exact limit of this coloration; a single cell having several yellow faces, while others were white, sometimes even one cell was party-colored in white and yellow. This distriution of colors could not be explained through the causes which we suspected of having influence. Honey and pollen would have uniformly tinted all the faces of a cell, up to the height of the liquid or of the coloring substance; the vapors of the hive likewise could have only a general influence upon the color of the combs; but it was necessary to ascertain more directly that these things had nothing to do with the observed effect.

It was first necessary to make sure whether cells that were kept from the contact of bees would preserve their whiteness; for this purpose, I used a hive with a division in the middle through which the bees could not pass. In this I enclosed a portion of comb of complete whiteness; it was exposed for a month to heat, moisture and all their atmospheric vapors, without alteration of color from any of those causes. Meanwhile the combs exposed to the contact of the bees yellowed more and more, but this coloring was partial and distributed irregularly, as in a striped manner; everything indicating that it was not due to exposure in the interior of the hives for more or less time, but to some direct action on the part of the bees.

We are not yet sure of the manner in which they give this tint to the combs. We have attributed it to two different maneuvers; first, the bees which appear to be resting upon the combs, or upon the glass or the wood of the hive, rub the tip of their mandibles against the object which they are supposed to varnish, moving their head back and forth; their jaws spread apart and come together successively, after each motion of the head; their front legs repeatedly rub with some speed the surface upon which they stand; the bee which is thus occupied walks right and left and continues this maneuver for a long time; the wall or the surface of the comb, to which they apply themselves, appears to change color, though we have not ascertained positively that it was in consequence of this work. We have noticed that there is always a little yellow substance in the cavity of the bees' teeth: but was this a substance which they were removing or which they were applying upon the wax? It appeared probable that it was being deposited, though while they rubbed both wood and glass in the same way, the glass did not secure any color, but the wood assumed a very pronounced tint.

The second process that we witnessed was performed with the trunk; this instrument acted like a slim and soft brush; it swept to the right and left the surface of the glass and appeared to leave upon it a few drops of a transparent liquid.

At each change of direction, we could see a bright and silvery liquid, flowing from the middle of the trunk and of the two longest palpi which surround it; this liquid was distributed from the end of the trunk upon the parts of cells for which it was intended; it was also deposited upon the glass, but not so as to tarnish it; for the opacity which glass sometimes acquires is not due to this cause; this happens only when the bees spread upon it parcels of wax which have been deposited upon its surface.

We shall not affirm which of these operations is the source of the yellowness of wax, but we incline to refer it to the first, because we often thought the color of certain cells altered, after the bees had rubbed them with their teeth and forelegs.

The bees do not restrict themselves to painting and varnishing the cells; they also give greater solidity to the edifice itself, by means of mortar which they know how to compose for that purpose.

The ancients, who had much studied these insects, knew some of the properties of propolis; they informed us that the bees mixed it with wax in several circumstances; they gave the name of *metis* or *pissoceron* to this substance, thus indicating its amalgamation with beeswax.

A test which I made with the propolis that coats the inside of beehives, indicated to me how well they had studied the subject, and that, although we may often reject their assertions, it would be a mistake to do so without previous examination.

Through my reported experiments, I had learned that ether dissolves propolis, and that it removes but a small fraction of the wax submitted to its action: so I took some fragments of this mortar from the walls of an old hive and steeped them in ether. Decanting it several times, I concluded that all the propolis was dissolved, when it ceased to color; the residue remaining in the vial was only the white wax which had been mixed by the bees with the gum-resin.

Pliny believed that these insects used a mixture of wax and propolis in constructing the braces and bases of the combs. Réaumur, on the contrary, thought it only pure wax. Perhaps the facts that I am about to relate may enable us to reconcile the opinions of these two great naturalists.

Shortly after the bees had finished the new combs, a manifest disorder and apparent agitation prevailed in the hive. The bees appeared directed by a sort of fury against their own combs; the cells of the first row, the structure of which we so greatly admired, were scarcely recognizable; thick and massive walls, heavy and shapeless pillars were substituted for the slight partitions which the bees had previously built with such regularity at the beginning; the substance of them had changed along with the form, being apparently composed of wax and propolis. From the perseverance of the workers in these devastations, we suspected that they intended some useful alteration in their architecture.

Our attention was drawn to the least damaged cells; some were still untouched, but the bees soon rushed precipitately upon them, destroyed the vertical walls of the cells, broke up the wax and cast aside the fragments. But we noticed that the trapezes of the bases of the first row were untouched; they did not tear down at the same time the corresponding cells on both faces of the comb; they labored alternately upon each of its faces, leaving to it a part of its natural supports, otherwise the combs would have fallen down, which was not their object; they wished, on the contrary, to provide a more solid base, and prevent their fall, by making these joints with a substance the tenacity of which infinitely surpasses that of beeswax.

The propolis which they used in this occasion had been deposited in a mass over a cleft of the hive, and had hardened in drying, which perhaps rendered it more suitable for the purpose intended than fresh propolis would have been.

These insects had some difficulty in removing it from the wall, on account of its hardness; we thought that they were impregnating it with the same frothy matter from the tongue, which they used to make wax more ductile, and that this process served to soften and detach it. Mr. de Réaumur had observed something similar in a like occasion.

We distinctly observed these bees mixing fragments of old wax with the propolis, kneading the two substances together to amalgamate them. They used this in rebuilding the cells that had been destroyed; but they did not follow the ordinary rules of their architecture; economy was entirely set aside; they were occupied alone with the solidity of their edifice; night intervening prevented us from following their maneuvers, but the following day we were able to judge of the result which confirmed what we have just mentioned.

These observations teach us that there is an epoch in the labor of bees, when the upper braces of their combs are constructed simply of wax, as Réaumur believed, and that after all the requisite conditions have been attained, the base is converted to a mixture of wax and propolis, as published by Pliny, so many centuries before us. (The change made in the structure of the cells of the first row does not take place at a particular time. It depends perhaps upon several circumstances which are not always together. We sometimes see the bees satisfied by bordering the edges of the upper cells with propolis without altering their shape and without adding to their thickness.)

This trait in the conduct of the bees explains the apparent contradiction, in the writings of these two naturalists. The first row of cells, built to serve as a base for the subsequent cells, was temporarily established, to carry the edifice, as long as the magazines were not quite full; but those light plates of wax would have been insufficient to sustain a weight of several pounds. The bees appear to anticipate the eventual inconvenience: so they soon destroy the too frail walls of the first row, leaving untouched the trapezes of their bases, and substitute, in the place of these light walls, strong pillars, heavy walls of a viscous and compact substance.

But this is not the utmost extent of their foresight. When they have enough wax, they make their combs of the breadth necessary to reach with their edges the vertical walls of the hive. They know how to solder them against the wood or the glass by structures approaching more or less the shape of cells, as circumstances admit. But if the supply of wax fails before they have been able to give a sufficient diameter to the combs whose edges are still rounded, these combs, being only fastened at the top, leave large voids between their oblique edges and the hive walls; they might break down by the weight of the honey, did not the bees provide against it, by building great pieces of wax, mixed with propolis, between their edges and the hive walls; these pieces are of irregular form, strangely hollowed out and their cavities are not symmetrical. The following happening, in which the instinct of bees is still better displayed, is a development of their particular art in solidifying their magazines.

During the winter, a comb of my bell-shaped glass hive, not having been sufficiently fastened in the building, fell between the other combs, still retaining its position parallel with the rest: the bees were unable to fill the vacuity between its upper edge and the ceiling, because they do not build combs of old wax[6] and no new wax could be then obtained. In a more favorable season, they would not have hesitated to graft a new comb upon the old one;

---

[6] Huber was mistaken in stating that bees do not build combs of old wax; they do not usually do it, but when circumstances of warmth are favorable, they can build quite a large amount of comb from old wax. In this instance it is probable that the conditions were unfavorable. The sentence which follows shows that bees do build combs from old wax. (Translator.)

but as their provision of honey could not then be spared to supply the elaboration of this substance, they provided the stability of the comb by another process.

They took wax from the bottom of other combs, and even from their faces by gnawing the orifices of the longest cells; they then gathered together in great numbers on the edges of the fallen comb, between it and the adjoining combs; they constructed there a number of irregular braces, pillars, buttresses, joists, arranged with art and adapted to localities.

They did not confine themselves to repairing this accident in their masonry, they apparently thought of those that might happen and profited by the warning which the fall of one comb had given them, by strengthening the others so as to prevent a second similar event.

The remaining combs had not been displaced, they appeared solid upon their bases, so we were greatly surprised to see the bees strengthen their principal fastenings with old wax, rendering them much thicker than before, and fabricated a number of new braces to unite them more closely together and more strongly to the walls of their home. All this passed in the middle of January, at a time when bees commonly keep themselves in the upper part of their hive, where such work is no longer seasonable.

I may restrain myself from reflections and commentaries, but I acknowledge that I could not suppress a sentiment of admiration for an action in which the brightest foresight was displayed.

CHAPTER VII.

On a New Enemy of the Bees.

Among the labors of insects, those that concern the defense of their habitations are perhaps not the least worthy of the attention of man, who is so often called on to provide himself against the enterprises of his enemies. If we compare the measures of security taken by these little animals against aggression, with our own tactics, if we establish a parallel between their policy and ours, we can better appreciate the relative height of their horizon. No other branch of their industry could be used with better success to indicate this gradation than natural protection; an impulse which is common to all species. In such circumstances, nature unfolds the most unexpected resources; in this it leaves the greatest freedom to the beings which it rules; for the chances of war are the object of one of those general laws concurring to the maintenance of universal order; without those alternatives of success and reverse, how could the equilibrium be maintained between the species? One of them would annihilate all those that are inferior to it in strength; nevertheless the most timid have subsisted since the origin of things: their tactics, their industry, their fecundity, or other circumstances peculiar to each kind, enable them to escape the extinction which seems to menace them.

Among the bees, as with the greater number of the hymenopters, the ordinary means of resistance are those poisoned darts with which they wound their enemies; the fate of war would be in their favor, on account of the greatness of their numbers, were not several of their antagonists still better armed than themselves; if others had not the art of evading their vigilance by surrounding themselves with a tissue that shelters them from their stings, and if there were not others still that profit by the weakness of some ill-peopled hive to gain a surreptitious entrance into it.

Wasps, hornets, moths and mice, have been known from all time by their ravages among hives; and as I have nothing to add to what every one knows on this matter, I shall confine myself to pointing out a new enemy of the bees, whose ravages I have already described in a special memoir (Brit. Lib. No. 213 and 214).

Towards the close of summer after the bees have stored up a part of their crop, we sometimes hear a surprising noise near their habitations; a multitude of workers issue during the night and escape in the air; the tumult frequently continues during several hours, and when we examine the effect of so great an agitation, in the morning, we see numbers of dead bees before the hive: for the most part it contains no more honey and sometimes it is entirely deserted.

In 1804, many of my farmer neighbors came to consult me on an occurrence of this kind; but I could not yet give them any explanations; notwithstanding my long practice concerning bees, I had never seen anything similar.

On visiting the scene, I found the phenomenon still subsisting and that it had been very accurately depicted; but the peasants attributed it to the introduction of bats into the hives, and I disagreed in crediting this supposition. Those flying mammifers are satisfied with seizing nocturnal insects in their flight, which are never wanting in summer. Bats do not eat honey; why therefore should they attack bees in their hive for the purpose of pillaging their stores?

If it was not the bats which attacked the bees, it might be some other animal. Therefore, having put my people in ambush, they soon brought to me, not bats, but sphinx atropos, great moths, better known under the name of *Death's head moths*. These sphinxes flew in great numbers about the hives; one was caught as it was about to enter in one of the least populous; its intention evidently was to penetrate within their home and live at the expense of the bees. From all quarters I learned of similar ravages committed by bats, as supposed. Cultivators who expected a plentiful harvest, found their hives as light as in the first days of spring, though they had recently been noticed well provisioned; at length the gigantic moth, which had caused the desertion of the bees, was surprised in several hives.

Such repeated proofs were required to convince me that a lepidopter, an insect without a sting, without any shield, and deprived of all other means of defense, could contend victoriously against thousands of bees; but these moths were so common during that year that it was easy to be convinced of the fact.

As the enterprises of the sphinx were constantly more disastrous to the bees, we resolved to contract their entrances to prevent the enemy's access. We manufactured a sort of grating, out of tin, the openings of which were only large enough to admit the bees, and we established it at the entrance of the hive; this process was completely successful, quiet was restored and the damage ceased.

The same precautions had not been universally taken; but we perceived that the bees, left to themselves, provided for their own security; without help, they barricaded themselves, by means of a thick wall made of wax and propolis, fitted behind the entrance of the hive, and sometimes in the entrance itself; it obstructed it entirely, but it was perforated by passages for one or two workers at a time.

Here the operations of man and bees completely met; the works which they had established at the entrance of their habitations were of varied forms; here, as I have just mentioned, was a single wall, whose openings were in arcades disposed in the higher part of the masonry; there several bulwarks behind each other recalled the bastions of our citadels; passages, masked by walls in front, opened upon the faces of the second row and did not correspond with the openings of the first; sometimes a series of intersecting arcades gave free egress to the bees, without permitting the entrance of their enemies; for these fortifications were massive, their substance being firm and solid.

The bees did not construct those casemated gates, without urgent necessity, so it is not a demonstration of general prudence prepared in advance to obviate inconveniences which the insect can neither know nor anticipate; it is when the danger is there, pressing and immediate, that the bee, compelled to seek an assured preservative, employs this last resource; it is curious to see so well armed an insect, supported by the advantage of numbers, conscious of its powerlessness, protecting itself by an admirable combination against the insufficiency of its arms and courage. So the art of war among bees is not restricted to attacking their enemies, they know also how to construct ramparts for shelter against their enterprises; from the role of simple soldiers, they pass to that of engineers; but it is not against the sphinx only that they must guard; weak hives are sometimes attacked by strange bees attracted by the odor of the honey and the hope of easy pillage.

The besieged bees being unable to defend themselves against such invasion, sometimes have recourse to a measure similar to that employed against the sphinx atropos; they also raise walls and leave but narrow openings through which a single bee can pass at a time; these are easily guarded.

But the time comes when these narrow passages are no longer sufficient for themselves; when the harvest is very abundant, the hive excessively populous, and the time comes of forming new colonies, they demolish these gates which they had erected at the hour of danger, and which now restrain their impetuosity; these safeguards have become inconvenient, and they discard them till new alarms demand their reconstruction.

The entrances built in 1804 were destroyed in the spring of 1805; the sphinxes did not appear that year, neither were they seen in the year following, but in the autumn of 1807 they were seen in great numbers. Immediately the bees barricaded themselves and prevented the threatening disasters. In May 1808, before the departure of swarms, they demolished these fortifications, whose narrow passages did not give sufficiently free passage to their multitude.

It is to be noticed that, when the entrance of their hive is naturally narrow, or when care has been taken to contract it soon enough to prevent the devastations of their enemies, the bees dispense with walling it.

This timeliness in their conduct can be explained only by admitting the development of their instinct according to the exigencies of the circumstances.

But how can a sphinx alarm such warlike colonies? Can this moth, the dread of superstitious people, also exercise a secret influence upon the bees, and have the power of paralyzing their courage? Does it perhaps emit some emanation pernicious to these insects?

Other sphinxes subsist upon the nectar of flowers only; they have a long, slender, flexible, spirally coiled trunk, and seek their food soon after sunset, but the atropos awakens later, it does not fly about the hive until night is farther advanced; it is armed with a very short, very large proboscis endowed with much strength; when it is seized some unknown organ emits an acute, stridulous sound. May not this sound, to which the vulgar attach sinister ideas, be also dreadful to the bees? May not its resemblance to the piping of the queens in captivity, which has the faculty of suspending the vigilance of the workers, explain the disorder observed in their hive on the approach of the sphinx? This is only a conjecture, founded on the analogy of sounds, to which I attach no importance. However, should the sphinx raise this piercing cry during its assaults, and should the bees then yield to it without resistance, this conjecture would acquire some weight.

Mr. de Réaumur attributed the sound produced by the death's head sphinx to the friction of the trunk against its sheaths, but we have ascertained that this takes place without the use of the trunk. Though many naturalists have sought its source, nothing satisfactory is yet known on the subject. It appears certain that the sphinx emits this sound at will, and particularly when affected by the apprehension of some danger.

The introduction of so large and so tangible a lepidopter as the sphinx atropos in a well populated hive, and the extraordinary consequences thence resulting, are phenomena the more difficult to explain, that the organization of this insect offers no indication of its being screened from the stings of bees.

We should have desired to observe this singular contest in our glass hives, but no opportunity has hitherto presented. However, to solve some of my doubts, I made a few experiments on the manner in which the sphinx is received in the nest of bumblebees.

I secured some atropos of the largest size, I introduced them at night-fall into a glass box, where I had established a nest of small bumblebees (muscorum).

The first that I brought to them did not appear to be affected by the odor of the honey, of which their cells were full; it first remained quiet in a corner of the box; but as it approached the nest and its inhabitants, it soon became the object, not of the dread, but of the wrath of the workers, they assailed it successively with fury, and gave it many stings; it sought to escape and ran with speed; at last, by a violent motion, it pushed away the glass which covered the apparatus and succeeded in escaping. It appeared to suffer but little of its wounds, remained quiet all night, and was still wonderfully well several days after.

I was unwilling to repeat this cruel experiment; captivity or some other circumstance evidently reduced this insect to too great a disadvantage to the bumblebees. Yet, after this attempt, it became still more difficult for me to conceive how it could introduce itself into the hives of common bees, whose stings are so much more dangerous, as well as their numbers incomparably greater. Was the light of the torch an obstacle to the development of the sphinx's means of attack? Possibly the success of its enterprises results from the faculty of seeing during the night, as with other moths of the same genus.

Another fruitless experiment was that of offering honey to these insects: I left two sphinxes beside a comb for a whole week, without their touching it: we vainly unfolded their proboscis, dipped it in the honey; this experiment, which succeeded perfectly with day butterflies, had no success with the sphinx atropos.

I might have entertained doubts of their fondness for this food, had I not had proofs of their avidity for it when in the natural state. A recent observation came to the support of the facts already related. When dissecting a large sphinx caught in the open air, we found its abdomen entirely filled with honey; the anterior cavity which occupies three-fourths of its abdomen was filled like a barrel; it might have filled a large tablespoon; this honey, of perfect purity, had the same consistency and the same taste as that of the bees. What appeared very singular was that this substance was not enclosed in a particular intestine, but occupied the space ordinarily reserved for air in the body of these insects. It is known that their abdomen is divided into a certain number of lodges, the walls of which, being exceedingly thin, have vertical membranes; all these membranes had disappeared; I could not affirm whether they had been ruptured by the quantity of honey with which the sphinx had gorged, or by our opening of its upper rings; one thing is certain, that in opening other sphinxes in the same manner, we always found these lodges well preserved though entirely empty.

These facts belong to the natural history of the sphinx, not to that of bees. Let us return to the means of preserving the latter from one of their most dangerous enemies.

I have already proposed to use, for this purpose, three different entrances according to the season. A horizontal strip pierced in its length with three sizes of openings, and placed as a slide between two stakes, may fulfill this purpose. These entrances must be proportioned to the requirements of the bees and fulfill the gradations which they establish themselves, when they seek to protect themselves from their enemies by similar means.

As they destroy their fortifications, in the spring, before the issue of the swarms, we should imitate them by leaving the hive entrance free: they have few enemies to fear at that time, their hive is well populated and can defend itself. After the issue of the swarms one should reduce the entrance, since the hive is weakened and strange bees and moths may enter. This proceeding is pointed out by the bees themselves when threatened with robbing. Each of the openings, left by them in the wax wall which is to protect them against outside dangers, can allow the passage of only one bee at a time. They are in proportion to the size of the insects that the bees dread.

In the middle of July, these entrances are enlarged by the bees to such an extent as to permit two or three workers to pass through them, and to allow the free egress of the males which are of larger size than the workers. At this epoch, therefore, we must change the slide before the entrance so as to permit the use of the larger openings, which must be cut in the upper part, with their convexity downwards.

Lastly, the crop being in full swing, in the months of August and September, the bees must not be too much impeded; those whose example we follow opened a third passage in the lower part of the wax wall; it was shaped like a very low vault; we should imitate this construction in the third row of holes; by this means the sphinx will be unable to enter the hive and the bees will issue freely. If the slide be made of tin instead of wood, it will exclude mice, one of the most dangerous enemies of bees.

When man takes possession of animals, he destroys in some measure the equilibrium which natural circumstances establish between rival species, and more or less diminishes their energy or vigilance; it is only by studying the peculiarities of their instinct that he may recognize certain features which subjection has lessened, which their new position has made less common, and in his turn he should partly compensate the advantages of which they have been deprived: he must do still more, if he wishes to augment their products, since he has to contend with nature which assigns limits to the multiplication of individuals; but this art demands a very profound knowledge of the wants of the creatures subjected to his dominion, and of the resources which providence has placed within their reach; for it is from them alone that we shall learn the art of governing them.

(The next chapter is the one entrusted to Graham-Burtt "On the respiration of bees.")

CHAPTER VIII.

On the Respiration of Bees.[7]

The air, though in time it destroys all, has nevertheless a healthful influence on living organisms. Even plants absorb it in their own way, and, like animals, owe to it the vital force of their existence. To all that has life it is an indispensable element; is the bee an exception to this universal law?

It is well known that all animals from the quadruped to the mollusc decompose the air, combining its respirable part with the carbon which is so abundant in nature, and breathing it out in the new form which it has received while in the lungs or gills: and that the heat necessary to life is generated by this process of combustion.

These laws are so widespread that they would not seem to admit of any exception. However one set of circumstances, as yet unconsidered, seem irreconcilable with them.

If a colony of insects could continue to live successfully and without any inconvenience to their well being, in an enclosed space, where air could only circulate with great difficulty, the scientist would be confronted with a new problem.

Now this is precisely the strange condition presented by bees. Their hive, the dimensions of which do not exceed one or two cubic feet, contains a multitude of individuals all living, active and industrious.

The entrance, always very small, and often obstructed by the crowd of bees which come and go during the laborious days of summer, is the only opening by which air can be introduced, yet it suffices for their needs. Moreover the hive, coated on the inside with wax and propolis by the bees themselves, and on the outside plastered with lime by the care of their owner, does not furnish any of the conditions necessary for the establishment of a natural current of air. Public halls offer, in proportion, far less obstruction to ventilation than a hive of bees, for air cannot circulate in a place which possesses only a single opening, and this moreover not favorably situated for the purpose. The following experiment will show that even

---

[7] It may add to the interest of the following chapter to recall the fact that Huber lived during the period when the foundations of modern scientific knowledge were being laid. Lavoisier in France, Priestley in England, and Scheele in Sweden had, within his life time, made their discoveries as to the nature of the atmosphere, the laws governing combustion and their application to living beings. Thus though his work on this subject may seem elementary to us in reality he was amongst the most advanced scientists of his age and was applying the newly discovered laws to his own particular hobby.

were the opening much larger, the air would not penetrate from the outside except by artificial means.

Take a box or bell-glass of the size of a hive and place it, with the opening at the bottom, on a board in which is cut a groove wider than a hive entrance. Introduce under this glass a lighted candle. In a few minutes the flame will flicker, become bluish, and die out. Air does not enter the vessel fast enough to sustain combustion, since there is no means of setting up a through current. The effect on any living things shut up in large numbers in such a glass would be analogous to that on the lighted candle.

Why then is not the same result shown in a hive inhabited by bees? Why do they not perish, when a candle flame cannot continue to burn? Are they so unlike all else in nature? Do they breathe differently from other animals, or do they not breathe at all?

I could not admit a deduction so opposed to general laws. I therefore wished to find out if these questions appeared of equal interest to persons more enlightened than myself.

I first put the problem to Mr. Charles Bonnet, who, struck by its singularity, warmly encouraged me to investigate it. But his death having unfortunately deprived me of the satisfaction which I found in sending him my results, I approached an eminent scientist whose approval was alone sufficient to incite me to new efforts. M. de Saussure listened with interest to the details of my experiments, and his conversation gave me greater confidence and eagerness to continue the work which I had undertaken.

But, inexperienced as I was in the analysis of gases, I should have had difficulty in attaining my end if I had not been aided, as I have said elsewhere, by M. Senebier, who kindly took an active part in my experiments, and gave a part of his time to the actual scientific tests which my investigations needed. M. Senebier as the colleague of Spallanzani, who was researching on the breathing of insects,[8] had the advantage which I had not of knowing the similarity which was shown between his records and mine.

The Professor of Pavia, with the ingenuity for which he is distinguished, investigated the breathing of insects and reptiles, compared the results, examined the influence which the life and even the death of these animals had on the composition of the atmosphere, and observed them in a state of suspended animation as in sleep, etc., etc.

All his work went to prove that insects breathe, that they corrupt the atmosphere (of which they consume more in proportion than other animals), and that their bodies after death still render up carbonic acid gas.

The experiments which I on my part made with bees, had the advantage that I was able to work on a larger scale owing to the ease with which I could introduce a considerable number into the same receptacle. They offered circumstances which gave me special problems to be solved, and led me to results as satisfactory to my mind as the more general ones of the Italian author.

---

8 "Memorandum on Respiration," by Spallanzani, 4 volumes, 8 vo., obtainable from J. J. Paschoud, publisher, Geneva and Paris.

PART II

EXPERIMENTS ON THE RESPIRATION OF BEES.

Proceeding systematically in our researches, we began by observing the effect of different gases on adult bees. We repeated the same tests on larvæ and nymphs and came to the conclusion that it was necessary to examine with greater care than heretofore the external organs of respiration.

The first tentative experiments were designed to discover whether bees are differently formed in this respect from other animals. If they are not under the necessity of breathing, they should be able to withstand a vacuum. They should be able to live as well in hermetically sealed jars as in ordinary air: in short their relation to the atmosphere ought to make little or no difference to their existence.

FIRST EXPERIMENT.

We introduced some bees into a receptacle connected with a vacuum pump. The first few strokes of the pump did not appear to make any appreciable difference to them. They walked and flew for some time, but when the mercury in the pressure gauge had dropped to within a quarter of an inch of the level they fell on their sides and remained motionless. They were however only rendered senseless, and on air being readmitted they were soon completely restored. The experiments which followed also showed without doubt that a certain amount of air is indispensable to these insects.

SECOND EXPERIMENT.

I wished to ascertain the effect on bees of keeping them in an enclosed space, and to note at the same time whether any alterations took place in the air with which they had been in contact. We took three sixteen-ounce flasks which contained ordinary air and introduced 250 worker bees into the first, the same number into the second, and 150 drones into the third. The first and the third were carefully sealed. The second, destined to serve, as a basis for comparison, was only closed in such a way as to prevent the escape of the bees inside.

The experiment began at midday. At first there appeared to be no difference between the bees in the sealed flasks and those in the unsealed one. Some seemed to show signs of impatience with their captivity, but without giving any sign of discomfort. At a quarter past twelve those in the sealed flask began to show signs of suffering. Their rings contracted and dilated with greater rapidity, they breathed more heavily, and seemed to undergo a great change for they licked up the moisture from the sides of the flask.

At half past twelve the cluster, till then hanging around a straw smeared with honey, suddenly gave way, and the bees composing it fell to the bottom of the flask and were not able to rise again. At a quarter to one they were all asphyxiated. We then took them out of their prison into the fresh air, and a few minutes afterwards they regained the use of their powers. The drones suffered the most tragic results from the confinement to which we had condemned them, as none of them came back to life. The bees shut up in the second flask with free access to the air had not suffered at all.

We next examined the state of the air in the sealed flasks and found it greatly altered. Other bees introduced into it were quickly suffocated. A lighted candle would not burn in it and a sample shaken with water showed a decrease in volume of 14%. It precipitated chalk from lime water, lettuce seeds would not germinate in it, and lastly, tests with nitrous oxide showed the total absence of oxygen.[9]

THIRD EXPERIMENT.

In order to learn whether the absence of the last named gas was the cause of the collapse of the bees, and whether I ought to attribute their return to life when restored to liberty to its presence, I made the following experiment. We took a ten ounce jar and poured into it nine ounces of water; the tenth part was reserved for the bees, and a layer of cork separated them from the liquid: the bees were therefore in ordinary air, and we had only to seal the opening.

In this experiment as in the preceding one the air was consumed by the bees who were quickly suffocated. We then opened the lower part of the jar under water and introduced one ounce of oxygen.[10]

The result was very satisfactory. Hardly had the oxygen reached the part of the jar occupied by the bees when we noticed slight movements in their proboscis and antennæ: next the rings of the abdomen resumed their normal functions, and a further dose of the life-giving fluid completely restored the insects to the full use of their powers.

FOURTH EXPERIMENT.

When other bees were placed in an atmosphere of pure oxygen they lived eight times as long as in ordinary air, a very striking result. However in the end they also died of suffocation, all the oxygen having been converted into carbonic acid gas.[10a]

The production of carbon dioxide from the breathing of 50 bees in oxygen during five hours may be put at 2 cu. ins., the lime precipitated from lime water being about 2¼ grains. To these tests we added sundry others on the effects produced on bees by various harmful gases.

[9] Endiometric tests:
    Ordinary air 1 part, nitrous oxide 1 part, residue 0.99.
    Air consumed by workers 1 part, nitrous oxide 1 part, residue 1.93.
    Air consumed by drones 1 part, nitrous oxide 1 part, residue 1.85.

[10] The method employed for measuring the consumption of oxygen was the one used by Priestley of absorbing the remaining oxygen with vitrous oxide and measuring the loss in volume.

[10a] Endiometric tests:
    Ordinary air 1 part, nitrous oxide 1 part, residue 0.99.
    Oxygen 1 part, nitrous oxide 3 parts, residue 1.98.
    Oxygen consumed by bees 1 part, nitrous oxide 1 part, residue 1.58.

FIFTH EXPERIMENT.

In carbonic acid gas prepared from chalk, they immediately lost the use of their powers, but regained them at once in the air.

SIXTH EXPERIMENT.

In nitrogen prepared from a mixture of sulphur and moistened iron filings, the bees perished at once and did not recover.

SEVENTH EXPERIMENT.

The same result followed their introduction into hydrogen prepared from zinc.

EIGHTH AND NINTH EXPERIMENTS.

We introduced bees into an artificial atmosphere composed of three parts of hydrogen and one of vital air, the two gases together having a volume equal to six ounces of water. During the first fifteen minutes there was no change in the state of the bees, but after that their powers began to fail and at the end of an hour they were without movement or life. Lastly in a mixture of three parts of nitrogen with one part of oxygen the bees perished immediately.

Perhaps it was superfluous to search for further proofs that bees breathe: but before leaving the subject we wished to assure ourselves of the effects which the same gases would have on them in a state of torpor.

TENTH EXPERIMENT.

We shut some bees in a glass receptacle surrounded by crushed ice. A thermometer placed in the same vessel fell from 140° R (the temperature of the surrounding air) to 6° (about 45° F.), when the bees became numb. They were then lifted out of the receptacle to be shut in tubes filled with the gases which had had such disastrous effects in the preceding experiments. They were left for three hours and when they were taken out they came to life in my hand, the warmth of which restored them, and they seemed to enjoy the full use of their faculties.

This experiment was very conclusive. It was not the contact of the poisonous gases which caused the death of the bees in the previous experiments, for in this case they had suffered no harm, but the introduction of the gases into their breathing tubes. This was proved by the preservation of their life in the midst of these gases when subjection to cold had arrested their vital functions.

ELEVENTH EXPERIMENT.

We repeated with the eggs, larvæ, and nymphs of bees the same tests as those applied to the adults. The results were entirely analogous; showing the consumption of oxygen and the formation of carbonic acid gas. The larvæ consumed more than the eggs and the nymphs more than the larvæ, and the nymphs were the only ones which succumbed.

TWELFTH EXPERIMENT.

Two larvæ placed in nitrogen and carbonic acid gas lived several seconds longer than adult bees had done.

THIRTEENTH EXPERIMENT.

Nymphs subjected to the same tests did not survive more than a few seconds.[11]

FOURTEENTH EXPERIMENT.

Eggs placed in air which had been altered by the breathing of bees did not develop, but larvæ and nymphs numbed by cold were not affected when kept for some hours in these harmful gases.

These experiments proved that the breathing of bees in all their stages is subject to the same laws. It should be borne in mind that Swammerdam had discovered three pairs of breathing orifices in the thorax, and seven on the abdomen of nymphs.

It therefore seemed to me of some importance to ascertain whether the same organs were also to be found in the adult insects, and my experiments in this direction yielded results which I am about to give. I employed the well known method of immersion in water, but to avoid the complication which might arise through numbness, I used water slightly warmed.

FIFTEENTH EXPERIMENT.

I will give here only the principal results of my experiments. When only the head of a bee was immersed in water or mercury for a period of half an hour she did not seem to be affected.

SIXTEENTH EXPERIMENT.

If on the contrary the head only was left outside the liquid the insect unrolled her tongue and quickly became suffocated.

SEVENTEENTH EXPERIMENT.

If the head and thorax were immersed leaving the abdomen in the air, the bee struggled several seconds, but very soon ceased to show signs of life.

EIGHTEENTH EXPERIMENT.

As the head and abdomen seem insufficient to supply bees with the air they need, the breathing apparatus should be found in the thorax. This was

[11] Endiometric tests:
   Ordinary air 1 part, nitrous oxide 1 part, residue 1.03.
   Air shut up with eggs 1 part, residue 1.08.
   Air shut up with larvæ 1 part, residue 1.31.
   Air shut up with nymphs, 1 part, residue 1.90.
   Air shut up with empty cells 1 part, residue 1.04.
   Air shut up with royal jelly 1 part, residue 1.09.

demonstrated by immersing the head and the abdomen at the same time, and leaving only the thorax out of water. The bee bore this uncomfortable attitude fairly patiently, and when released took to flight.

NINETEENTH EXPERIMENT.

When wholly immersed in water, a bee quickly suffocates, but it is then that the working of the orifices or stigmata can best be seen. Four air bubbles appear, two between the neck and the base of the wings, the third on the neck at the base of the proboscis, and the fourth at the opposite extremity of the thorax just above its junction with the abdomen. These bubbles do not immediately rise to the surface of the water for the bee seems to wish to retain them, as they are partially drawn in again several times. They only escape at last when they have grown large enough to overcome the resistance caused by the breathing organ, or alternatively by the adherence of the air to the walls of the orifice. The two last named bubbles show the existence of stigmata which had escaped the attention of Swammerdam.

TWENTIETH EXPERIMENT.

In other experiments we submerged each of the orifices in turn, leaving the others outside the water. We discovered that one only of the orifices is sufficient to maintain respiration, and we noticed that in each case the other orifices did not release bubbles, which in my opinion shows the existence of intercommunication.

TWENTY-FIRST EXPERIMENT.

The same test repeated with lime water proved that the formation of carbonic acid gas in the preceding experiments was in a great measure due to the respiration of the bees, for the bubbles escaping from their bodies made the liquid milky by precipitating the chalk.

PART III.

EXPERIMENTS ON THE VENTILATION OF HIVES.

We had thought to explain the existence of bees in their hive by supposing them equipped in such a manner as to have no need of breathing. As however we are now convinced of the fallacy of this hypothesis, the difficulty remains, for it is impossible to believe that the air could keep itself pure enough to maintain life in so confined a space. Moreover the number of bees may rise even to 25,000—30,000 or more.

However as we could only determine by experiment whether the air had or had not been altered, we judged it necessary to analyze it, and for this purpose we made the following preparations.

FIRST EXPERIMENT.

We prepared a large cylindrical receptacle to serve as a hive. In it we placed a swarm and gave it time to establish itself and build several combs so that the conditions might be those of a normal colony. We then connected up a flask with a tap arranged in such a way as to permit the introduction of air from the cylinder. This air, displaced by the fall of water or mercury contained in the flask, mounted into it when the communicating taps were opened, and these were closed again with all the necessary precautions. The mercury or water used in this experiment was received in a funnel which conducted it into a basin situated at the bottom of the hive so that the bees did not suffer any inconvenience.

The air of the hive, taken at different times of the day, was analysed by M. Senebier by means of nitrous oxide. The results were very different from those we had expected, for he found the air nearly as pure as that of the atmosphere. In the evening he found a slight alteration but this was not appreciable and could be explained in other ways.[12]

In another experiment a flask was connected with the hive for a period of six hours and when the air was analysed it was found as pure as that of the atmosphere.[13]

Have the bees then either in themselves or in their hive any means of supplying oxygen? One of our experiments showed that neither wax nor pollen produced it.

Empty cells of 82 grains in weight, also the same quantity filled with pollen were shut for 12 hours in a six ounce flask at the temperature of the hive and did not make the air any richer in oxygen. It even seemed slightly poorer.

Not yet satisfied that I had found any solution to my problem I decided to try an experiment which seemed more promising. I thought that if the bees had in their hive any source of oxygen capable of supplying their needs, it should be a matter of indifference whether the door of the hive were open or closed, which we could try by sealing them in their hive and testing the air inside. This test would overcome all objections which could be raised to the preceding experiments: for by separating bees from their fellows, their larvæ, and their hive we might have indirectly exercised an influence on them.

SECOND EXPERIMENT.

It was only necessary to shut the bees in a hive with transparent walls which would permit observation of what passed inside. For this experiment I made use of my swarm living in the cylinder.

---

12 Endiometric tests:
 Ordinary air 1 part, nitrous oxide 1 part, residue 1.05.
 Air taken from the hive at 9 a. m., residue 1.10.
 At 10 a. m. 1.12, at 2 p. m. 1.13, 6 p. m. 1.16.
 At 11 a. m. 1.13, at 3 p. m. 1.13, 7 p. m. 1.15.
 Midday 1.13, at 4 p. m. 1.13, at 8 p. m. 1.16.
 1 p. m. 1.13, at 5 p. m. 1.13.

13 Endiometric tests:
 Ordinary air 1 part, nitrous oxide 1 part, residue 1.02.
 Air from the hive, 1.05
 Air from the hive, 1.06.

Immense activity reigned in their busy world. Approaching within ten steps we could hear a loud hum. For carrying out the experiment we chose a rainy day so that all the bees might be in the hive. The experiment commenced at 3 p. m. We closed the entrance carefully and, not without misgiving, watched the effects. In a quarter of an hour the bees began to show signs of discomfort. Till then they had appeared to ignore their imprisonment, but now all work was suspended and the hive entirely changed its aspect. Soon we heard an extraordinary noise. All the bees, both those covering the surfaces of the combs and those which were clustered beneath, stopped work and beat the air vigorously with their wings. This continued for about ten minutes. The movement of the wings became less continuous and less rapid. At thirty-seven minutes past three they had entirely lost their powers and could no longer cling on with their legs. This state was quickly followed by collapse.

The numbers of bees on the floor of the hive rapidly increased until there were thousands of both workers and drones. There did not remain a single one on the combs. Three minutes later the whole colony was apparently suffocated. The hive suddenly became colder, and from 28 R. (about 95 F.) the temperature dropped to that of the outside air.

We hoped to restore life and warmth to the suffocated bees by giving them pure air again. We opened the door of the hive and also the tap fixed to the flask. The effect of the current of air thus established was striking. In a few minutes the bees recommenced breathing. The rings of the abdomen resumed their normal play, the bees simultaneously started to beat their wings, a very remarkable circumstance, which we had noticed, as we have said when the lack of air first began to make itself felt in the hive.

Soon the bees climbed up onto their combs, the temperature rose to normal, and by four p. m. order was re-established.

This experiment shows without doubt that bees have not in their hive any means of supplying oxygen, which therefore comes to them from the outside.

PART IV

RESEARCHES ON THE METHOD OF RENEWING THE AIR IN HIVES.

Renewal of the air inside hives is absolutely necessary to the existence of bees and certainly takes place. Fresh air must come from outside as the bees perish so soon as the entrance is hermetically sealed. How does this come about?

We thought at first that the natural heat of the bees might have enough influence to establish a current between the inside and the outside air by upsetting the equilibrium between them. However we soon gave up this idea as we called to mind the experiment in which we had placed a lighted candle under a bell-jar. The bell-jar had an opening larger than that of a beehive but the candle went out for lack of air though the temperature of the jar was raised as high as 50° R (144° F).

There remained only one hypothesis to explain the purity of the air contained in the hive, namely to admit that the bees possess the extraordinary faculty of being able to draw fresh air into the hive and at the same time to expel that used up by their breathing.

We had therefore to find out whether their activities offer any special circumstance which would explain this phenomenon. Not finding any satisfactory explanation our attention was again drawn to the possible connection between the circulation of the air and the fanning of the wings which we had previously noticed and which produced a continual hum from the interior of the hive. We surmised that the motion of the wings being pronounced enough to produce a definite sound, might also be sufficient to replace the air used up in breathing.

But could so apparently slight a thing dispose of the waste air resulting from the respiration of the bees? At first sight in seems difficult to believe, but on considering how continuous and energetic is the fanning of the bees it seems to offer a simple and satisfactory explanation of the problem. Anyone who places his hand near a bee when in the action of fanning will notice that she sets up an appreciable current, her wings moving so rapidly that one can scarcely distinguish them. United at their edges by little hooks the two wings at each side make a very effective fan, the more so as they are slightly concave. The movement of the wings is through an angle of 90° which can be easily verified as they move so rapidly that they can be seen in all positions practically simultaneously.

The bees brace themselves firmly against the floor of the hive: the first pair of legs are stretched out in front, the second are spread to the right and left of the body, while the third, very close to one another, and immediately beneath the abdomen, enable the insect to raise and lower itself.

During the summer a certain number of bees may always be seen beating their wings in this manner in front of the hive door, and others can be observed within, most commonly stationed on the floor of the hive. All those thus occupied, whether inside or out face towards the interior of the hive.

It is evident that the bees place themselves in order so that they may fan with greater effect: they form themselves into rows, often converging towards the door. This however is not necessarily the case owing probably to the necessity of the fanners giving place to the foraging bees whose rapid coming and going might knock them over at every moment were they not ranged in rows.

Sometimes as many as 20 bees or more are fanning within the hive. At other times their number is more limited. Each bee fans for more or less time. We have watched individuals at work for as much as 25 minutes during which time they did not stop at all though several times they seemed to take breath ceasing the vibration of their wings for a fraction of a second. As soon as any cease to fan, others replace them, so that there is never any interruption in the hum of a well inhabited hive.

If in winter they are obliged to fan near to the center of the cluster, doubtless they perform this important function between the irregular combs whose surfaces leave between them enough space to permit the movement of the wings, for there must be a space of at least half an inch to allow free movement.

A further question is whether ventilation is necessary for bees in their wild state as for those in hives. Dwelling as they do in hollow trees and in holes in rocks, their different circumstances might give rise to variation in their method of renewing the air of the hive. Consequently we sought to imitate natural conditions by placing bees in a hive five feet high. It was glazed the whole height so that it was easy to see on all sides the cone shaped cluster which hung from the combs at the top of the hive. The door was placed at the bottom as in ordinary hives.

We saw that there were only a few bees fanning near the entrance, the majority being always on the side of the hive and that the one nearest the cluster. They were spaced only a short distance from one another in the same path as that of the foragers returning from the field.

This ventilation by the bees or the humming which is the indication of it, manifests itself not only in the heat of summer, but throughout the year. It even appears at times to be more marked in the middle of the winter than when the temperature is more moderate. An action which so continuously occupies a certain number of bees must have a very marked effect on the atmosphere. The equilibrium once being upset, a current should be established and the air thus renewed.

But so remarkable a result cannot come about without some outward sign, and nothing is easier than to show this. For this purpose we fixed a small indicator (lit: anenometer) in front of the hive entrance. It must be very light—of paper, feathers, or cotton wool, and this should show us whether there is any appreciable current of air passing in or out of the hive door and if so what is its strength?

For this experiment we chose a calm day and a time when the bees were all in their hive, taking the precaution to fix a screen at some distance from the entrance in order not to be confused by any chance current from outside.

The indicators were scarcely in place when they began to move. Sometimes they seemed to precipitate themselves towards the door, and stop for a moment, sometimes they were repelled with the same rapidity and held themselves in the air as much as one or two inches out of the perpendicular. The amount of motion appeared to be proportionate to the number of bees fanning. Sometimes there was less movement but they were never entirely stopped.

This experiment therefore demonstrates the existence of a current of air at the door of the hive: It shows that the air corrupted by the bees is at once replaced by external air, thus explaining the purity which we had previously noted.

It may possibly be objected that it is the custom of some beekeepers to close the doors of their hives during winter, apparently without harm. Assuredly if, by this method, entry of air were completely prevented it would be obvious that the bees could do without it. But this practice is only followed by skeppists and skeps are very difficult to close entirely as the air can penetrate through their joints.

For the rest we can affirm nothing of the winter as we only made a single experiment, though it certainly seemed sufficient to set our minds at rest on this point. It was again to Burnens that we entrusted the care of the experiment. He had by this time left us and sent the following letter on the subject:

Sir:

I have just carried out, at the request of M. Senebier, the experiment which we made in the summer.

I chose for it a skep which was well populated, and one in which the bees seemed to be full of life and activity. After having fixed the edge of the skep to its floor, I placed through the top a fairly strong wire ending in a hook from which I suspended a loop made in the end of a hair. This carried a small square of the thinnest paper I could find, which was placed level with the door of the hive and at a distance of about an inch from it.

As soon as the apparatus was in position, I noticed that my indicator began to move. To measure the movement I had placed at the junction of the hair and the paper a small horizontal rule graduated in lignes[14] of the Paris foot. The paper moved backwards and forwards a number of times, and the greatest movements were an inch out of the perpendicular.

I tried putting the paper at a great distance from the opening, but the oscillations no longer took place, and the apparatus remained motionless.

Following your suggestion I made an opening in the upper part of the skep and ran in some honey. Very soon afterwards the bees started humming. Then the hum became louder, and several bees emerged. I watched the apparatus carefully, and saw that the movement of the paper was more frequent than before the introduction of the honey, and that it had a greater intensity: for when I fixed the hair fifteen lignes from the entrance, the paper was definitely moved to and fro several times. I endeavored to see whether the movement would take place at a greater distance, but the paper remained motionless.

All that remains is for me to report on the temperature. I had an alcohol thermometer which registered a shade temperature of 5¼°R. (just over 43¾°F). There was bright sunshine, and the experiment was made at 3 p. m.

If you wish for any further work be so good as to tell me of it, and I will fulfill your behests with the greatest pleasure.

I have the honour to be Sir,

Your most humble and obedient servant,

F. BURNENS.

PART. V.

Proofs Taken From the Results of a Mechanical Ventilator.

The preceding experiments left me in no doubt as to the object of ventilation. One could no longer hold the theory that the air was produced by chemical changes within the hive. I had shown that the used air could not

14 The twelfth part of an inch.

by its own change in weight set up the ventilation which is so essential to the bees. However not daring to trust entirely to my own judgment I wished again to consult M. Saussure before establishing an hypothesis which in many ways is of interest to scientists. This learned man was interested in the results of my experiments and being struck by the originality of the means employed by Nature to preserve bees from a certain death, suggested to me a test which would do away with all doubts on the matter.

He saw only one way of deciding whether the renewal of air in the hives could be attributed to natural ventilation, and this was to imitate the movements of bees by a mechanical action under conditions similar to those of an ordinary hive, all other possible sources of ventilation being cut off. He suggested that I should use a mechanical ventilator, the wings of which would vibrate at a speed fast enough to reproduce the movement of fanning bees. One of my friends[15], a skillful mechanic and clever scientist, helped me to make this instrument, and assisted also in the various experiments for which it was destined.

In place of a number of small ventilators we constructed a tin windmill having eighteen wings. We adapted this to fit a large cylindrical vessel of which the capacity was increased by a super on which it was solidly fastened. An opening in the super of suitable size, which could be completely closed, served to introduce a candle into the bell jar. The ventilator was placed above the super and fixed in place. On one side of this box we had arranged another opening.

This part of the apparatus communicated with the upper vessel, but was arranged to prevent a direct draught, so that the ventilator should not itself blow out the candle. We suspended light substances in front of the opening of the box, and started with the following experiment in which the mill was not put into action.

FIRST EXPERIMENT.

We introduced a candle into the bell jar, the hole corresponding to the door of the hive being left open. The flame did not long maintain its first brilliancy. It soon diminished, and at the end of 8 mins. went out, although the capacity of the vessel was about 3228 cubic ins. The upper part of the bell jar was warm, and the indicators gave no sign of any current of air.

SECOND EXPERIMENT.

After having renewed the air which had been consumed, we repeated the experiment. The candle went out after the same length of time, showing that one opening only is not sufficient for circulation of air, unless it is put in motion by some outside agency.

THIRD EXPERIMENT.

Having again renewed the air of the vessel, we replaced the candle, and hung several indicators near the door. When these preparations were made

---

[15] M. Schwepp, inventor of the process for making aerated waters.

we started the ventilator. At once two currents of air were established: the indicators showed this clearly, swinging to and from the door, and the brilliancy of the light did not diminish at all during the course of the experiment, which could be prolonged indefinitely. A thermometer placed at the lower part of the apparatus registered 40°R. (122°F.), and the temperature in the upper part was evidently higher.

FOURTH EXPERIMENT.

I wished to see whether my ventilator would provide enough air for two lighted candles. They burnt for 15 minutes and then went out together. In another test where the mill had not been started, they burned for 3 minutes only.

FIFTH EXPERIMENT.

We tried increasing the number of openings in the side of the box, but were not successful. One of the two candles went out at the end of 8 minutes. The other kept alight as long as the ventilator was in motion. I had therefore not obtained a stronger air current by multiplying the openings.

These experiments show that in a place with an opening only on one side, air can renew itself when there is some mechanical cause tending to displace it, and this seems to confirm our conjecture on the effect which the fanning of bees has on the hive.

ARTICLE VI.

IMMEDIATE CAUSES OF VENTILATION.

We shall misconstrue Nature if we suppose that the real objects of any given actions are always those which appear on the surface. This line of thought, which is capable of great development, is one of those which best show that invisible power which governs the universe. The bees in beating the air with their wings little realize the object which they achieve. Perhaps some simple desire or need makes itself felt, and instinct prompts them to fan their wings which seem to have been given them for flying only. This is without doubt a natural reaction to the stimulus of some particular sensation, for one cannot credit them with the knowledge which would lead us to act were we in an analogous position. Nevertheless it is interesting to note the characteristics with which Nature endows them; lower orders though they be, since they achieve the end which they set out to accomplish.

The first idea which occurs to us is that the bees do not fan except to procure a sensation of freshness, and an experiment will easily convince us that this motive may be one of the actual causes of fanning. We opened the shutter of a glazed hive: the sun's rays beat on the combs covered with bees. Soon those which first felt the influence of the heat started to hum, while those still in the shade remained quiet. An observation which one can make any day confirms the result of this experiment: the cluster of bees one sees in front of the hive during the summer, feeling the heat of the sun, fan with the greatest energy, but if an intervening body shade a part of the cluster, the fanning ceases in the shaded part, while it continues in that which is in the sun.

The same fact may be noticed with insects similar to bees. The velvet coated bumble bees whose nest we kept on a window sill, ordinarily became very active when the sun heated the box which held them, and all beat their wings, making a loud humming.

Sometimes one hears the same noise in nests of wasps or hornets. Thus it seems a constant law that heat will cause bees or other insects to fan.

But the remarkable point about bees is that they fan in the depth of winter, and that this noise is often the sign by which one tells that they are alive during that season. Heat is therefore only a secondary cause which in summer augments this habit of the bees. It is necessary to seek other causes. We tried surrounding bees with various obnoxious gases and found that several of these stimulated them to fan. We separated a number of bees from their hive, leaving them with some honey, and then placed some cotton wool soaked in methylated spirit near to them while they took their food. The wool had to be placed quite close to their heads before they noticed it, but then the effect was striking. The bees at once moved away, returning again shortly to the honey. As soon as they had come back we recommenced the experiment. They moved away once more, but this time without entirely rolling up their tongues, contenting themselves with beating their wings while feeding. Several times however the insects too close to the disagreeable odours moved away immediately and took to flight. Sometimes a bee turned her back to the honey, fanned until the odour was diminished, and then turned back to partake again of the repast we had provided.

These experiments succeeded best at the door of the hive, as the bees, held by the double attraction of honey and their home, were less disposed to escape by flight from the smell with which we were testing them. The humble bees, of which we have already spoken, act in the same manner when confronted by harmful odours, but a point which is very remarkable and emphasizes to a certain extent the importance of fanning, is that the drones and queens, though very sensitive to strong smells, do not know how to preserve themselves as do the workers.

Ventilation is therefore one of the labours of the hive undertaken only by the workers. The Almighty, in assigning to these insects a dwelling place into which air could only penetrate with difficulty, also gave them a means to overcome the sad effects which might result from the alteration of their atmosphere.

Of all the animal world the bees are perhaps the only creatures to which the care of so important a function is given, and incidentally this indicates the perfection of their organisation. An indirect consequence of this ventilation is the high temperature which bees sustain without effort in their hives. It results from their breathing as is the case with all other living beings. This heat, which one writer has attributed to the fermentation of honey, is certainly derived from the gathering together of a number of bees in the same place. It is so absolutely essential to them and their brood that it should be independent of the temperature of the outside air.

The very existence of the bees is therefore in direct dependence on the continuity of their fanning. Though called to so many different labours, each of these insects must occupy itself constantly in the duty of maintaining the air at the necessary degree of purity. This function, exercised by a number of individuals each in their turn, does not exempt any of them from the other work of the hive which has to be performed.

Thus the social organisation of these insects permits them to fulfill in turn the different functions imposed on the entire population.

CHAPTER IX.

On the Senses of Bees and Especially That of Smell.

The infinite variety of habits exhibited by the different races of insects and animals, gives rise to the very natural idea that physical objects do not procure them sensations similar to those of man; their faculties not being the same, and their nature admitting not the light of reason, they must be directed by other agents. Perhaps the idea which we form of their senses, founded upon those which were given to ourselves, is incorrect; senses of a more subtle kind or modified otherwise, may present objects under an aspect unknown to us, and cause impressions which are foreign to us; were they only better developed than ours, they would open a new field to our observations. Thus what man discovers with the help of enlarging glasses still belongs to eyesight, although the ancients had no idea of the objects which we perceive since progress came in the art of optics.

Can we not admit that the intelligence which dispenses to each animal the organization suitable to its tastes and habits has the power to modify its senses beyond any knowledge that art gives us?

Cannot the same regulator who created for us those five grand avenues, whereby our mind gains its notions of the physical world, open up to beings less favored with judgment channels more secure, more direct, or more numerous, the branches of which extend in the entire domain assigned to them?

Art enables us to determine regarding objects not so immediately within the sphere of the senses, where judgment is more particularly required; as physics and chemistry prove in a thousand examples; thermometers, menstrua, and reagents by the means of which we detect the most intimate nature of objects which elude our senses, as so many new organs. Thus there may be other means of viewing objects, those which we invent speak only to the mind; but when nature establishes communications between the physical and the spiritual, it does so through sentiment or sensations, and it is not repugnant to admit the possibility of its having created other sensations for beings which differ from us in so many other respects.

Insects living in a republic, among which bees certainly occupy the highest rank, often exhibit traits inexpicable, even supposing these small beings to be endowed with the same senses as ourselves, which renders it so difficult to penetrate the secret impulse actuating them. However they possess sensations of a less subtle nature, and as it is advisable to gain as much knowledge of their powers' as possible, it would be wrong to neglect the study of the outward displays that are within our reach, whereby we can judge at least of their appetites and their aversions.

Sight, feeling, smell and taste are the senses most generally ascribed to bees; hitherto we have no proof that they enjoy the sense of hearing, although a custom very prevalent among the country people seems to support a contrary opinion; I allude to the practice of striking a sonorous instrument, at the time of issue of a swarm, to prevent it from flying away; but in compensation, how great is the perfection of their organ of sight! How easily a bee recognizes her habitation amidst an apiary of numerous boxes all similar to its own! She returns to it in a straight line and with extreme speed, which indicates that she distinguishes it from the others from afar by marks escaping our notice. The bee departs and flies straight to the most flowery field; having ascertained her course, she is seen traversing it by a path as direct as the flight of a bullet escaping from the barrel of a musket: her harvest being made, she rises aloft to recognize her hive and returns with the rapidity of lightning. (Since Huber wrote the above, it has been ascertained that the so-called beeline is more or less wavy, probably owing to the currents of air and the breeze. Translator).

Their sense of feeling is perhaps still more admirable, it is substituted for, and completely supplies the want of sight within the hive: the bee constructs her combs in darkness, pours her honey into the magazines, feeds the young, judges of their age and necessities, recognizes her queen, all by means of the antennæ, the shape of which are much less adapted for *knowledge* than our hands; shall we not therefore grant to this sense modifications and perfections unknown to the touch of man? Had we but two fingers to measure and compare so many divers things, what subtility would they not require to perform the same service?[16]

The sense of taste is perhaps the least perfect of all the senses of the bee; for this sense in general admits of selection in its object, but contrary to the received opinion the bee certainly displays little choice in the honey that it collects. Plants whose odor and savor appear to us most disagreeable do not repulse them. Poisonous flowers are not excluded from her choice, and it is said that the honey harvested in certain provinces of America is a rather violent poison; aside from this, bees do not despise the secretions of aphides under the form of honeydew, in spite of the impurity of its origin; we see them even quite tolerant concerning the quality of the water which they drink; that of ponds and of the foulest ditches is seemingly preferred to the most limpid stream and to dew itself.

Nothing therefore is more unequal than the quality of honey: that of one district does not have similar flavor to that of another; that of spring is unlike that of autumn; the honey of one hive does not always resemble that of the hive adjoining.

Thus it is true that the bee does not select her food; but if she is not particular as to the quality of the honey, she is not indifferent as to the quantity contained in flowers. They constantly resort where most is to be found; they issue from their hive much less in regard to the temperature than according to their expectation of a more plentiful or scanty harvest. When the basswood (tilia) or buckwheat are in bloom, they brave the rain, they depart before sunrise, and return later than ordinary; but this effervescence relaxes as soon as the flowers fade, and when the scythe has cut

---

[16] The three ocelli on the head of the bee are generally believed now to serve them in the darkness of the hive, at very short range.

down those which adorned the meadows, the bees remain in the hive, however brilliant the sunshine. To what shall we ascribe the knowledge of the greater or less abundance of honey in the flowers of the country which bees appear to possess, without leaving their home? Does one sense, more subtile than the others, that of smell, warn them of it?

There are odors repugnant to bees; others attract them; the smoke of tobacco and every other kind of smoke displease them. Human industry turns to its benefit their aversion as well as their liking; but it is satisfied with reaching the desired aim and does not invade the domain of philosophical inquiry.

Led by other motives, we will endeavor to find how different odors affect the bees, to what degree they are attracted by some and repulsed by others; this is within our reach; perhaps some day the growth of progress will permit us to go beyond.

Of all odorous substances, honey is that which most powerfully attracts bees; other odors have the same faculty perhaps only as far as they suggest to them the presence of a liquid which seems so valuable to them.

To ascertain whether it was the odor of honey and not the sight of flowers only which apprises bees of its presence, we must hide this substance where their eyes could not see it; for this purpose, we first placed honey near the apiary, in a window, where the shutters almost closed still allowed their passage if they chose; in less than a quarter of an hour, four bees, a butterfly and some house-flies insinuated themselves between the shutter and the window, and we found them feeding on it. Although this observation was sufficiently conclusive, I wished it better confirmed: we took boxes of different sizes, colors and forms, we adjusted to them small card valves corresponding with apertures in their covers; honey being put into them, they were placed two hundred paces from my apiary.

In half an hour bees were seen arriving, they carefully inspected the boxes, and soon discovering the openings through which they could enter we saw them press against the valves and reach the honey.

One may thence judge of the extreme delicacy of smelling of these insects; not only was the honey quite concealed from view, but its emanations could not be much diffused, since it was covered and disguised in the experiment.

Flowers frequently exhibit an organization resembling our valves: the nectary of several classes is situated at the bottom of a tube, enclosed or concealed by the petals; nevertheless the bees find it; but its instinct, less refined than that of the bumblebee (Bremus), affords less resource; the latter, when unable to penetrate the flowers by their natural cavity, knows how to make an aperture at the base of the corolla, or even of the calyx, to insert its proboscis at the place where nature has located the reservoir of honey; by means of this stratagem and the length of its tongue, the bumblebee can obtain honey where the domestic bee would reach it with great difficulty. From the difference of the honey produced by these two insects, one might conjecture that they do not harvest it from the same flowers.

The honeybee, however, is as much attracted by the honey of the bumblebee as by her own. In a time of scarcity, we have seen them pillage, a nest of bumblebees which had been placed in an open box near an apiary; they had taken almost entire possession of it: a few bumblebees, remaining in spite of the disaster to the nest, still repaired to the fields and brought back the surplus of their needs to their ancient asylum; but the plundering bees, trailing them, accompanied them home and never quitted them until having obtained the fruits of their harvest; they licked them, held out their trunks, surrounded them and did not release them until they had obtained the saccharine fluid of which they were the depositaries: they did not try to kill the insect which thus afforded them their repast; the sting was never unsheathed, and the bumblebee itself was accustomed to these exactions, it yielded its honey and resumed its flight: this new-fashioned domestic economy lasted above three weeks; wasps, attracted by the same cause, did not become so familiar with the original proprietors of the nest; at night the bumblebees remained alone; they finally disappeared and the parasites did not return.

We have been assured that the same scene happens between robber bees and those of weak hives, which is less astonishing.

Not only have the bees a very acute sense of smell, but to this advantage is added the recollection of sensations; here is an example. Honey had been placed in a window in autumn, bees came to it in multitudes; the honey was removed and the shutters closed during the winter; but when opened again, on the return of spring, the bees came back, though no honey was there; doubtless they remembered that some had been there before; thus an interval of several months did not obliterate the impression received.

Let us now seek the site or the organ of this sense, whose existence has been so well proved.

Nostrils have not yet been recognized in insects, nor do we know in what part of the body these, or any organs corresponding to them are placed, in this class of beings. Probably odors reach the sensorium, by a mechanism similar to the one given to us; that is, the air is introduced into some opening at the termination of the olfactory nerves; hence we must ascertain whether the stigmata do not perform this function, whether the organ which we seek is situated in the head or in some other part of the body.

FIRST EXPERIMENT.

A pencil dipped in turpentine, one of the substances most formidable to insects, was presented successfully to all parts of the body of a bee, but whether it was brought to the abdomen, the thorax, the head, or the stigmata of the thorax, the bee which was busy eating did not seem to be in the least affected.

SECOND EXPERIMENT.

From the uselessness of the first test, we concluded that it was necessary to bring the pencil successively to all parts of the head: so we took a very fine pencil, to avoid touching more than one spot each time. The bee, busy with her meal, held her trunk protruding forward; we brought the pencil near the eyes, the antennæ, the trunk, in vain; it was otherwise when we placed it near the cavity of the mouth, above the insertion of the proboscis.

At that instant the bee receded, left the honey, and beat its wings while walking with much agitation; she would have taken flight had not the pencil been withdrawn; she resumed her eating and we again presented the turpentine, still placing it near her mouth; the bee then turned away from the honey, clung to the table and fanned herself during some minutes. A similar test, with oil of marjoram produced the same effect, but in a more speedy and constant manner.

This experiment seems to indicate, therefore, that the organ of smell, in these insects, resides in the mouth or in the parts depending on it.

Bees not occupied in feeding appeared more sensible of this odor, they perceived it at a greater distance, and speedily took flight, whereas, when their trunk was dipped in honey, several parts of the body might be touched without disturbing them from this occupation.

Were they absorbed by their love for honey and distracted by its smell, or were their organs less exposed? This could be ascertained in two ways, either by covering all parts of the body with varnish, leaving only the sensitive organ bare, or by cementing up the part wherein the seat of this sense was supposed to be located, leaving the other parts completely free.

The latter method appearing the more positive and practicable, we seized several bees and, compelling them to unfold their trunks, filled their mouths with flour paste; when this coating was dry enough to prevent them from divesting themselves of it, they were freed; this process did not seem to incommode them, they breathed and moved as easily as their companions.

Honey was offered to them, but they did not appear to be attracted by its presence, nor did they appear affected by odors most offensive to them. Pencils were dipped in oil of turpentine, and of cloves, in ether, in fixed and volatile alkalis, and in nitrous acid, and their points insinuated very near the mouth; but these odors, which would have caused a sudden aversion to them in their ordinary condition, had no sensible effect upon any of them. On the contrary, several of them mounted upon the poisoned pencils, and traveled upon them as if unimpregnated with any of these substances.

These bees had therefore temporarily lost the sense of smell, and it appeared to us sufficiently demonstrated that it had its seat in the cavity of the mouth.

We also wished to investigate in what manner bees would be affected by different odors.

Mineral acids and volatile alkali, presented on a pencil at the opening of the mouth, made upon these insects the same impression as the spirit of turpentine, but with greater energy; other substances did not have so pronounced an effect. On presenting musk to bees feeding at the entrance of the hive, they ceased and dispersed a little, but without precipitation or beating of wings; we scattered pulverized musk on a drop of honey; they thrust their tongues into it, but as if by stealth, keeping as far from the honey as possible; this drop of honey, which would have disappeared in a few minutes, had it not been covered with musk, suffered no sensible diminution in a quarter of an hour, although the bees had many times plunged their trunks into it.

Mr. Senebier having called my attention upon certain odors which might affect the bees, because they vitiate the air, and not because of any direct action upon their nerves, I thought of making similar experiments with substances which do not perceptibly vitiate it, such as camphor, assa-fetida, &c.

THIRD EXPERIMENT.

We mixed pulverized assa-fetida with honey, and put it at the entrance of a hive; but this substance whose odor is insupportable to us, did not appear to annoy the bees; they took greedily all the honey which was in contact with the extraneous molecules; they did not seek to withdraw, did not vibrate their wings, and of the mixture they left only the particles of assa-fetida.

FOURTH EXPERIMENT.

I placed some camphor at the entrance of a hive, and I noticed that the bees, both in coming home and going to the field, turned aside in the air to avoid passing directly over this material. I attracted some with honey upon a card; while their trunks were all dipped into the honey, I brought the camphor towards their mouths and all took flight. They flew about some time in my cabinet, and at last settled beside the honey; while they were sucking it with their trunks, I threw fragments of camphor into it; they receded a little, still keeping the end of the trunk in the honey, and we observed that they first took that which was not covered with camphor. One of them vibrated her wings while feeding, others agitated them seldom and others not at all. Wishing to see what a greater quantity of camphor would cause, I covered the honey entirely with it, and the bees took flight instantly. I carried the card to my hives, to ascertain whether other bees would be less attracted by the odor of the honey than repulsed by the odor of the camphor; and I also placed pure honey within their reach on another card; the latter was soon discovered and the honey consumed in a few minutes. An hour elapsed before a single worker approached the cam-phorated card; at length one or two bees alighted upon it and thrust their trunks into the edge of the drop of honey. Their number gradually aug-mented, and two hours after it was covered by them, all the honey was carried off and only the camphor remained, on the card.

These experiments prove that although camphor displeases bees, their attraction to honey destroys the effect of this repugnance, and that there are odors which repel them without vitiating the air.

A great number of experiments convinced me also that the influence of odors on the nervous system of bees is incomparably more active in a closed vessel than in the open air; of this I will cite but one example.

I knew already that the odor of spirits of wine was disagreeable to them, and that they vibrated their wings to get rid of it; but I had not yet made this test in a closed vessel.

FIFTH EXPERIMENT.

I put spirits of wine in a small glass under a receiver, I left it uncov-ered so that this liquid could evaporate; but arranged it so that the bees could not fall into it, in case they fell upon the glass; I then gave honey to a bee and when she had enough I placed her under the receiver; she traveled about in every direction, trying to escape; for an hour she did nothing but vibrate her wings and seek an exit; I then perceived a continuous tremor of her legs, trunk and wings; she soon lost the ability of standing on her legs, lay supine, and we saw her move in a singular manner; advancing on the table in this position, using the four wings like oars or feet, and all the honey swallowed, before exposure to the vapor of the spirit of wine, was disgorged by her at different times. As water, by combining with the spirit of wine might destroy its effect and bring about the recovery of this bee, I immersed her twice in cold water; the bath benefited her without giving her any strength; vinegar appeared to revive her, but its effect was not sustained and she soon perished.

House flies and wood bugs also lost their life when exposed to similar effluvia; but a large spider sustained the test without appearing affected.

SIXTH EXPERIMENT.

As the poison of the bee exhales a penetrating odor, I was curious to ascertain its effects upon the bees themselves; this experiment yielded a lively result.

We took with pincers the sting of a bee with its appendages saturated with poison; we presented this object to worker bees which were resting in a tranquil state before their entrance; emotion instantly spread in the little throng; none fled away, but two or three darted against the sting, and another wrathfully attacked us. It was not the threatening apparatus of this experiment, however, which had irritated them; for when the poison had coagulated on the point of the sting, and on its appendages, we could offer it to them with impunity; they did not seem to notice it. The following experiment proves still better that the odor of the poison alone is sufficient to anger them.

We placed a few bees in a glass tube closed only at one end; we rendered them half torpid, so that they might not escape at the open end. They were gradually revived by the heat of the sun. They were afterwards irritated by touching them with the barbs of an ear of wheat; all protruded their sting, upon which appeared drops of poison.

Their first signs of life were therefore demonstrations of anger, and I doubt not that they would have pierced each other or would have rushed upon the observer, had they been at liberty; but they could neither move nor escape against my wishes from the tube.

I took them out one by one with pincers, and confined them within a receiver, that my experiment might not be disturbed. They had left in the tube a disagreeable odor, that of the poison darted against its inner walls. I presented its open extremity to groups of bees in front of their hive. They became agitated as soon as they smelled the odor of the poison, but this emotion was not that of fear; they testified their anger in the same manner as on the former trial.

Thus, certain odors not only act physically, but have a moral influence upon them.

Here doubtless commences a series of sensations of a particular class, eluding our researches, and of which we can form but a confused idea; animals possess a sort of superiority over us in this regard. What varieties of impressions are produced by smell on the hunting dog! A sense developed to so high a degree awakening in its imagination ideas of fear, anger or love, instructs the animal upon anything which may affect its security, its inclinations or its industry.

In accounting for the conduct of insects in some circumstances, we must appreciate the influence of different sensations, which without drawing them out of their natural sphere, combine with their habits and momentarily modify them.

Certain odors, or too high a temperature, impel the bees to flight; but if some other cause, such as the attraction of honey, acts in a contrary sense and induces them to remain, they know how to preserve their present enjoyment, and shelter themselves from disagreeable sensations, by agitating the air about them. Retained in their hive by all the attractions which nature has there combined for them, and unable to withdraw from the mephitic gas, without abandoning their young and their amassed stores, bees have recourse to the ingenious means of ventilation, for the renewal of air.

But why do not all the bees which are affected in the same manner, vibrate their wings at the same time? To what can we ascribe the general tranquility of the swarm, when a few individuals are occupied in procuring a salubrious atmosphere? Are there sensations of a sufficiently subtile nature to warn them that their turn has come to vibrate their wings?

We cannot suppose only a portion of them affected by a cause which has no operation on the greatest number; but perhaps this depends upon a temporary more or less favorable disposition.

We have seen all the bees of a hive vibrating their wings at once, when the air of their hive, too tightly enclosed, was not renewed at their will; but so urgent a case does not occur in a state of nature, and we usually see but a small number of bees occupied with ventilation.

Insects of the same species, although excited by the same causes, are not usually affected in so uniform a manner, that we may not perceive differences in the result of experiments to which they are submitted.

Some are influenced more promptly than others, as circumstances or occupations render them more or less sensitive, and it is only when the cause is carried to an extreme degree that we see its action in full force.

Thus it may be that as soon as a certain number of ventilating bees have succeeded in bringing the air to sufficient purity; the others, not experiencing the sensation of its impurity to an equal extent, abstain from vibrating their wings and yield to more pressing occupations. Should the number of ventilating bees momentarily diminish, the first workers that would experience the alteration of the air would begin to ventilate, and their number would increase, until their united exertions restored to this element the degree of purity essential to the breathing of so many thousands of individuals.

Such is the mode which we conceive of the establishment of this perpetual chain of ventilating bees; for no communication is observed between them. This hypothesis presumes a very delicate organization in the bees; it is evident that the continuation of their life, depending upon the care with which they renew the air, they must be provided with senses sufficiently subtile to detect the smallest alteration in the fluid which they breathe.

The air may lose many degrees of its purity, before we are aware of it, though proving very noxious to our health; but nature has not placed us in circumstances similar to those of the bees, and we should never need to provide for the inconveniences of confined air, if we did not depart from the conditions adapted to our physical constitution.

CHAPTER X.

Researches Upon the Use of the Antennæ in Some Complicated Operations of Bees.

We have examined the general relation of the senses of bees, to objects of immediate utility; but it is very probable that the sphere of their activity is not restricted to distinguishing odors and the substances they have to collect; the act of gathering and using those materials is only one branch of the history of bees; their conduct as a great society whose prosperity depends upon more or less variable elements, should offer civil connections, so to speak, between all the members of the swarm.

Their senses must undoubtedly have a large share in the operations resulting from this state of things. It is essential to determine by experiments what degree of influence should be ascribed to them in the developments where instinct appears adapted to the most complicated circumstances.

One of the facts which appear the most deserving of meditation and research, is the formation of a queen in a hive that has lost its own by accident. If we take time to consider what an operation it is, for insects, to promote one of their brood to a different destiny from that which was intended, we are astonished at the hardihood of the undertaking; whether the worker be aware or not of the result to be secured in changing the food and the form of the cell destined for a royal worm, her conduct certainly displays a refinement of instinct, of which we could not believe an insect capable.

In given circumstances, though very rarely, the colony runs the danger of speedy destruction, by losing its queen; nature instructs the bees to avert so dire a disaster, by lavishing upon some worker larvæ the attentions which are usually reserved for royal larvæ. These attentions produce the desired effect; but how are the bees induced to do this; how can the absence of a queen guide them to so complex, so remarkable a proceeding, as choosing larvæ of the proper age to fulfill the purpose to be secured?

Did the absence of the queen alone produce these effects, we should observe them constructing new cells immediately after her disappearance; but on the contrary, when we remove a queen from her native hive, the bees at first do not seem to miss her; the work of every kind advances, order and tranquility are uninterrupted; it is only an hour after the departure of the queen that disquiet commences to be manifested among the workers; the care of the young no longer seems to occupy them; they go back and forth with activity; yet these first symptoms of agitation are not felt throughout the hive at once. They originate on a single portion of a comb; the disturbed bees soon quit their little circle, and when meeting their companions, the antennæ are reciprocally crossed and they strike them lightly. The bees receiving the blow of the antennæ become agitated in their turn, and carry trouble and confusion to other places; the disorder augments in rapid progression, gains the opposite side of the comb, and at length the entire colony; we see the workers then run over the combs, rush against each other, hurry to the entrance and impetuously depart from the hive; they scatter about, go in and out repeatedly; the buzzing is very great within the hive, increasing with the agitation of the bees; it lasts two or three hours, seldom four or five, but never longer.

What impression may cause and stop this effervescence; why do the bees recover gradually their natural state and resume interest in all that seemed to have become indifferent to them? Why does a spontaneous action recall them to their young which they had abandoned for some hours? And whence comes the inducement afterwards to visit the larvæ of different ages and to select among them some to be reared to the dignity of queens?

If we examine this hive twenty-four hours after the departure of the common mother, we see that the bees have been working to repair their loss; we will readily distinguish those of their brood which they intend to rear as queens, yet their form has not been altered, but those cells, which are always of the smaller diameter, are already distinguished by the quantity of pap in them, which infinitely exceeds the portion in the cells of worker larvæ. It follows that, from this profusion of food, the selected larvæ intended to replace their queen, instead of being lodged at the bottom of the cells in which they were born, are now brought very near to the orifice.

It is probably for that purpose that the bees accumulate the pap behind them; and place them on this high bed; this is evidenced by the fact that this large bed of pap is not necessary for their food, for we still find it in the cell after the worm has descended into the pyramidal prolongation by which the workers terminate its abode.

We may therefore know what larvæ are destined for queens, by the aspect of the cells occupied by them, even previous to their enlargement and their change into a pyramidal shape. From this observation it was easy to ascertain, at the end of twenty-four hours whether the bees had resolved to replace their queen. Among the great number of mysteries which surround this great trait of their instinct, there is one which I hoped to discover and which would appear to lead to the clearing of other points equally obscure.

It had always seemed difficult to explain how the bees ascertain the absence of their queen, when she has been removed, for those that are placed in the far corners or even only on the other side of the comb upon which she was, should not take note of her disappearance; yet it was evident, from previous observations, that within an hour they were all informed of it; that this condition caused sadness among them, that they manifested a great agitation and appeared to seek for the object of their solicitude.

How, then, did they make sure of the loss of their queen? Was it by means of smell or by feeling; should we attribute to some unknown sense the discovery of the critical condition of the colony, or must we suppose that these insects can communicate to one another, through some signs, such important information? I did not wish to conjecture upon a question which experience and observation might decide.

When I was called upon to remove a queen, I perceived that this could not be done without causing agitation among the bees; in such an operation one is always compelled to open the hive and consequently throw upon the combs the light of day and outside air which differs much in temperature from that of their hive. There is no resistance from the bees when we put out the hand to seize the queen, but the bees surrounding her might be affected by this removal: in order to dispel all doubts and all exciting circumstances I employed a process which would leave no uncertainty.

I divided the hive into two equal parts by means of a grated partition; this was done with so much celerity and care that no disturbance was noticed at the time of this operation, and that not a single bee was wounded. The bars of this grating were too close for passage of the bees from one to the other side; but admitted the free circulation of air in all parts of the hive. I did not know which half contained the queen, but the tumult and the buzzing in N° 1 soon apprized me that she was in N° 2, where tranquility prevailed. I then closed the entrances of both, so that the bees seeking their queen should not find her, but I made sure that outside air should continue to circulate in the hives.

At the end of two hours the bees calmed and order was restored.

On the 14th, we visited hive N° 1 and found 3 royal cells begun. On the 15th we opened the entrances of both hives; the bees went to the field and we noticed that they did not mix, upon their return, and that those of each half kept to their respective hives. On the 24th we found two dead queens at the entrance of hive N° 1, and in examining the combs we found the young queen that had killed them. On the 30th, she emerged from the hive and was fecundated and thenceforth the success of the swarm was assured.

The apertures which I had preserved in the partition allowed the bees of hive N° 1 to communicate with their old queen by means of smell, hearing or any unknown sense; they were separated from her only by a space not exceeding a third or a fourth of an inch, which they could not pass, yet they had become agitated, had constructed royal cells and reared young queens, therefore they had conducted themselves just as if their queen had been truly taken away and lost to them forever. This observation proves that it is not by means of sight, hearing or smell that the bees notice the presence of their queen; another sense is necessary; but since the grating used in this occasion had only removed the contact with her, is it not probable that they must touch her with their antennæ in order to make sure of her presence among them, and that it is through the use of this organ that the feeling of their combs, of their companions, of their brood and of their queen is communicated to them?

However in order to obtain complete satisfaction on this point, it was necessary to know whether the bees would become agitated in case the meshes of the grating were of such condition as to allow them to pass their antennæ into the part in which the queen was confined.

For this purpose we removed a pane from one of my glass hives and substituted a box of equal dimension, closed on the hive side with a grating that would not enable them to pass their heads through, but would allow the passage of the antennæ. The other side of the box was closed by a movable glass partition.

As we did not wish to excite the bees, instead of opening the hive to remove the queen, we waited until she placed herself on a comb in view; we then opened the glass partition and took her from among her escort without alarming them. She was immediately confined in the glass box destined to receive her; but in order that she might not suffer from a condition so different from what she had been accustomed to, some bees of the same hive were enclosed with her, from which she received the ordinary care.

We remarked from the first that the distress commonly following the departure or loss of the queen was not manifested in this occasion; everything remained in order; the bees did not forsake their brood a single instant; their labors were not interrupted; and when we opened the hive, 48 hours later, we did not find any royal cells begun; the bees had made no arrangements to procure another queen. Thus all the bees knew that they had no need to replace her, that she was not lost, and when we returned her to them they did not treat her as a stranger, but seemed to recognize her at once and we saw her lay eggs in the midst of a surrounding circle of workers.

The means of communication with the queen that these bees employed were very remarkable; an infinite number of antennæ thrust through the screen and turning in all directions plainly indicated that the workers were concerned about their mother; she acknowledged their eagerness in the most decided manner; she was nearly always fixed on the grating, crossing her antennæ with those so evidently seeking her; the bees attempted to pull her through; their legs passed through the meshes seized those of the queen and firmly held them; we even saw their trunks introduced through the meshes so that she was fed by her subjects from within the hive.

How can we doubt, after this, that the queen and the workers preserved a communication by the mutual touch of the antennæ, and that, knowing she was so near, the latter felt that there was no necessity of providing another queen.

It seems impossible now to assert that her odor had indicated her presence to the bees; however in order to acquire additional evidence I repeated the same expriment by enclosing the queen so that her odor only could reach them.

I took the queen of one of my leaf hives and had her introduced into a box composed of a double screen the meshes of which were too distant for the operation of the antennæ; the result was such as we had foreseen; after an hour of quiet the bees became agitated, abandoned their labors and their young, emerged from the hive and afterwards returned, and tranquility was restored after two or three hours. On the day following, we examined the combs and recognized the rudiments of eight or ten royal cells, which had been commenced the preceding evening; demonstrating that the bees had believed their queen lost, though she was among them. Her emanations, therefore, had not been sufficient to undeceive them; they required actual contact with her to be assured of her presence.

But since every bee cannot be in all parts of the hive, we must admit likewise that they communicate their disquiet to each other and labor in common to repair their loss.

If we could still be in doubt about the part that touch fills in the labors of the hive and the intercommunications of these insects, it would only be necessary to read the following experiments. Those which we had attempted upon the antennæ of the queen will be recollected. The amputation of a single one of those organs brought no change in their behavior, but when both antennæ were cut off at their base, those beings so privileged, those mothers so much the object of consideration in their homes lost all their influence, even the instinct of maternity disappeared; instead of laying their eggs in the cells they dropped them here and there, they forgot their mutual hate, queens deprived of their antennæ passed by one another without recognizing each other, and the workers themselves seemed to participate in their indifference, as if nothing but the agitation of the queen had warned them of the danger to the colony.

It was no less interesting to learn the moral effect of the amputation of the antennæ upon drones and workers: for this purpose we mutilated two hundred workers and three hundred drones; the former being released at once re-entered the hive, but we noticed that they did not climb upon the combs and that they no longer shared in the common household duties; they pertinaciously remained in the lower part of the hive which received light from the entrance; light alone seemed to attract them; they soon emerged from the hive and returned no more.

The same effects were produced upon the males by the amputation of the antennæ; they likewise returned to the hive, but could not find the internal passages; they rushed towards the open shutter where the light was admitted and sought an exit there. We saw some of them begging for food from the workers, but in vain, they could no longer direct their proboscis, carrying it awkwardly upon their head or their thorax, thus obtaining no relief; when we closed the shutter, they rushed out of the hive although it was 6 o'clock, when no males issued from other hives. Thus their departure was to be ascribed to the loss of that sense which guides them in darkness.

We have stated that the deprivation of a single antenna produced no perceptible effect upon the instinct of a queen; neither had it any influence upon the males or the workers. The amputation of a small part of this organ did not impair their faculty of recognizing objects, for we saw them remain in the hive and pursue their usual labors. Therefore the conduct of the bees deprived of their antennæ cannot be ascribed to pain, it must be due to the impossibility for them to guide themselves in obscurity and communicate with the other members of the colony.

Weight is added to these conjectures by the fact that bees use their antennæ particularly in the night; to ascertain this it is only necessary to watch their actions by the light of the moon, when they watch at the entrance of their hive to prevent the entrance of moths then flying about; it is curious to observe how artfully the moth profits of the disadvantage of the bees which require much light for seeing objects, and the tactics used by the latter to recognize and drive away so dangerous an enemy; vigilant sentinels, the bees roam around their entrance, their antennæ always stretched forward, directed alternately to the right and to the left. Woe to the moth if it does not manage to escape their contact: it tries to glide along between them, carefully avoiding the touch of this flexible organ, as if aware that its safety depended upon this caution. We do not wish to assert that these insects possess the sense of hearing, yet we acknowledge that we have often been tempted to believe it.

Bees watching during night at the entrance of their hive often produce a short, light rustling sound; but if a strange insect, or any enemy happens to touch their antennæ, the guard is aroused, the sound assumes a different character from that produced by the bees while buzzing or in flight, and the enemy is assailed by several workers coming from the inside.

Should we strike the alighting board of a hive, the bees at once put their wings in motion; but if we breathe through a cleft of the hive they inhabit, we hear some of them produce with their wings sharp and interrupted sounds, and we then observe other workers in agitation directing themselves towards the side where the air has entered.

These observations seem to correspond with the effect of the queen's song, in leading us to admit a sense in bees analogous to hearing. Yet it must be observed that sounds which are not relative to their instinct produce no noticeable effect upon them.

Thunder, the discharge of firearms, do not seem to affect them. Thus the sense of hearing, if it exists in these small beings, is differently modified from the same sense among beings of a higher order.

We shall then restrict ourselves to observing that certain sounds produced by bees apparently serve as a signal to their companions, and are followed by fairly regular effects: these additional means of communication may be added to those afforded by the antennæ.

This memoir appears to give sufficient proofs of the existence of a language among these insects; there is nothing repugnant to the idea of a language among beings whose instinct is as developed as that of bees, whose life is very active, whose conduct is compounded of a thousand circumstances, and which, living together in great numbers, cannot share their respective labors, or aid each other properly without the means of mutual communication.

This observation applies to all insects that live in association, as well as those large animals whose existence is subjected to similar conditions.

CONFIRMATION OF SCHIRACH'S DISCOVERY.

Perhaps it may seem extraordinary to recur to facts with which we have already entertained our readers in the first volume, and apparently corroborated by our own observations. But those mentioned in the fourth letter are of such great importance in the history of bees and animal physiology, that the reader will not be unwilling to have us speak of them here with more thoroughness than at first; and, besides the interest of truth, we must take the defence of a faithful observer, to whom the science of bees is indebted for its greatest progress, and whose reputation has recently been so outrageously assailed by an Italian writer.

For a long time it was affirmed, as a fact beyond doubt, that worker bees had no sex. The observations of Swammerdam reduced them to the condition of neuters. Réaumur and Maraldi concurred in this opinion; most of the writers had ranked them in a distinct order; but Schirach's discoveries began to sap the foundations of this opinion.

By repeated experiments he proved that bees at all times can procure a queen, when their own is removed, if they have comb of common cells containing larvæ three days old. Hence he concluded that worker bees were of the female sex, and that nothing but certain physical conditions, such as a special food and a more spacious lodging, was needed for them to become real queens.

Views so adverse to those generally entertained were received with enthusiasm on the one hand and with distrust on the other; it was not denied that bees could procure a queen when they had brood of all ages, since Schirach had secured this result in numerous experiments, made with care, in the presence of worthy and intelligent persons; but the conversion of a worker worm into a royal larva was denied. They asserted that there must be some royal eggs in worker cells and that it was such eggs that the bees confined by Mr. Schirach had promoted to the royal rank; vainly did he repeat his experiments, vainly did he oppose the improbability of such a supposition, the objection remained in full force: although aided by the best microscopes he could perceive no difference between the larvæ from which he could produce at will either a queen or a worker.

Mr. Schirach, anxiously desirous of the support of a great philosopher, wrote several letters to Mr. Bonnet, in which he described his discovery with such details as should have secured his assistance; but he found in him a zealous supporter of the views of Réaumur, and it was only after sending him numerous evidences of the correctness of his assertions that he finally succeeded in weakening his opinion; but he nevertheless did not succeed in convincing him fully.

Being requested by Mr. Bonnet to repeat the experiments of the Lusatian observer, I recognized the correctness of his assertions; I added new developments and gave very strong proofs of the disputed conversion, but I felt with him that the establishment of such important facts rested upon the material demonstration of the sex of the workers; I was still in hopes of some day solving this great question.

The discovery of fertile workers, by Mr. Riem, confirmed by my own observations, led me to anticipate that the whole class of workers belong to the female sex. Nature does nothing by leaps: fertile workers lay none but male eggs, in this resembling queens whose fecundation has been retarded; advancing another step, they may remain absolutely sterile, while none the less females originally. I could not admit the worker bees to be monsters or imperfect beings; too many marvels are the result of their instinct and of their organization to consider them as the outcasts of the species, or as imperfect bees when compared with the queens; it seemed to me that an enlightened philosophy might conciliate all these difficulties.

Nothing is more repugnant to reason than the hypothesis of an actual transformation; all those that were formerly admitted by credulity have been reduced by the observations of the great anatomists of the 16th and 17th centuries, to simple developments still more admirable. At first view the following question seems to indicate the idea of transformation. Will the worm that is to hatch from this egg become a prodigiously prolific queen, unfit for any of the work observed among the bees, or will it become a sterile worker, capable of the greatest industry? These two modes of existence exclude one another. The worker has organs appropriate to her destination which the queen who gave her birth does not possess; strong jaws, a palet and pincers of peculiar shape, which we have described, wax organs, a longer tongue, wings proportionately longer, &c. Although the queen possesses the same organs, they are modified in such way as to be unable to fulfill the functions of workers. As long as we see fit to suppose that in order to convert a worker larva into a queen larva we must admit an exchange of these organs, we shall consider such a conversion impossible, and we will be correct. If, as I presume, these two beings are identical originally and have similar individuality, we may readily believe that they are as likely to produce a queen as a worker bee. Some will say that the queen was in the egg and that a peculiar circumstance has made a worker of her; others may equally assert that the worker was the original insect from which the queen has been produced through some modifications, for we cannot avoid thinking that the faculties and organs peculiar to the common bee pre-exist their development. We are then bound to conclude that this being which as yet is neither worker nor queen; that the worm, before three days elapse, contains alike the germs of the insect which shall prove industrious, and of the insect susceptible of fecundity; the germs of the organs of the two beings, the instinct of the common bee and that of the queen not developed, but capable of being so, according to the direction given by the circumstances of its rearing. In the one case the productive faculties will be repressed or will remain undeveloped; in the other the same thing will happen with the industrial faculties.

Perhaps between these two extremes, will nature present some mixed beings, participating of the essence of queens and of the qualities of workers; and hence the fertile common bees observed by Needham. It is easier to conceive how certain faculties and their corresponding organs may be annihilated, than how they may be spontaneously created; it is on this that my explanation is founded.

However, I wish to anticipate an objection that might be raised against this theory: how can we explain the opposite instincts of the workers and the queen, in the same hive, in relation to other queens; for the workers entertain a kind of love for their mother, and render her the most assiduous attention, whereas queens are animated towards each other by the most implacable hate?

But do we know in what degree any sensation may be developed in insects by circumstances? I shall cite but one example, published in the transactions of the Linnean Society of London (6th volume). It is known that there are three sorts of individuals among the humblebees as among the domestic bees. In one of these republics which we observed, some very remarkable facts happened; several of the workers which, until a certain epoch, had lived in the best intelligence with the mother of the colony, having become fertile, they exhibited symptoms of the most violent jealousy; some fell victims to the rage of others, and we saw the principal female perish by the stings of the workers which she had produced; therefore, if such rivalry may arise among workers after they become fertile; if their affection for their companions and for their mother may in an instant change into hatred, the objection that we might draw from the different instinct of queens and of workers, the strongest that may be urged against their primitive identity, is reduced to its proper value; such a trait shows us that the germ of passions is only waiting for its development until circumstances harmonize with them; after this who will deny the mobility of instinct?

My conjectures regarding the sex of workers at length received the most unexpected confirmation; a singular fact, which was a striking example of the possible modification in bees, led us into researches the results of which appear of the utmost importance.

HISTORY OF SOME BLACK BEES.

In 1809, we remarked something peculiar in the treatment of certain bees by their companions at the entrance of their hive. On the 20th of June, a cluster of workers attracted our attention; the bees composing it were so irritated that we durst not separate them; night approaching prevented us from ascertaining the cause of this assemblage; but on the subsequent days, we frequently observed bees occupied in defending the entrance of the same hive against some individuals whose external appearance was absolutely similar to that of ordinary workers, a few of them were seized: their difference consisted only in color, they were less downy on the thorax and abdomen, which gave them a blacker aspect; but as to the limbs, antennæ, jaws, body and size, the whole external form presented perfect resemblance to common bees.

Each day we saw some of these black bees at the entrance of the hive; it was evident that the workers expelled them; they had combats in which the ordinary worker always had the better; she soon killed her adversary or reduced it to such a state of weakness that it could not resist: she then would carry it off in her teeth to a great distance from the hive. We caught a number of the black bees and introduced them into a vase; but they speedily darted upon each other and were reciprocally killed; others were confined in a glass sand-box with workers from the same hive; but no sooner had the latter observed them than they were attacked and destroyed.

Each day we noticed a greater number of these proscribed bees; once driven from their native hive they never returned; so that when the sting spared them they perished of hunger.

This singular scene continued during the whole remaining part of the good season; sometimes the black bees did not appear to be so cruelly treated by the workers; and they seemed modified a little from the former; their hate had lessened and they did not repeat their mutual encounters; but the rigor of the common bees soon resumed against them, and they were again expelled.

We were not able to ascertain whether all the brood of this hive was attacked by the malady, or by the peculiar condition which rendered them odious to their companions, and as we saw their number augment successively for several weeks, we had cause to fear that the entire offspring of the queen was affected. But at the end of September, black bees were no longer noticed; the colony had apparently suffered from the exile of so many individuals; it was weaker than previously; yet we were encouraged as to the condition of the colony when we satisfied ourselves that the queen had not lost the faculty of laying eggs which produced workers perfect in every particular.

From the month of April of the following year, we watched this colony and did not see a single black bee appear; the increase of workers was so great as to make us hope that it would swarm; but it did not happen that year (1810); we were then fully convinced that this anomaly, whatever it be, had affected only a part of the eggs of this queen.

Several other questions presented themselves here; was the queen entirely cured of this disposition to produce monstrous individuals? Was this vice hereditary? What would be the consequences upon the queens produced from her?

Observation taught us that she was not cured without relapse; for in 1811; that is two years after the birth of the black bees observed, others appeared in great numbers, in the same circumstances, and under the same character; lastly in the past year of 1812, this hive cast a fine swarm: as the old queen always follows the first swarm, we were not long in noticing defective bees at the entrance of her habitation.

But it was more singular still to witness the same phenomenon in both hives at once; the old one had swarmed on the 3d of June, and on the 2d of July we noticed defective bees at the entrance, which evidently could not belong to the brood of the queen that had passed into the new hive[17] and this fact convinced us that the trouble was hereditary in her race.[18]

This subject is only sketched here, our aim being to arouse the attention of observers, in order to obtain a combination of facts necessary to complete the history of the defective bees.

The desire of discovering the cause of the extermination of the black bees, led me to examine whether there was anything internal or external that would indicate a development of sexual organs in them; for I conceived that if they were real females, they might disquiet the common bees in respect to their queen, and that perhaps it was to protect her against such rivals that they expelled them from the hive.

There was but one way to discover whether there was any ground for my suspicions, it was to dissect these bees with particular care. I had no one near me nor in my family with enough experience in the difficult art of dissection to fulfill my views; such researches required extensive knowledge and great dexterity: but I remembered with gratitude what I already owed to the friendship and complaisance of a young lady who was alike distinguished by the combination of rare qualities, of striking virtue, of superior talent, who directing her ability in a manner corresponding with the tastes of a beloved father to whom several sciences are indebted, had devoted to natural history her leisure and all the gifts which she had received from nature; she was as expert in painting the picture of insects

---

[17] Such bees could easily be from that queen.

[18] This year (1813) we have again seen some black bees maltreated at the entrances of both of these hives, but in small number.

and of their most delicate parts, as to discover the secrets of their organs; being at the same time a rival of Lyonnet and of Mérian: such was the one whom we were to lose so soon, such was she whose loss natural history was to regret for so many reasons, and who, shortly before that fatal time displayed her talent through discoveries that had escaped Swammerdam and Réaumur. It was to Miss Jurine that I entrusted the important research in which so many anatomists had failed, the finding of organs that were to furnish evidence of a still unknown truth.

The first point was to discover whether the defective bees exhibited in their structure any difference from the common workers; Miss Jurine proceeded upon this research with her peculiar sagacity.

The exterior appearance of those bees indicated nothing to her that we had not already noticed; excepting, as had occurred to ourselves, a less quantity of down upon the corslet, she found no difference between them and the common bees; similar shape of thorax, head and abdomen; the legs, the jaws, formed in the same shape, same length in all the parts; complete external identity.

But when this expert naturalist extended her researches farther and removed the outer teguments of the black bees, after spreading apart the muscles and properly preparing the internal parts of the body of these bees, she discovered two very distinct ovaries, in which no eggs were perceptible indeed, but analogous in substance and form to the ovaries of queens, though more difficult to distinguish; we show the figure of them, on plate XI (aa) made by the same hand that dissected those bees; it also shows the sting (c), the poison sack (d), and a part of the spinal marrow (b).

At first we concluded that a solution of the question had been obtained; we did not anticipate that this would lead us to a more important discovery which was to overturn our conjectures as to the cause of the persecution of the black bees; but which would unveil a mystery long sought by the naturalists.

As Miss Jurine was desirous of carrying farther the comparison between the defective workers and the common bees, she dissected some of the latter with the same care and in the same manner, and she ascertained that all the workers had ovaries which had escaped the scalpel and the microscope of Swammerdam: this discovery was principally due to the precaution which the Dutch naturalist had probably not taken, but which was very important, of keeping the open abdomen of the bee for two days in brandy; the advantage of this process is to give greater opacity to these transparent membranes which would otherwise be blended with the fluids. Miss Jurine dissected a great number of bees taken at random at the entrance of a hive and found in all of them ovaries formed like those of the black bees: she exhibited them to her father who assured us that they could even be distinguished with the naked eye.

Thus the existence of those black bees led us to a discovery the importance of which will be appreciated by all those who have followed the progress and the vicissitudes of the history of bees, and by all those who have read the objections which Schirach's antagonists opposed to his theory; which objections were based upon the supposed absence of ovaries in the workers.

Thus the theory of neuters among bees vanishes, and the organization of those insects that have so excited our admiration exhibits one of the most remarkable physiological phenomena.[19]

The system which we have thus established on a solid foundation must extend to all insects, among which neuters have been observed; that is bumblebees, wasps and ants, for according to the observation of a great naturalist, the more important an organ in the animal economy, the more general must be its existence.

We will now examine whether this rule permits exceptions in the present case, or whether we again find here the uniformity observed in other works of creation.

We could not decide on the sex of the whole species from the fertility of a few, until we discovered the ovaries of worker bees; but since these two peculiarities are co-existent in the bees, wherever one shall manifest itself under the same circumstances, the existence of the other may be presumed from analogy.

According to Riem's observations, there are sometimes fertile workers in the hives, but those individuals never lay except the eggs of males.

I believe I have given evidence of this fact in the former part of this work, and I have shown also the cause to which we should ascribe their existence: a nutriment resembling that which is given to the queens produces this remarkable change in their constitution. It would be of the greatest interest to observe in details the actions of those half-fertile bees, of those females whose external characters are the same as those of the workers; but the smallness of their number renders this almost impossible; perhaps if we should rear some in a box similar to that which Schirach used for producing queens, and if we removed the royal cells in time, we might observe their habits amidst a very few workers; we have not yet attempted this but it is one of the things which we propose to execute as soon as the season becomes favorable; at the same time we may examine whether the fecundation of workers is attended by the same circumstances as that of queens; all these researches are important in the history of bees, and that of the generation and the development of the faculties and of the organs in the insects. It is necessary to show that this phenomenon recurs in the entire class of insects that live in association. In the memoir already mentioned, we explained the existence of fertile workers in the bumblebees; we described the jealousy awakened in these individuals by the sentiment of maternity, their rivalry, their anger and all the details of their laying. In comparing these small mothers with the true females, we found no difference except in their size; but having been unable to discover whether the fertile workers had a progeny of both sexes, we later engaged in researches which gain in importance by their connection with the actions of the fertile workers among domestic bees.

We established a nest of red and black bumblebees (hemoroidalis Lin.)

---

[19] Mr. Cuvier says that the oviduct of queens has a vesicle and a long canal; and numerous chaplets on each side; "I observed," said he, "very small ones in the neuter bees, which would confirm the idea that they are undeveloped females."—Lessons on Comparative Anatomy, Vol. V, page 198.

in an ordinary box, in a window; we soon perceived that the mother of the colony was not the only fertile bee; the motion and agitation of these bees every afternoon, their rivalry, their laying, demonstrated it; it would have seemed easy to ascertain the result of their fecundity, but it was necessary to avoid a certain possibility, which would lead us into error.

The mother bee often laid eggs in the same cells as the workers: so it was not possible to ascertain which individuals were produced by the one or the others, without completely separating them: we used the following process, which succeeded fully.

A fragment containing no brood was detached from the nest and placed in an open box at the spot where the bumblebees were accustomed to retire into their nest: and the mother, with a number of the bees were transported with the other portion to a distant window. I calculated upon the bees now foraging in the country to people the portion wanting inhabitants. In fact they did so and lodged themselves upon the isolated fragment which had been substituted for combs and brood, although they appeared to notice the change. I was in hopes that some of these workers might prove fertile, nor was my expectation disappointed, for in the afternoon of the same day in which we made this artificial swarm, the workers prepared a cell for receiving their eggs and I saw several of them lay. The number of eggs multiplied daily; larvæ were soon hatched, transformed into nymphs, which at the end of a month became bumblebees. I observed these individuals with the greatest care and all were males.

These males were in every respect similar to those originating from the laying of a female; they were equally large and colored in the same manner. I had selected the red and black bumblebees for this experiment because their males are more readily distinguished than those of any other species, having bands of green hairs upon the thorax and a spot of similar color on the front; so I could not be mistaken regarding this fact, and I can affirm that neither worker nor female was produced in this nest while the other had as many females as males. Here, therefore, is seen a great analogy with the domestic bees; I must add to this that most of the workers of that nest were fertile, except a few very small ones, at least I did not catch them in the act, but most of the others laid eggs in my sight.

Here is another striking example of the generality of the law which proves that nature does not produce true neuters. Mr. Perrot, who has already furnished to us some interesting facts, permits us to use an observation which supports ours.

Studying a hanging wasp's nest with that scrupulous attention which denotes the genuine naturalist, he saw one of the workers laying eggs several times; he was impatiently awaiting the transformation of those eggs when an accident to the wasp nest prevented him from following their full development, however he became convinced that they were all of the male sex; we will not take the liberty of publishing the interesting facts which enabled him to discover the sex of the workers and of their masculine progeny; but they confirm the relations which exist between bees, bumblebees and wasps.

Ants likewise afford a striking analogy; we have never seen the workers lay but we have witnessed their mating. This fact could be attested by several members of the Geneva Society of Natural History, to whom we exhibited it; the death of the worker always follows the approaches of the male; therefore their conformation does not permit of their becoming mothers, but the instinct of the male proves them to be females.

All these facts concur in demonstrating that there are no neuters in this class of insects, which would interrupt the continuity of nature, for I do not know that they exist in any other kind: in other beings we sometimes see both sexes conjoined in one individual, but neuters seem monstrous and adverse to nature.

Who will be able to explain the singular peculiarity that the workers of insects in a republic lay none but the eggs of males, when they are fertile? Who can account for such a fact? They have ovaries similar to those of the queens or the mothers that gave them birth, yet they possess only a semi-fertility; it is no easier to conceive why the queens that have been impregnated later than three weeks after their birth produce only male eggs. Doubtless there is a connection between these two facts.[20]

If we accept the opinion of a great physiologist, the seminal liquid is but a special stimulant acting upon the germs as a very substantial food suitable for their development; Mr. Bonnet, in trying to explain Schirach's theory, used the following hypothesis, he writes: "I have established on apparently solid evidence, that the seminal liquid is a nourishing fluid and a stimulant, I have shown how it is able to produce the greatest changes in the interior part of the embryos; therefore it does not appear impossible that a certain and more abundant food should cause the development, in the larvæ of bees, of organs that could never have developed without it; it is unimportant that this particular food should reach the organs through the intestines or by another route, it is sufficient that it has the property of extending them: it is for those organs an appropriate fecundation just as efficacious as that which gives birth to the animal itself."

Is it impossible that this kind of food, so substantial and so different from what is received by the common larvæ, being administered too late or too sparingly to the larvæ originating near the royal cells, may have consequences similar to the retarded fecundation of queens? Have not the fibres of the ovaries attained too great rigidity, to permit the development of some of the eggs, when the semen of the male, or the royal pap does not produce enough energy to act in the opposite way and destroy the equilibrium? While giving these conjectures, I do not pretend to explain everything, I feel that they may be overthrown as well as defended, but I have thought best to suggest them, as they may open a new path to the meditations and the experiments of physiologists.

The sex of worker bees having been demonstrated as clearly as it is possible to do, we will investigate the reproaches addressed to Mr. Schirach by Mr. Monticelli, a professor of Naples, author of a work entitled: "Of the Treatment of Bees at Favignana." This writer accuses the Dutch

---

[20] Huber almost pointed to parthenogenesis in the above words. The student knows that parthenogenesis was discovered by Dzierzon a few years after Huber's death.—Translator.

philosopher with claiming the discovery of the formation of artificial swarms
and with having borrowed the idea of it from the customs of a small nation
inhabiting a cliff in the Mediterranean, near the coast of Sicily. Schirach
was far from giving himself out as the author of a method practised long
anterior to his own time in the country in which he lived. At all times
practice had preceded theory; it is success which leads to the discovery of
the truths upon which it is founded, and the knowledge of those truths in
its turn insures the wavering advance of the cultivators: assuredly no one
will claim the discovery of the theory which the Lusatian observer had so
much trouble in propagating, which appeared contrary to all accepted notions,
and concerning which Mr. Bonnet, so wise in his opinions, had warned
the members of the Lusatian association not to support the conversion of
worker larvæ in queens for fear of discrediting themselves completely in the
eyes of true naturalists.

It was only the passionate love of truth which led Mr. Schirach and his
supporters to espouse a cause so inauspicious; he describes his discovery
in the following words:

"I was compelled to use a large amount of smoke, for driving bees to
the top of their hive, in order to cut out some brood, on the 12th of May.
They were annoyed by it beyond my wishes; a number escaped from the hive
with the queen without my perceiving it; but my younger daughter who
assisted me in this operation warned me of it and her suspicion proved
correct.

"To hear the plaintive sounds of the bees that had remained in the hive,
one might have concluded that the subjects of this republic were unanimously
mourning the loss of a cherished queen; I sought the neighborhood, the
garden, the vegetable enclosure, even the meadows of the vicinity, without
having the good luck to discover the fugitives; thinking that this swarm was
lost without hope, I resolved to rear a new one by introducing into the hive
a comb containing all three kinds of cells, similar to the one of which I had
just deprived them.

"On the morning of the 13th, I prepared to clean the hives which I had
pruned on the preceding day, and which never failed to carry out the rubbish
during the night. I observed a cluster of bees of the size of an apple on the
support of the hive whose queen had fled. Being astonished at this sight,
I undertook to separate them to look for the lost queen; I did find her, placed
her at the entrance of the hive, and she was immediately surrounded with
bees: their extraordinary concourse, their activity, the pleasant humming
which succeeded their lugubrious sounds indicated that she was indeed their
queen; to make myself still better sure of it, I introduced her into the hive,
which was raised for that purpose. What was my astonishment when
wishing to introduce her among the combs, I saw that the bees remaining
had already outlined and almost finished three royal cells. Struck with the
activity and sagacity of these insects to save themselves from impending
destruction, I was filled with admiration and adored the infinite goodness
of God in the care that he deigns to take to perpetuate his works. Wishing
also to see whether the bees would continue their operations, I removed two
of the cells and left them but the third. The next morning I beheld with
the utmost surprise that they had removed all the food from the third worm

so as to prevent it from forming into a queen; a strange fact; is there anything more surprising, more remote from the simple mechanism? &c."

The discovery of this kind of transformation soon rendered the practice of artificial swarms easier and less expensive. Formerly they thought it necessary to give the bees large combs containing the three kinds of brood; Mr. Schirach showed that its success depended upon a single cell occupied by a worm three days old, and proposed several improvements in the process of swarm formation; but he never thought of claiming the invention of this method. In order to convince ourselves of this, it is only necessary to read a passage of a letter from his brother-in-law, Mr. Willelmi, who was not likely to yield to him on any point:

"Since a long time," he writes to Bonnet, "in these districts they make artificial swarms, in May, as soon as they discover brood in the hive; this method has been much improved by the researches of Mr. Schirach, as shown by the records of our society for the years 1766 and 1767."

The letters from which I have taken these quotations are found in the book of Mr. Schirach entitled "Natural History of the Queen Bee," translated by Blassière. Is it likely that he should have left, in a book translated under his name, authentic evidences of the ancientness of the process of artificial swarms, if he had desired to appropriate that discovery?

The Italian author wishing to gain credit to his country for the discovery of the artificial swarm method, and forgetting that the great community of science is less interested in disputes about inventions than in their utility and the perfecting of them, openly charges Mr. Schirach with borrowing the plan of artificial swarms from Favignana, a distant island where travelers land rarely. A connection between the name given by Columella to the brood of bees (pullus) and that used by the inhabitants of this island (pullo) induces him to believe that the Romans and perhaps the Greeks knew the Favignana method; another connection between the distance to which both Schirach and the inhabitants of this island carry the old hives in the operation of artificial swarming, appears to him as a sufficient demonstration of the plagiarism of the secretary of the Lusatian society: but we must read what he says concerning this matter:

"Urged by the desire of being useful to my fellow-men and especially to the Italians, I have concluded to describe in these memoirs the method by which the natives of Favignana manage the industry of bees; a method very different in several ways from that which is practiced in the Kingdom of Naples, and in the rest of Italy, and which, for this reason, deserves to be made known, especially as it unites the utility of transmigration of bees with the art of producing artificial swarms, known in Europe as the production and invention of Mr. Schirach, although the Favignanese practice it ordinarily in so ancient a manner that they have preserved the latin names in their process; we will thereby have an additional occasion to vindicate the honor of Italy, disparaged upon that point as upon many others, by clever strangers who, while traveling in our country, visiting our libraries, reading our authors, take from our books the finest inventions to adorn their own selves.

"Certainly, whoever shall read these memoirs and shall compare the artificial swarm method of Favignana, with that of Mr. Schirach, will not fail to recognize the origin of the latter in the former, as we shall prove in due time; I must however acknowledge that the Greeks and the Turks of the islands of the Ionian Sea make artificial swarms; which Mr. Schirach may have learned; but as the Favignana method is perfect, and of assured success it is but fair to grant to its inhabitants the honor of having preserved so useful a practice, which required as much perspicacity and thought in our ancestors as it showed correctness of bee observation in what was transmitted to us.

"Mr. Schirach passes among the people beyond the Alps as the inventor of the method of artificial swarms, which is still so noised about in Germany and in the North; the Favignanese knew this before Mr. Schirach and before the invasion of the barbarians; they have still preserved two methods, one of which, greater, more generally used and more perfect, is not known to Mr. Schirach who imitates the second method of the Favignanese, &c."

We shall not repeat all the assertions of this sort with which this work is filled and which indicate that the author did not read Schirach; we shall not even take notice of the darts personally addressed to us by Mr. Monticelli; it is evident that, blinded by national feelings he could not forgive us for rendering justice to the savant whom he tries to condemn as a plagiarist.

Had the love of truth induced this writer to verify for himself the facts which he denies, had he found errors in Burnens through his own observations, we could blame him only for the levity with which he expresses himself. But his incredulity relies upon the authority of a certain Father Tanoya, who may be a very respectable man, but with whom we cannot agree as does the Naples professor when he states that there are in each hive three kinds of bees, independent of each other, to wit: drones male and female, queens and workers of both sexes, each kind building its own particular cells, the queen building hers, the drones theirs, &c.; regardless of Réaumur, de Gers, Geoffroi, Linné, Buffon, Swammerdam, Latreille, &c. If they were not aware of the hypotheses of Father Tanoya, Mr. Monticelli challenges their reliability: we shall not complain of having to share the fate of all these observers; we must, on the contrary, thank the Napolitan professor for being kind enough to admit us into so honorable a proscription.

We cannot help regretting that these faults be found in the work of Mr. Monticelli, for it contains a fairly good practice in the art of caring for bees and of producing artificial swarms; it is written with interest and purity and contains a happy confirmation of the principles of Mr. Schirach and we are astonished that an author whose ideas of natural history appear to be taken from the best sources should have admitted in its notes the most absurd system.

The industrious Favignanese constructed their hives of wood: they are oblong square boxes, the ends of which are movable; the box itself is open at the bottom and rests upon its stand; it is with these hives that they practice artificial swarming in the manner following: As the spring is much earlier with them than with us they may begin as early as the month of March in the multiplication of hives; as soon as the bees bring back pellets of pollen they consider the time favorable for this operation; the hive is transported at some distance from the apiary; they open it from the farther end and the bees are driven with smoke to the forward part, when some of the combs commonly containing honey are cut out; next driving the bees to the posterior part, they take a certain number of combs from the anterior part, some of which are empty, some full of brood of all ages (worker brood which they call latin combs); these are then put into the new hive which they hold in an inverted position, and which is thus open from above; they establish them in it in the same order as found in the mother hive and fasten them with pegs driven in from the outside; this done, they carry the new hive to the spot occupied by the old one, and remove the latter fifty steps from the apiary; the bees that were in the field, coming home, find a hive similar to the one from which they had issued, lodge themselves there, rear the brood and prosper.

The success of this operation, which very much resembles Schirach's, amply confirms his theory.

This gives us occasion to mention a slightly different and very ingenious method, invented by Mr. Lombard, a great cultivator of bees and the author of an excellent treatise on their practical economy.

The Lombard process is the reverse of that of Favignana: instead of making an artificial swarm, he forms, so to speak, only an early natural swarm.

He carries the hive destined for this purpose to a dark place where he has already brought the one intended to receive the swarm; the cylindrical shape of his straw hives facilitates the work which consists in driving a part of the bees with the queen from the old hive to the new; the old hive is then returned to its stand so that it may be repeopled by all those returning from the fields, and the new one is established at a suitable distance from it in the apiary; this swarm has a queen and can prosper without help, and enjoys the advantage of the blooming of fruit trees, which is not usually enjoyed by natural swarms. For the details I refer to Lombard's work itself, which is of essential utility to every cultivator of bees.

This method being founded, as is shown, on the production of a queen in a hive containing only brood, farther confirms Schirach's doctrine, since its long practice has always been attended with success.

Thus experiment concurs with theory in demonstrating that the larva of a bee may become a queen or a worker, because in either of these modes, it is a female possessing either the physical qualities of maternity in the fecundity of queens, or the conservative properties, such as love, care and solicitude for the young displayed by the workers. This dividing of industry, and courage on one side, with prodigious fecundity on the other, this division originating from the mystery of the education of the larvæ, is one of the finest subjects for meditation which natural history affords; we owe to Mr. Schirach's perseverance and perspicacity one of the most curious discoveries that have brought honor upon science; this fact, of which we have given material proofs, throws a great light upon the phenomenon of the development of organs in living beings, and belongs with the greatest researches of physiologists.

LETTER UPON THE ANALYSIS OF WAX GLANDS

By Miss Jurine

Sir, You have desired me to seek in the bees the organs which produce wax; in order to inform you I had to examine the parts which rest upon the segments of the abdomen, where the wax plates are found; compare these parts with those of the female bumblebees (bremus) which also produce a waxy substance, without having, like the bees, glands in which it is moulded; establish a similar comparison with the females of some other hymenopters that do not secrete wax, and lastly ascertain whether there are any great differences between queens, males and workers in the structure of these organs.

On carefully removing the four wax segments of a worker, one discovers an adipose membrane, interspersed with tracheæ, and exactly similar to that which had been recognized by Swammerdam, under the upper segments of the abdomen; this membrane is held under each ring by six little bundles of muscles. Since this membrane is found under all the segments, while wax appears only in the lower ones, it is not presumed to be the secretory organ. To ascertain this, I examined the abdomen of the violet bee (sylocopa violacea), and of two species of wasps, and found this membrane existing in the same way.

I examined afterwards the internal surface of the wax segments, and discovered a whitish membrane which coated only the wax-producing parts; I removed this readily by maceration, and placing it under a microscope, it appeared to consist of a pretty net of very small hexagonal meshes, full of a liquid as thick as syrup. If this net work was the organ of wax secretion, I could expect to find it under the same segments of the abdomen of bumblebees, and it was there indeed; with this difference, that it occupied all their anterior half.

In order easily to perceive this membrane, which is sometimes indistinct, we must select bees that are building their combs; as it is so full of whitish matter, then, that it might be taken for scales of wax.

Detaching the net-work from the ring, to ascertain whether it contained real wax, or only a preliminary preparation for it, I placed it in a vessel, in order to compare it with scales of wax placed into another vessel; and poured boiling water over both; the scales of wax melted while no waxy particle escaped from the former; being but little pleased with this experiment I repeated it twice; but the result was the same, although I had broken the meshes of this net-work in several places. If the existence of this net-work was to be considered as an initial step towards the discovery of the wax-secreting organs, it was necessary to discover the vessels communicating with it, and how the wax transuded from the abdomen; for this purpose I dissected a great number of bees, and could only see minute tracheæ, communicating immediately with the net-work. In the hope of succeeding better with another plan, I fed some bees on honey colored with lac, but this substance did not reach farther than the digestive organs. I tried injections of mercury in these same organs, with no better success; unable to discover any other vessel, I conjectured that the material of which wax was formed might be supplied by a transudation of the juices of the stomach, which is very much gorged when bees work in wax. To clear my doubts, I examined it in several wax workers, and by repeatedly and gently pressing it, while I avoided rupturing it, I succeeded in causing half of its contents to flow into the abdominal cavity; I tasted this and found in it a sweet and saccharine flavor: these bees having been afterwards exposed to the heat of a moderate fire, this liquid assumed the consistence of dried syrup. Bees having several means of obtaining such a pressure upon their stomach, may it not be attained with similar effects, and may not this liquid reach the hexagonal net-work where it receives a preparation suitable for its conversion into wax?

The researches which I made, to discern how the wax or the liquid found within the hexagonal net-work passed from the inside to the outside of the body, had no greater success; I could not find any opening, either in the horny part of the segment which is lined with this net or in the membrane which unites the rings; but although I had not seen such an opening, should I conclude that there was none? In this uncertainty I made the following experiments: Among some bees that had just been killed by a brimstone fumigation, I selected such as showed scales of wax; after having fastened them on their back on a board, I stretched their abdomen in order to remove the wax plates more easily; then, pressing the wax producing segments repeatedly with the head of a needle, I saw their receptacle insensibly moistened with a liquid, of the consistence of syrup, observed nowhere besides: when the bees in this condition were exposed to moderate heat, it acquired still greater consistence, however without assuming a waxy appearance.

I repeated this experiment on bees that had been dead several days, and were somewhat dried; the scales broke into fragments when I tried to remove them; by the simple expedient of pressing the wax segments several times, I succeeded in obtaining them entire, which I could ascribe only to the oozing of the syrupy matter which I had noticed in the previous experiment.

The comparison of the abdomen of the queens with that of the workers yielded the following modifications: The reticulated membrane, which in the latter occupies only the wax segments, is replaced in the queens by a membrane which extends over the anterior two-thirds of each segment; its consistency is so fine and delicate that it may only be seen with a microscope; after having removed it, I noticed that the scale exhibited a hexagonal tissue much more decided in the half of the segment corresponding with the wax organs of the worker than in the posterior half. While trying to remove what I thought to be a second membrane, I ascertained that it was the scale itself which was thus organized; this led me to a closer inspection of the scale of the wax segments of the worker which I found perfectly smooth in the part where the wax receptacles are situated, and resembling that of the queen throughout the rest of the segment.

As to the difference between the males and the workers, it consists in the following: The drones are entirely deprived of the fatty membrane and the hexagonal net-work; in their place one sees only very thick muscular fibres, through which tracheæ exist which are disposed as in the worker; the scale of the male segments displays the same hexagonal tissue as that of the queen.[21]

[21]   See Plate III. A is a worker segment, B that of a queen, C that of a drone. Figs. 4, 5, 6, show the same segments in profile.

EXTRACT FROM THE MEMOIR BY JOHN HUNTER

On Beeswax, Translated From the English.

"In explaining in a new way the formation of beeswax, I shall prove that it could not have the origin which it was supposed to have. I shall first remark that the materials from which the combs are composed are in a different state from that of the stamen dust of any vegetable whatever.

"The substance which the bees bring home on their legs, and which is the fecundating dust of flowers, has always been considered as the material from which wax is composed; some authors have even called *wax* the little pellets which our bees bring in from the fields.

"Réaumur was of that opinion; I made several experiments in order to ascertain whether there was in this product a quantity of oil sufficient to account for the quantity of wax formed from it, and to learn whether it actually contained oil; I held one near a candle; it burnt but without the smell of wax, and emitted the same smell as stamen dust when exposed to fire.

"I remarked that this substance was of different colors on the legs of different bees; but always of the same color on both legs of the same bee; whereas the shade of a new made comb is uniform. I observed that the bees of old hives where the combs are complete, gather this substance with more activity, than those inhabiting new hives where they are only begun, which would hardly be the case were it the elements of wax. We may observe also that, when we place bees in a new hive, they spend two or three days before bringing any pellets on their legs, and that it is only after that interval of time that they gather it. Why? Because during those first days they have had time to build cells in which this substance may be stored; a few eggs have been laid and after they are hatched the worms will need this food which will be ready for them, and which will not be lacking if the weather should be moist and the bees became unable to gather it outside.

"I have also observed that, when the weather was so cold or so wet in June, as to prevent a young swarm from going abroad, as much comb was constructed, nevertheless, as might have been built, if they had been able to fly about the fields.

"Wax is formed by the bees themselves; it may be called an external secretion of oil and originates between each plate of the underside of the belly. On first observing it, in examining a worker, I was embarrassed to explain its appearance, and doubted whether new scales were forming, and whether bees cast the old ones like the shells of lobsters, but I soon discovered that this substance could be found only between the scales of the belly. When examining the workers climbing on the inside of the panes of glass hives, I saw that most of them exhibited this substance; it gave the lower and posterior edge of the scales the appearance of being double, or there

229

seemed to be double scales; but I ascertained that this substance was loose and did not adhere.

"Having proved that the pellets brought on their limbs were farina from the stamens, apparently destined for the food of the larvæ and not for wax making, and having found nothing else which could be supposed to be wax, I conjectured that these scales might be wax itself. I placed several of them on the point of a needle, which I held to the flame of a candle; they melted and formed a globule. I doubted no longer of this being wax and made sure of it in a more positive way by ascertaining that they are never found except during the season that bees construct their combs."

In the remainder of the paragraph the author relates having made useless efforts to seize the moment when they detached the scales from themselves.

He afterwards affirms that it is with this material, transuded through the rings of their abdomen, that they build their combs, but he believes that they add to it a little of the fecundating dust of the stamens, when the wax secretion is not sufficiently abundant for their work.

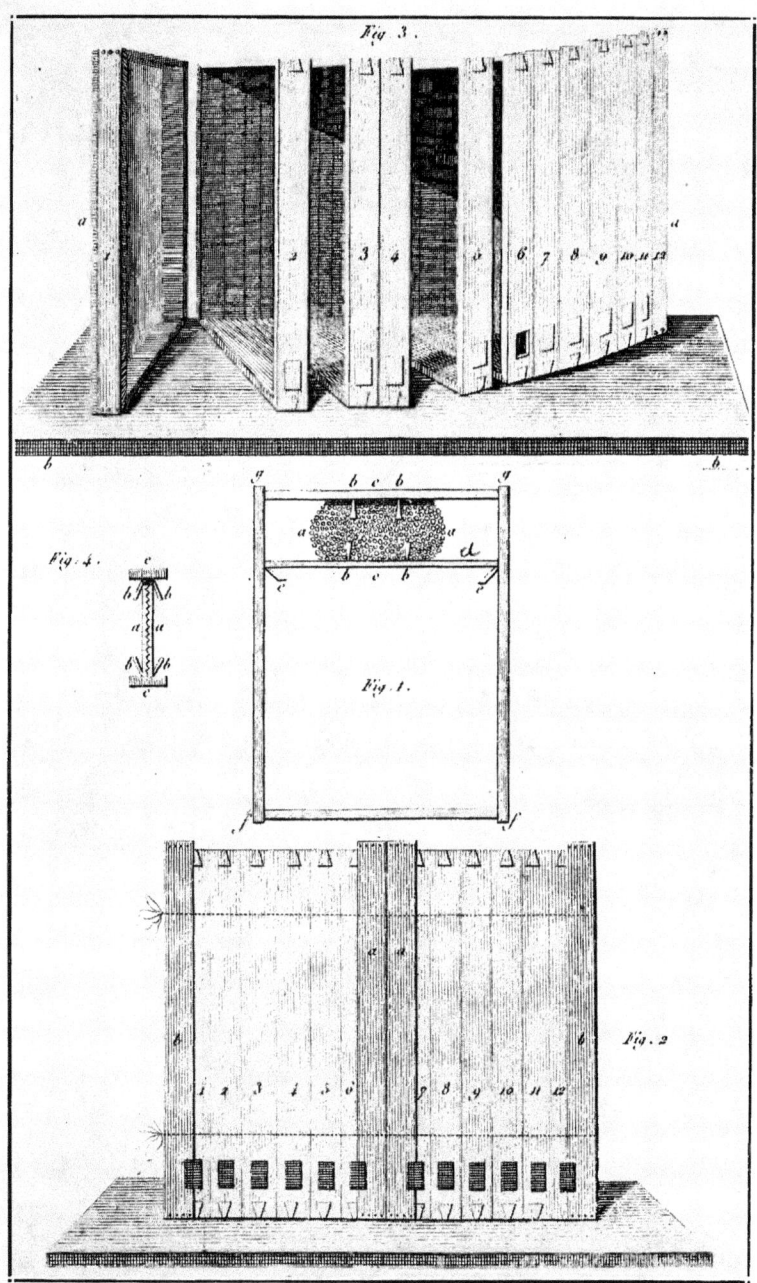

VOLUME 1—PLATE 1.

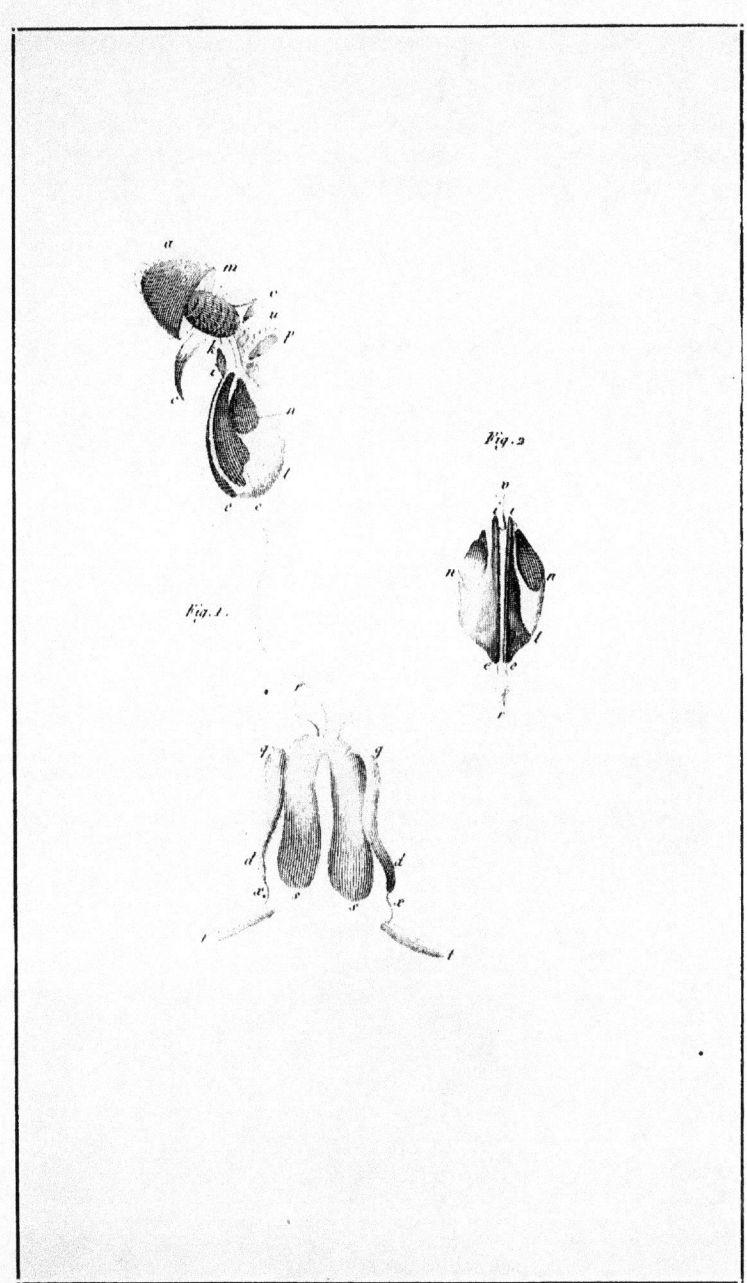

Fig. 2.

Fig. 1.

VOLUME 1—PLATE 2.

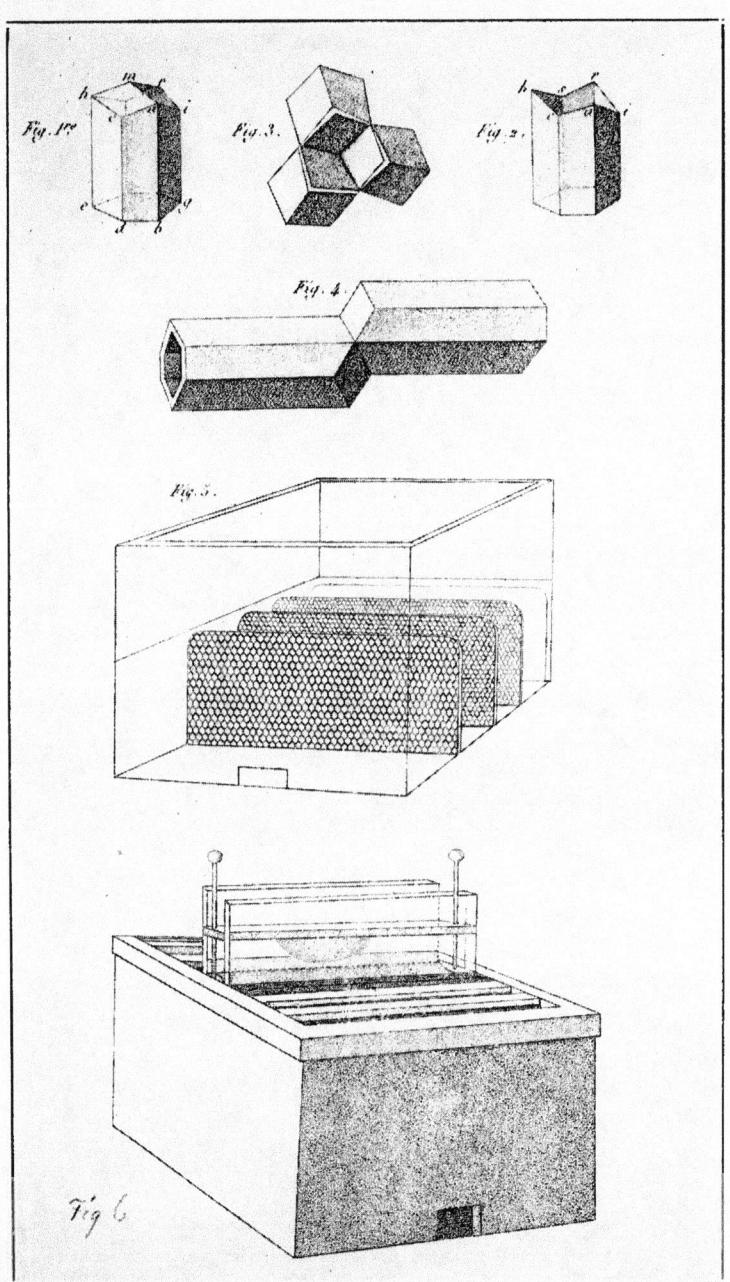

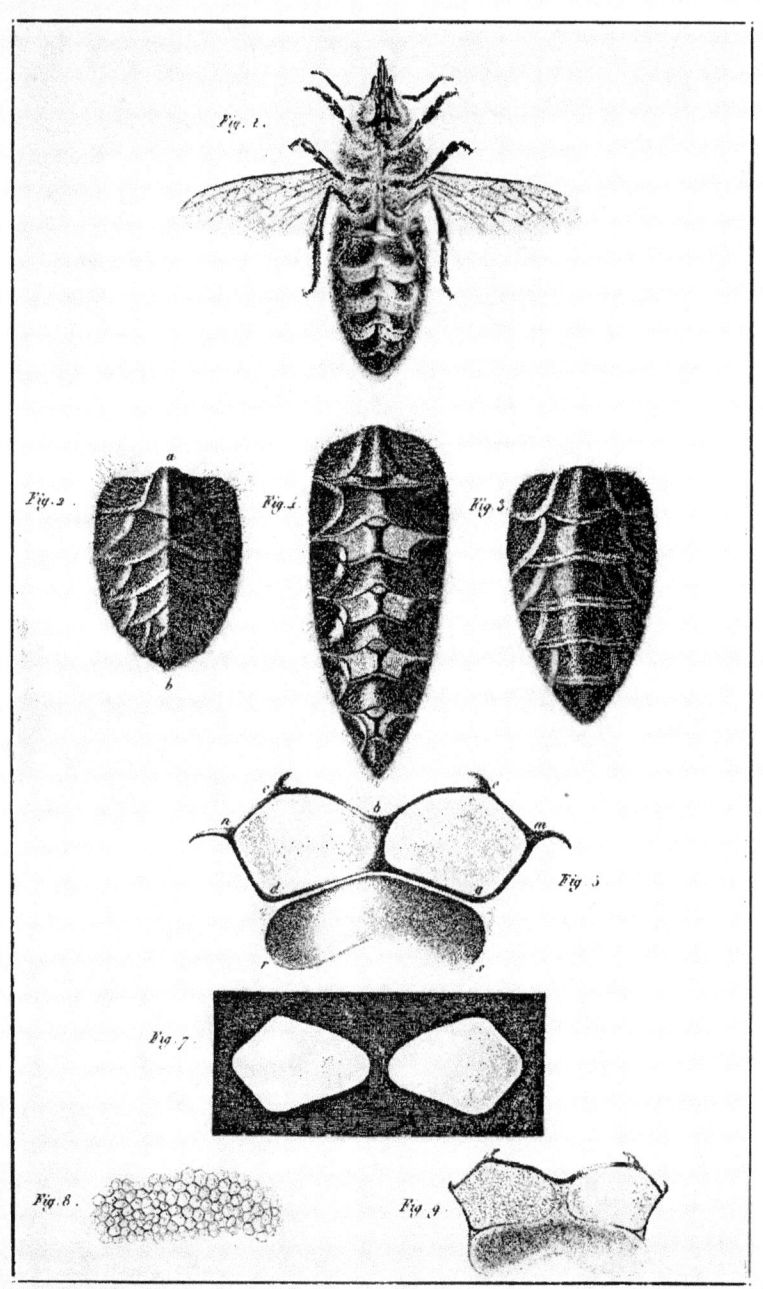

VOLUME 2—PLATE 2.

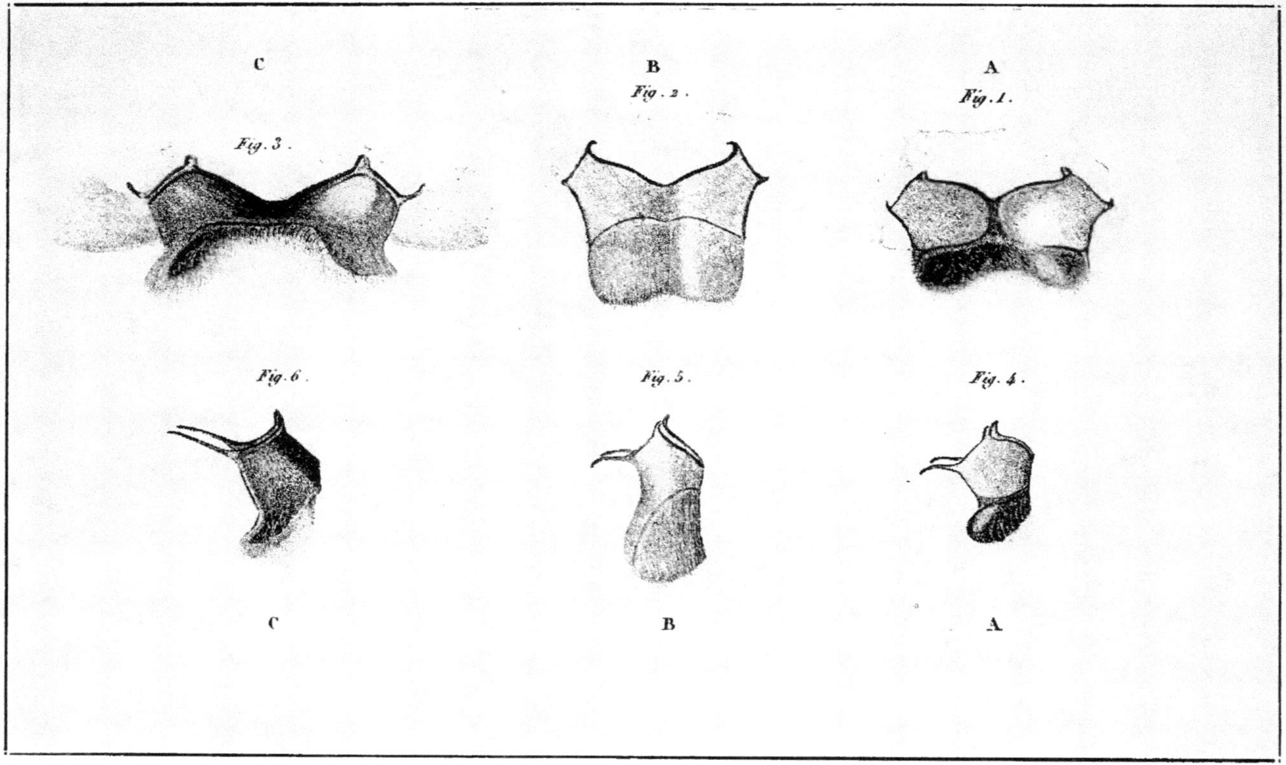

A
Fig. 1.

B
Fig. 2.

C
Fig. 3.

Fig. 4.
A

Fig. 5.
B

Fig. 6.
C

VOLUME 2—PLATE 3.

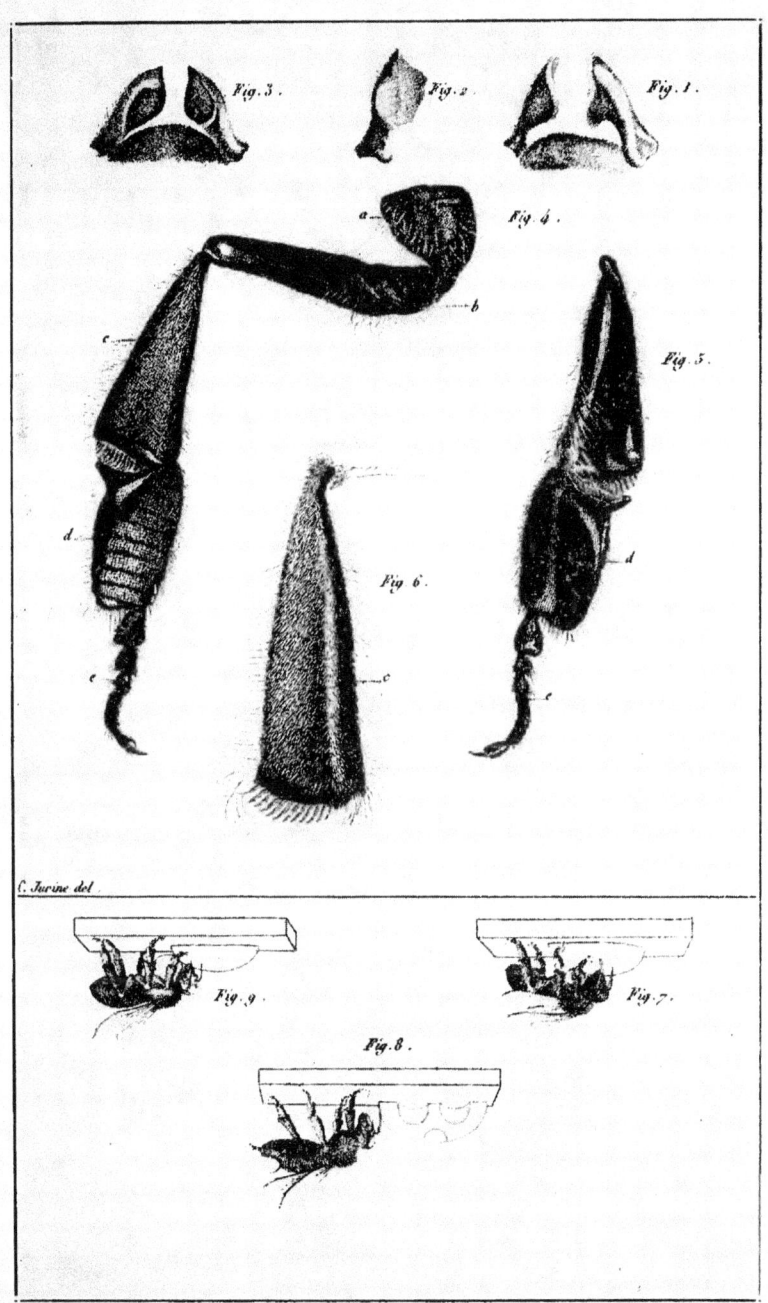

Fig. 3.

Fig. 2.

Fig. 1.

Fig. 4.

a

b

c

Fig. 5.

d

d

Fig. 6.

e

c

e

C. Jurine del.

Fig. 9.

Fig. 7.

Fig. 8.

VOLUME 2—PLATE 4.

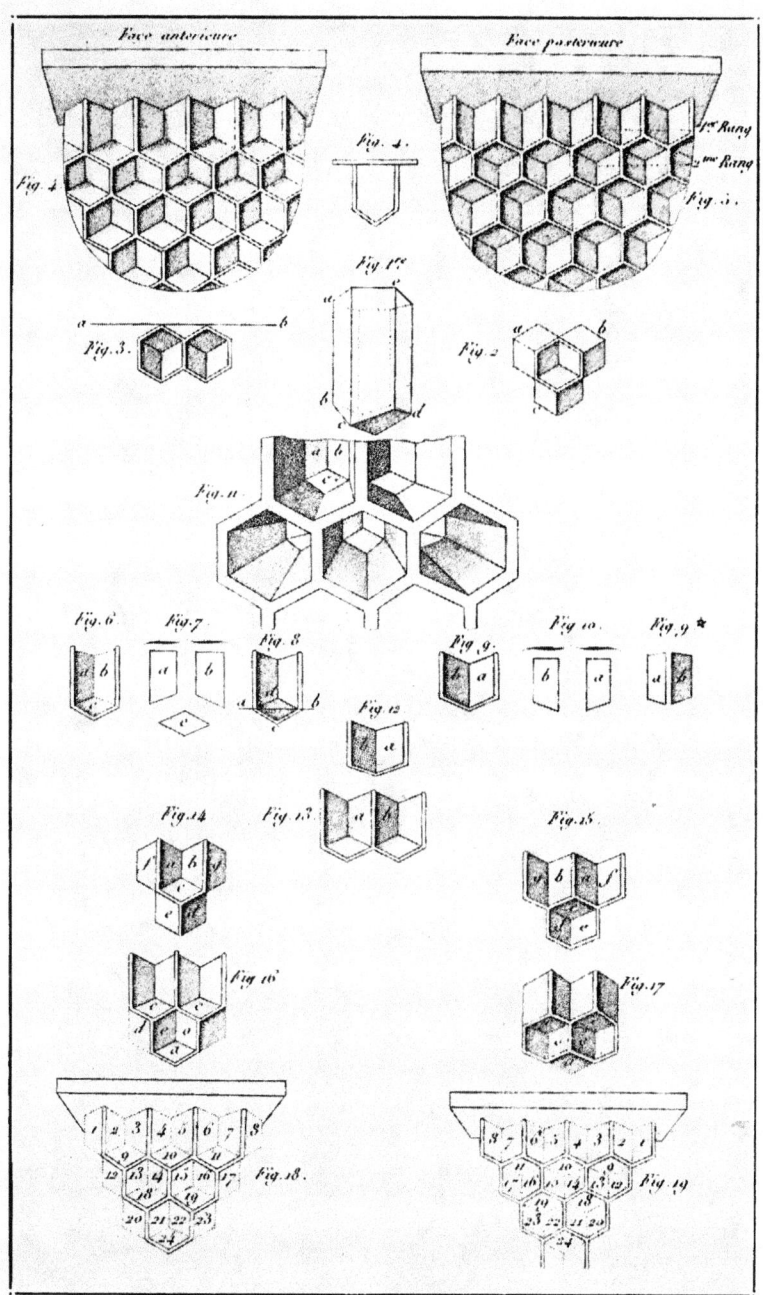

Face antérieure

Face postérieure

Fig. 4.

Fig. 4.

Fig. 5.

1er Rang

2me Rang

Fig. 5.

Fig. 1re

a ——————— b

Fig. 3.

Fig. 2.

Fig. 11.

Fig. 6. Fig. 7. Fig. 8. Fig. 9. Fig. 10. Fig. 9.

Fig. 12.

Fig. 14. Fig. 13. Fig. 15.

Fig. 16. Fig. 17.

Fig. 18. Fig. 19.

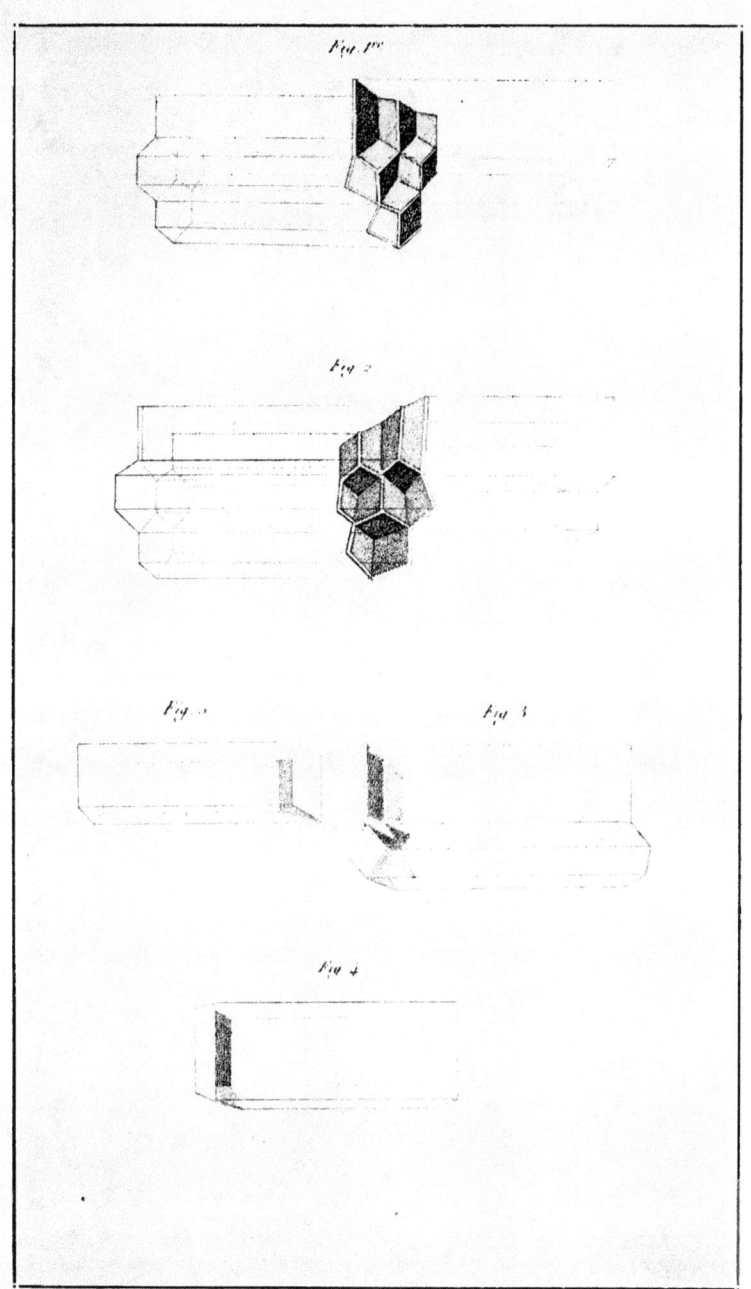

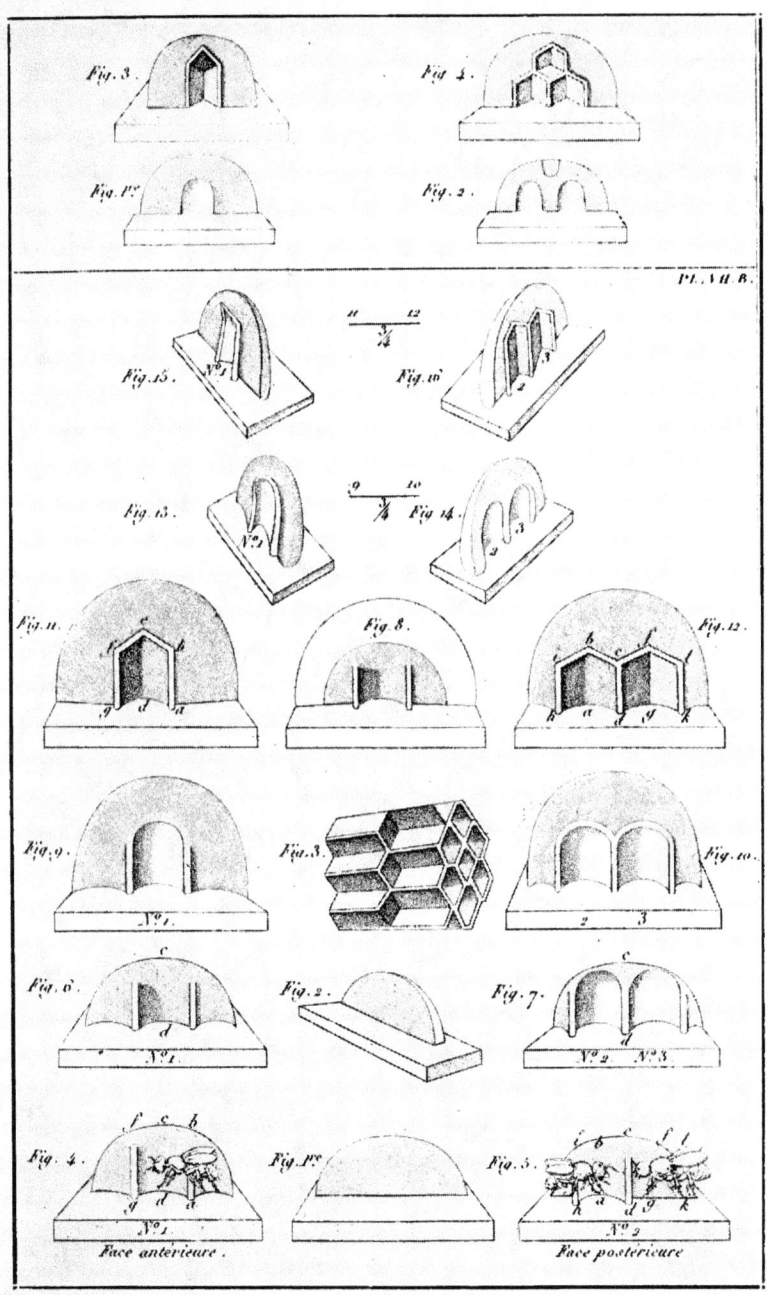

Face antérieure.

Face postérieure

VOLUME 2—PLATE 7.

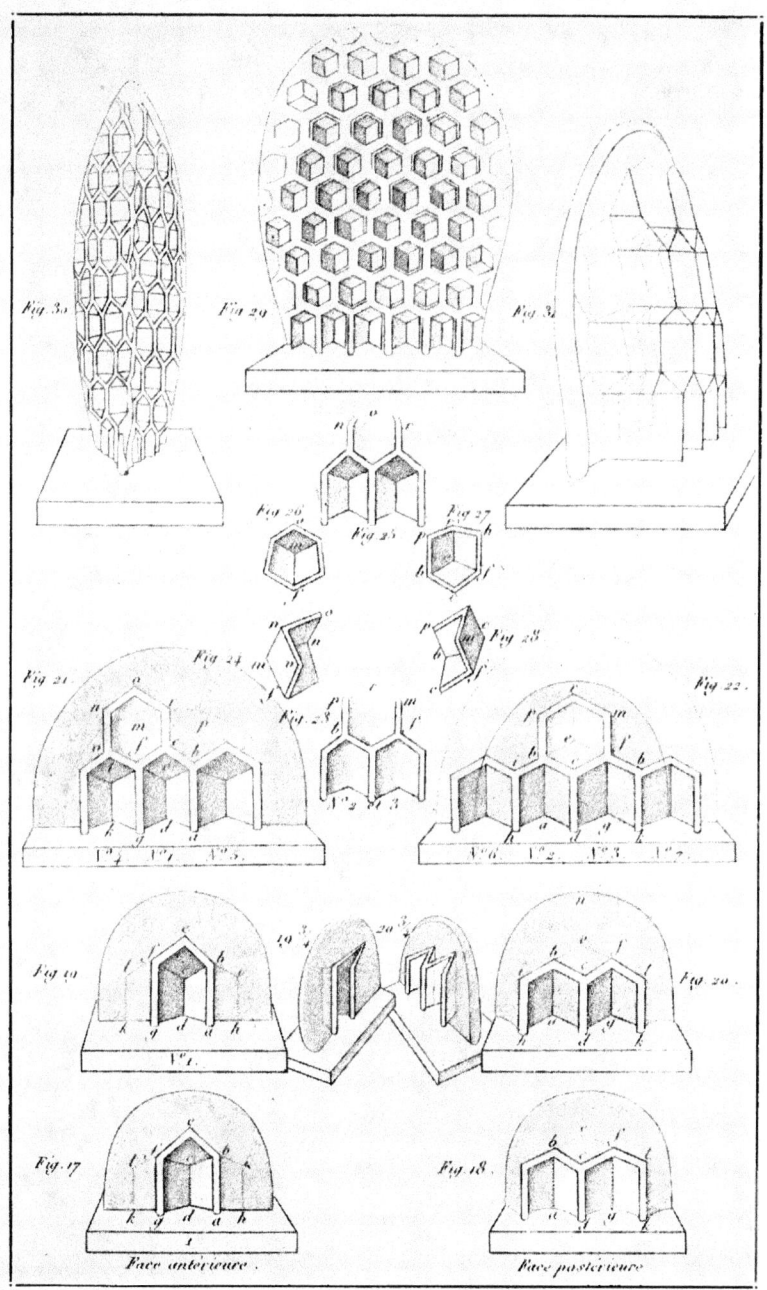

Fig. 30   Fig. 29   Fig. 31

Fig. 26   Fig. 25   Fig. 27

Fig. 24   Fig. 28

Fig. 21   Fig. 23   Fig. 22

Fig. 19   Fig. 20

Fig. 17   Fig. 18

Face antérieure.   Face postérieure

VOLUME 2—PLATE 8.

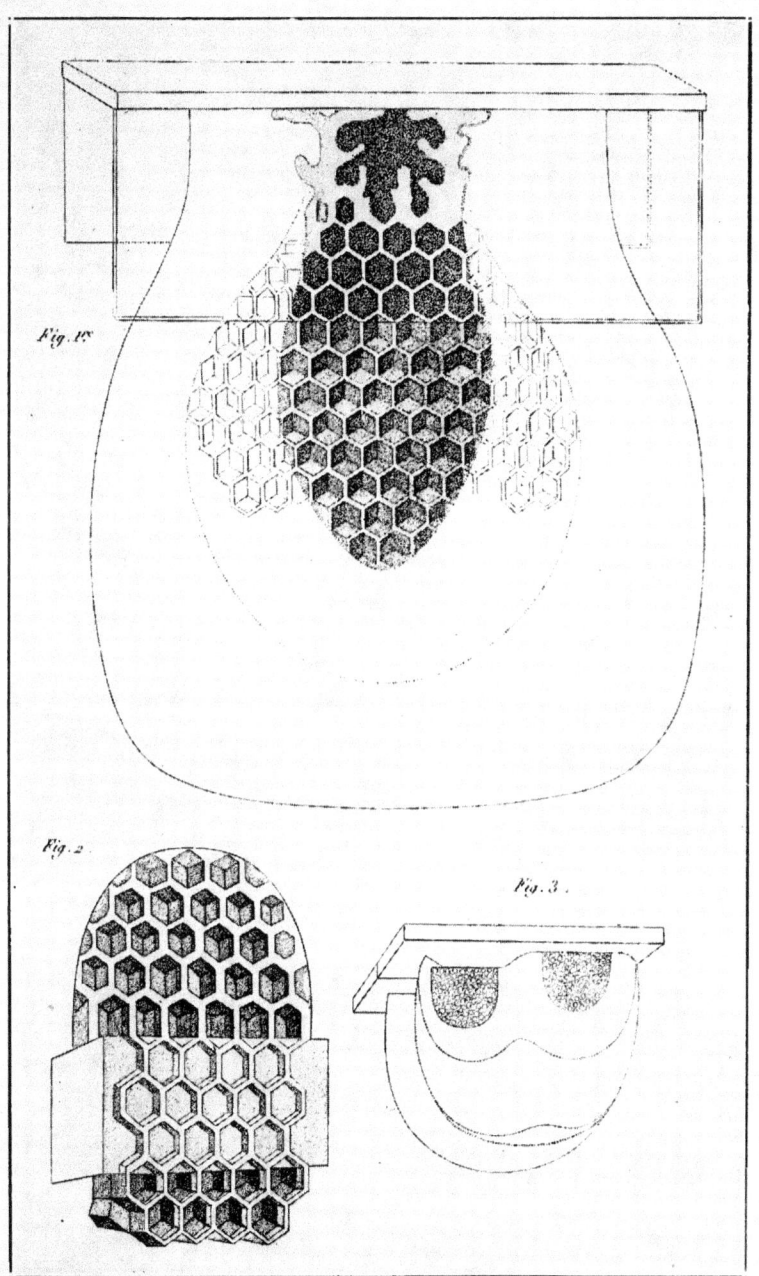

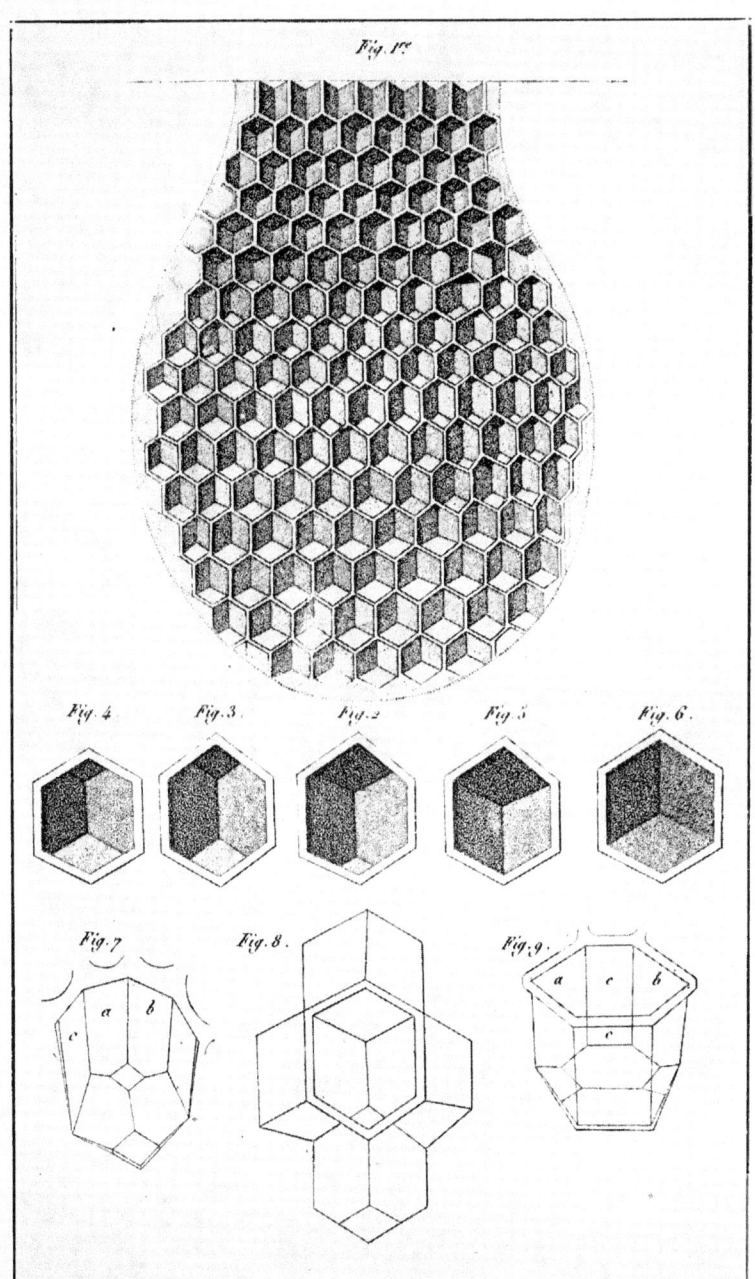

Fig. 1ᵉʳ

Fig. 4   Fig. 3.   Fig. 2   Fig. 5   Fig. 6.

Fig. 7   Fig. 8.   Fig. 9.

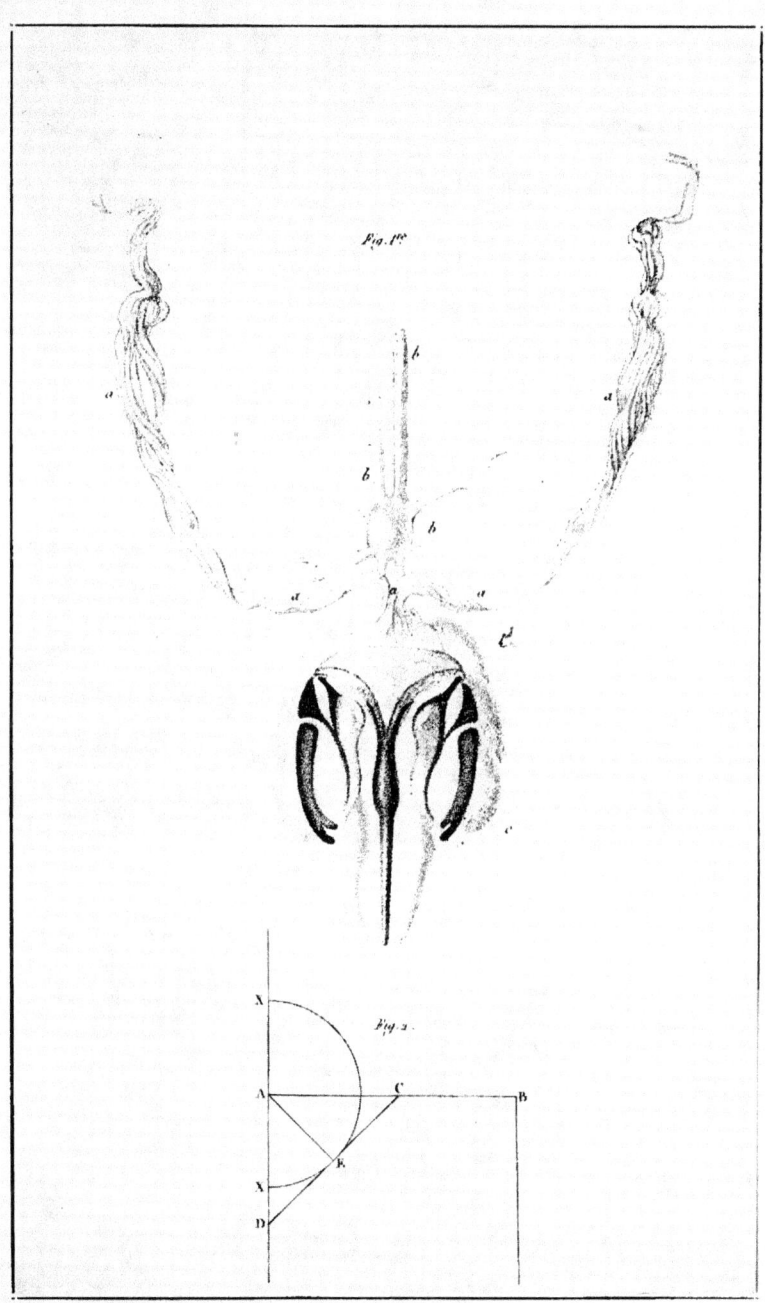

Fig. 1re

Fig. 2

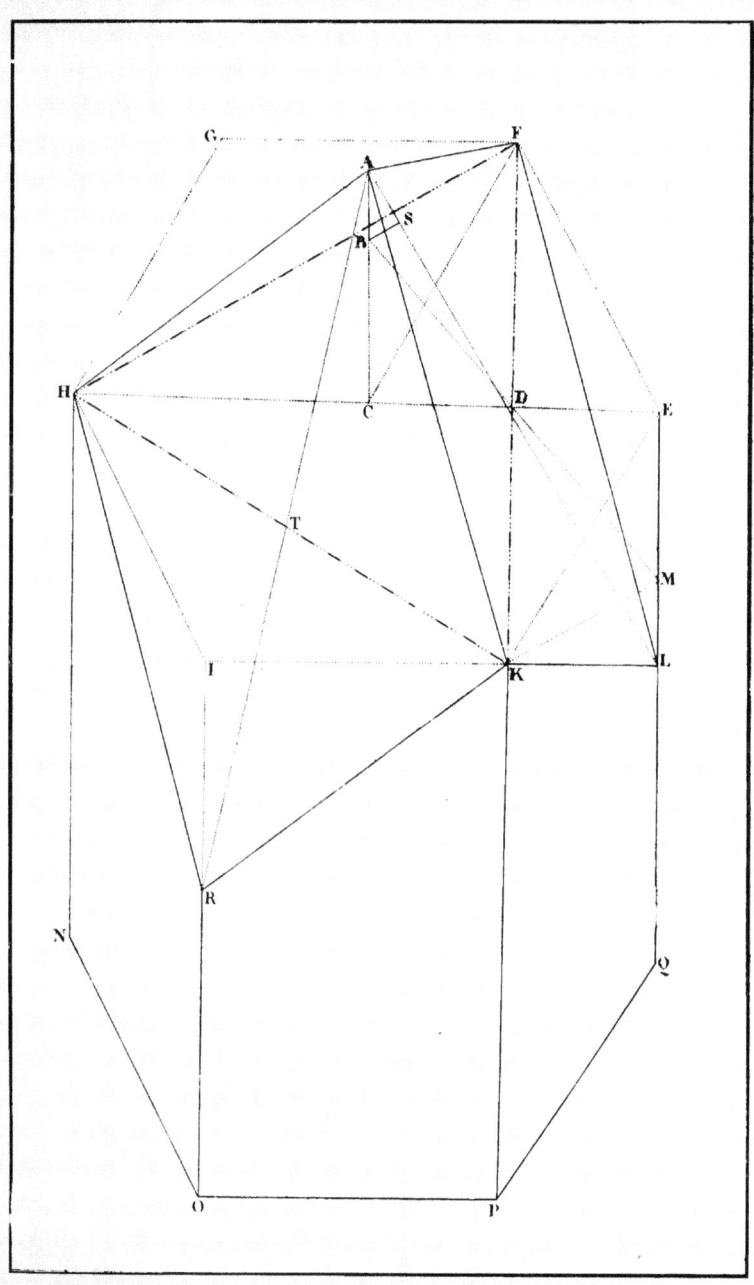